ROUTLEDGE LIBRARY EDITIONS:
SOVIET SOCIETY

Volume 2

I0105038

AN INTRODUCTION TO
THE SOVIET LEGAL SYSTEM

AN INTRODUCTION TO
THE SOVIET LEGAL SYSTEM

E. L. JOHNSON

Routledge
Taylor & Francis Group

LONDON AND NEW YORK

First published in 1969 by Methuen & Co Ltd

This edition first published in 2025
by Routledge
4 Park Square, Milton Park, Abingdon, Oxon OX14 4RN

and by Routledge
605 Third Avenue, New York, NY 10158

Routledge is an imprint of the Taylor & Francis Group, an informa business

British Library Cataloguing in Publication Data
A catalogue record for this book is available from the British Library

ISBN: 978-1-032-86028-2 (Set)
ISBN: 978-1-032-88608-4 (Volume 2) (hbk)
ISBN: 978-1-032-88632-9 (Volume 2) (pbk)
ISBN: 978-1-003-53875-2 (Volume 2) (ebk)

DOI: 10.4324/9781003538752

Publisher's Note
The publisher has gone to great lengths to ensure the quality of this reprint but
points out that some imperfections in the original copies may be apparent.

Disclaimer
The publisher has made every effort to trace copyright holders and would
welcome correspondence from those they have been unable to trace.

AN INTRODUCTION TO THE
SOVIET LEGAL SYSTEM

E. L. JOHNSON

METHUEN & CO LTD
11 NEW FETTER LANE · LONDON EC4

First published by Methuen & Co Ltd 1969
© 1969 The Administrators of
the Estate of the Late E. L. Johnson

SBN 416 13230 8

Printed in Great Britain by
Butler & Tanner Ltd
Frome and London

Distributed in the USA by
Barnes & Noble Inc.

Contents

CONTENTS [vii

Preface

This book is based on a course of public lectures which I gave at University College London during the session 1963-4 and which was repeated the following session. The lectures have been thoroughly revised, expanded and brought up to date for publication in book form, but the book is intended to serve the same purpose as the lectures did, namely to provide an Introduction to the Soviet Legal System for students of Soviet affairs who are not trained lawyers. This explains why I have dealt with Criminal Procedure and Family Law in some detail whereas the technicalities of property, succession, contract and tort have received comparatively brief treatment: I have tried to deal with those aspects of the Soviet Legal System which interest the ordinary educated citizen rather than those which are of interest primarily to lawyers. For similar reasons I have included a certain amount of general background material which seems essential to a proper understanding of the legal provisions; some of this is perhaps rather elementary, and I therefore ask the indulgence of those who are already well informed about general conditions in the Soviet Union. Translation of Russian terms commonly presents difficulties, and where any misunderstanding might arise I have given the original Russian word; this may be of assistance to readers who have some knowledge of the Russian language. For those who wish to make a deeper study of the matters treated in this book I have provided a short general bibliography of works in English dealing with the Soviet Legal System as a whole, and at the end of each chapter there are further lists of books and articles of a more specialized character.

Every worker in this field owes an immense debt to those indefatigable American scholars, Harold J. Berman and John N. Hazard, whose researches have done so much to throw light in dark places; without their pioneer labours, this book could never have been written, and their influence will be seen on many of its pages. Apart from the

English translations of Soviet books, published by the Foreign Languages Publishing House, Moscow, which appear in the General Bibliography and suggestions for further reading, I have not indicated the Soviet sources on which I have drawn for information: full references to Soviet sources will, however, be found in the books and articles referred to in the General Bibliography and the suggestions for further reading at the end of each chapter.

In view of the several references to roubles in the book it may be stated that the Soviet rouble now has an exchange value of approximately one United States dollar or about nine shillings sterling. The 'old rouble' in use before the currency reform of 1961 had one-tenth the value of the present rouble.

E. L. JOHNSON

University College London
September 1968

General Bibliography

H. J. Berman, *Justice in the U.S.S.R.*, Cambridge, Mass., 1963.

L. Daiches, *Russians at Law*, London, 1960.

G. Feifer, *Justice in Moscow*, London, 1964.

J. N. Hazard and I. Shapiro, *The Soviet Legal System*, New York, 1962.

W. R. LaFave (ed.), *Law in the Soviet Society*, Urbana, Ill., 1965.

P. S. Romashkin (ed.), *Fundamentals of Soviet Law*, Moscow, 1962.

Table of Statutes

This table includes all enactments ('Statutes' proper, decrees, instructions, etc.) given in the text with the date of promulgation where known. Only the short English title is given here, and in the majority of citations, no distinction is made as to *ukaz, zakon, postanovlenie*, etc., nor as to the source of the enactment (Supreme Soviet, Council of Ministers, etc.).

The following abbreviations are used:

OGPU   All-Union State Political Board
RSFSR   Russian Socialist Federative Republic
USSR   Union of Soviet Socialist Republics

Main entries are indicated in italic.

CHAPTER ONE

Introduction

SOVIET LAW – A CIVIL OR ROMANISTIC SYSTEM

As every sovereign state is entitled to enact such laws as it thinks fit, and as the historical, geographical, religious and economic circumstances in each state are so different, it might be thought at first sight that it would be difficult to classify the various legal systems of the world. Yet in fact the similarities are often more striking than the differences, even though these may be considerable. An Englishman who knows no German and a German who knows no English cannot, unless they should happen to have some third language in common, converse with each other; the differences in their respective languages are too great for mutual comprehension. Yet the philologist recognizes both German and English as Germanic languages, for he has been trained to see the similarities between these languages, which put them in a distinct group which may be distinguished, for example, from the Latin languages such as French, Spanish and Italian, and the Slavonic languages such as Russian, Polish and Czech. Moreover, the philologist sees the resemblances between the Germanic, the Latin and the Slavonic languages which enable them to be placed, together with other languages and groups of languages, such as Greek and the Celtic languages (Welsh, Gaelic, Breton, Irish), in a more comprehensive grouping, that of the Indo-European language group, which has its own special characteristics which become obvious when the languages constituting this linguistic family are compared, for example, with the languages of Africa or South-East Asia.

Just as the philologist seeks and finds basic similarities between languages, and proceeds to classify them into groups and families, while noting the special features and characteristics of each individual language within a group, so the jurist finds basic resemblances between many of the world's legal systems, despite their many individual features. And in fact he finds two major groups of legal systems, which

B

are usually termed the common law systems and the civil law systems.[1]

The common law systems are ultimately based on the rules, principles and practices elaborated by the mediaeval common law courts at Westminster, and the particularly English method of thinking about law and dealing with legal problems was taken by British colonists to most parts of the English-speaking world. If we speak of common law systems, we are thinking of the legal systems of England, of both jurisdictions in Ireland, of Australia, New Zealand, the United States of America (except the state of Louisiana), Canada (except the Province of Quebec), and also of many parts of Africa and Asia to which the common law was extended, in whole or in part, by British Imperial rule, and where it has survived and flourished despite the granting of independence to former colonial possessions. With the exceptions of Scotland, Louisiana, South Africa and Rhodesia, the English-speaking world generally is governed by legal systems of the common law family.

The civil law systems are ultimately derived from the rules, principles and practices elaborated in the ancient Roman Forum. When we speak of civil law systems, we are thinking of those of continental Europe and Latin America, and of those African and Asian countries formerly dependencies of continental European powers. Japan, and with some reservations China, would also be included, for in legal matters they have borrowed much from continental Europe.

British Imperial rule, however, did not force the common law on countries where there was already an established civilized system of law in force, and for that reason the Province of Quebec in Canada retained its former French system of law, and South Africa retained the system of Roman-Dutch law in force there at the time of its cession to Britain; from South Africa, Roman-Dutch law was extended to Rhodesia. For similar reasons Roman-Dutch law provides the basis of the legal system of Ceylon. French law remained in force in Louisiana when the territory was acquired from France by the United States in 1803.

Besides the two major groups of common law and civil law systems there are also certain other well-developed legal systems, which, however, have little in common among themselves apart from being closely

[1] The term 'civil law' has several meanings. Sometimes it is used, as here, to denote Roman law and the modern law derived from it, and it is then contrasted with common law. Sometimes civil law means private law among citizens in contrast to criminal law, or military law, or ecclesiastical law. Only the context will show its sense, but the most usual use of the term in common-law countries is that in which it means 'the whole of the law of a particular country except its law relating to crimes and criminal procedure'. It has a much narrower sense in modern Soviet usage, as will appear later.

connected with a particular religion. Among these may be mentioned Hindu law, Mohammedan law, and Jewish law.[1]

Soviet law, like Imperial Russian law (at any rate after 1864), clearly falls within the civil law group of legal systems. This presents particular problems for Anglo-American students of the Soviet system, whereas for the continental students, there is much, especially in the way of principle and terminology, that a French or Dutch student may be able to take for granted; he is, in effect, enabled to concentrate on the differences between Soviet law and his own system, just by reason of the fact that certain basic assumptions and, in particular, certain matters of terminology are similar. The French research worker, for example, who finds some Soviet rule, institution, or juridical technique that differs from his own, will usually want to find out whether that particular rule, institution or technique was paralleled in the Imperial Russian legal system, for only then can he decide whether it is to be regarded as a specific feature of the Soviet legal system or whether it is part of the Russian legal heritage acquired and taken over, perhaps with modifications, by the Soviets. In other words, he asks himself, does this rule or institution have a specifically Soviet or a specifically Russian character? The Anglo-American lawyer researching into Soviet law, however, who finds some rule or institution of an unfamiliar nature, has first to pose a preliminary question; is this rule or feature a common characteristic of civil law systems in general, as distinct from common law systems? Only when he is satisfied that it is not can he go on to consider whether he is dealing with some specifically Russian or specifically Soviet rule or institution.

It is difficult to convey in a short form the basic distinctions between common law and civil law systems. There may still perhaps be some truth in the old view that civil law encouraged political autocracy, on the grounds that, whereas the principle of the common law was *rex non debet esse sub homine sed sub Deo et lege*,[2] the maxim of the civil law was *quod principi placuit legis habet vigorem*.[3] But this is far from being the whole truth; the Swiss have deep-rooted traditions of democracy, though the Swiss legal system is a civil law one. Again, there is much truth in

---

[1] These religious systems deal, in the main, with matters of family law and succession. Thus in India, Hindus and Mohammedans are governed by Hindu and Mohammedan law as far as family law and succession are concerned, but by the Indian Contract Act, 1872, a codification of the English common law of contract, in matters of contract law.

[2] 'The king should not be under any man but under God and the Law.'

[3] 'The will of the sovereign has the force of law.'

the statement that whereas common law is based on precedents established in cases in the courts, modern civil law systems are based on comprehensive Codes; but it is still far from the whole truth, for the Roman-Dutch law of South Africa and Ceylon is uncodified, and so is Scots law. To a considerable extent, the difference is one of terminology; the common law systems all use the English language and English legal terminology, and it is often difficult, if not impossible, to translate an English statute into language that is meaningful to a civil lawyer. The difficulty of translating, say, French legal material into German or Russian, is minimal compared with that of translating English legal material into continental languages. Generally speaking, however, one may say that the civil law systems seem to give a greater authority and prestige to state officials, and that there is greater reliance placed on official documents and reports than in common law systems. This last point is interesting, for the modern civil law systems are attacked by Soviet jurists for insisting on a sharp division between public law and private law, and they appear to regard this distinction as typical of 'bourgeois' law; in their view, all law is, or ought to be, public. Yet from the other side Anglo-American jurists have attacked this civil law distinction on the grounds that it gives too much power and immunity to state officials; they feel that civil servants should be subject to the same obligations as ordinary citizens; in other words, the feeling is that all law ought, as far as possible, to be private law.

The American lawyer is used to a system under which law may be federal law, applying throughout the United States, or state law, applying only within one particular state and therefore he has little of the difficulty that the English lawyer, used to a unitary system of law, would encounter in understanding that Soviet law consists both of All-Union or federal law, applying throughout the USSR, and Republican law, the law of one particular Republic in the Union. In fact, however, the differences between the laws of the different Soviet Socialist Republics forming the USSR are insignificant when compared with the differences between the laws of the individual states of the USA, and indeed are deliberately kept so, for in many fields the Soviet practice is for 'basic principles' to be enacted on an All-Union basis, and for these basic principles to be elaborated in detail in the codes of the various Union Republics.

However, although we correctly place Soviet law within the civil law group of legal systems, there is another factor of the greatest importance to be considered, for Soviet law claims to be an entirely new type of legal system based on the Marxist political philosophy and the socialist type of economy. In this respect Soviet law has no resemblance to French or Italian law; indeed, so far as the legal system purports to be nothing more than the legal expression of a particular ideology or outlook on life, the comparison of Soviet law with a religious system such as Mohammedan law does not seem too far-fetched. Soviet law undoubtedly has different aims and purposes than those of the legal systems of capitalist states, and it must be conceded that it is the first legal system in the world to be based on the philosophical and economic principles of socialism; to this extent, those who assert its originality are justified.[1] On the other hand, in so far as Soviet law uses legal techniques common to other civil law systems (though in many cases quite different from the techniques of the common law) those who deny its originality are justified. In the early years of the present century the Austrian jurist, Karl Renner (who became President of the Austrian Republic after the Second World War), elaborated a doctrine of the 'neutrality of legal concepts'. In his view, legal concepts and techniques were like bricks, which could be and were put to use for the construction of buildings serving very different purposes, such as dwellinghouses, warehouses, prisons, concert halls, and so on. In the same way, the same legal concepts may serve for the construction of legal systems, based on different economic and political systems, such as feudalism, capitalism, monarchy, aristocracy and democracy. The fact that the traditional civil law concepts have now been used for the purpose of constructing a system based on Marxist philosophy and socialist economics will seem to many a striking justification of Renner's thesis. This point should be seriously considered by socialists in common law countries, for if any common law country were to adopt socialist or Marxist economic policies, the question would arise whether Soviet legislation should be copied, or whether the existing common law techniques should be used to effect the transition. With the partial exception of China, every country which has so far adopted Marxist principles has been within the civil law orbit, and most have, to a very considerable extent, been able to adopt Soviet enactments with some modifications. Whether this would be possible or practicable in a country with common law traditions may well be open to doubt.

[1] Soviet jurists pay very little attention to the distinction between common law and civil law systems; they classify legal systems according to the economic bases of their respective societies, and so they distinguish between 1. systems based on slavery, i.e. the legal systems of the ancient world and pre-eminently Roman law, 2. systems based on feudalism, 3. systems based on capitalism, and 4. systems based on socialism. This classification is based on the purposes of the different systems and not on the techniques employed.

THE STRUCTURE OF THE SOVIET LEGAL SYSTEM

Officially Soviet law is divided into twelve branches:

1. Constitutional Law. This deals with the structure of the State, the basic principles governing the State, the powers of various important State authorities, and the basic rights and duties of citizens. It is contained primarily in the Constitution of the USSR and the Constitutions of the Union Republics.

2. Administrative Law. This deals with the details of matters of administration, regulates procedures for disputes between citizens and administrative authorities, and defines the powers and duties of various classes of administrative officials. The border-line between administrative law and constitutional law is not a very clear one, but in general it can be said that matters dealt with in the Constitutions of the USSR and of the Union Republics are regarded as matters of constitutional law, and less important matters as matters of administrative law. The rights and powers of the Supreme Soviet, the Supreme Court of the USSR, the Procurator's Office, dealt with in the Constitution, are matters of constitutional law: the rights and duties of postmasters, inspectors of weights and measures, and so on, are matters within the sphere of administrative law.

3. Civil Law. Civil law governs relations between citizens themselves, and also between citizens and public corporations. It covers legal capacity, property law, the law of contract, the law of civil wrongs (torts) and the law of succession on death (i.e. the law governing wills and intestate succession).

4. Labour Law. This governs the rights and duties of employees and employers, such as rights to pay, sick pay, holidays, maternity leave, and also with qualifications, rights to promotion and the settlement of labour disputes. Each Republic has its own Labour Code, and new Basic Principles of Labour Law are in the course of preparation.

5. Land Law. This governs rights to use land, and rights over land occupied by someone else.

6. Collective Farm Law. This includes the law governing the structure and management of collective farms, and the rights and duties of collective farmers.

7. Revenue Law. This deals with the law governing taxation, and the distribution of public financial resources. It also covers the law relating to the budgets of the USSR and of the Union Republics.

8. Family Law. Matters concerning marriage and divorce, rights and

duties of parent and child and adoption come within the sphere of family law, and here again, each Union Republic has its own Code, and Basic Principles of Family Law apply throughout the Union.

9. Criminal Law. This deals with the general principles of the law relating to crime and defines criminal offences and punishments.

10. Criminal Procedure. This governs matters such as arrest, preliminary investigation, procedure at criminal trials, evidence, appeals, and reviews.

11. Civil Procedure. This governs procedure in the civil courts, and deals with matters such as service of process on the defendant, procedure at the trial, appeals and reviews, and the enforcement of judgments.

12. The structure of the courts, or the judicial system. This covers the rules relating to the courts and the administration of justice.

To these twelve branches of law another is often added, namely, Economic Law. Economic Law governs the structure of public corporations engaged in production and distribution and with their relations to each other. It is, in effect, the Soviet equivalent of Commercial Law. There have been a number of disputes about the position of Economic Law in the Soviet legal system and these were particularly strong during the discussion of the Draft Basic Principles of Civil Law during the period 1960–2; the basic question was whether Economic Law should be regarded as a separate branch of law or not. The official view which ultimately prevailed was that Economic Law is not a separate branch of law, for the rules of so-called Economic Law really come either under Administrative Law or under Civil Law. The dispute was not a purely academic one of classification; it concerned the question of whether public corporations in their contracts with each other should be subject to the same rules of contract law that govern contracts between private individuals. In England we would take it as a matter almost for granted that a contract, say, by a Regional Coal Board to supply the Railway Executive with coal would, in principle, be governed by the same legal rules as a contract by an individual to buy coal from a coal merchant. The law of contract is the same for all, and it makes no difference that one or both parties may be public corporations. And indeed this is the attitude that has now been officially adopted in the USSR; but there has been a good deal of controversy about it, and the controversy may break out again at any time. Strictly speaking therefore, Economic Law is not an official branch of Soviet law, but in practice it is often regarded as though it were. At any rate there is a difference of jurisdiction, for whatever the substantive law may be, disputes between public corporations themselves (for example a claim by a railway corporation against a coal-supplying organization for breach of a contract to deliver coal of the proper quality) would come before a special state arbitration tribunal, and not before an ordinary civil court.

The importance of these different branches of law lies in the fact that the procedures for enforcement of rights given by a particular branch of law vary. Labour disputes, for example, can only come before the courts after certain procedures aimed at conciliation have failed to produce any result. Matters within the sphere of administrative law must be dealt with by administrative procedures and are quite outside the jurisdiction of the civil courts. This does not mean that there are no opportunities for complaint or getting administrative decisions reversed, but that the courts are not the proper channel for dealing with these matters.

For the foreign student of the Soviet system, some branches of the law are more interesting than others, and therefore in this book we shall, after considering the historical background of Soviet law and some of its special features at the present time (in chapters II and III), consider its foundations in chapter IV; much of this will be Constitutional Law. Criminal Procedure and Criminal Law are dealt with in chapters V and VI, and chapter VII, 'Contracts and Torts', covers part of the field of Civil Law. Succession on death, also part of civil law, is dealt with in chapter VIII, as is Family Law. Chapter IX is devoted to Labour Law, and chapter X to Collective Farm Law. Chapter XI is mainly concerned with Economic Law. Chapter XII deals with the legal profession in the Soviet Union. Thus certain branches of Soviet law, namely Administrative Law, Land Law, Revenue Law and Civil Procedure are not covered, though some points will be dealt with incidentally while dealing with other matters. The omission of these branches of Soviet law is due partly to considerations of space and partly to the fact that their details are of lesser interest to the general reader or to the student of Soviet affairs.

FURTHER READING

F. H. Lawson, *A Common Lawyer looks at the Civil Law*, University of Michigan Law School, Ann Arbor, 1953.

CHAPTER TWO

The Historical Background

THE TSARIST LEGAL LEGACY

In any country the laws in force are to some considerable extent the product of that particular nation's historical experience and present needs, and if we are usefully to compare the legal system of the USSR with those of other countries it becomes important to know something of Russian legal history. Formally speaking, the Russian Revolution of 1917 effected a complete break with the past: the old laws no longer existed, for the state and society which had brought them into being had passed away. Nevertheless, despite the complete break with the past formally effected by the Russian Revolution, and despite the intention of the Soviet authorities to make a completely new start, there were certain traditions, the residue of historical experiences, that they could not eradicate, and by which the Soviet leaders themselves were still influenced, probably in many cases quite unconsciously. Even if we were to take at face value the Soviet claim that 1917 was a completely new start, we should still have to admit that the new start was based on the Revolution, and to understand the Russian Revolution it is important to understand the conditions against which the Bolsheviks were reacting.

Revolutionaries, in making a break with the immediate past, sometimes tend to revert, consciously or unconsciously, to a more remote past; for example, the English revolutionaries of the seventeenth century deliberately appealed to the legal precepts and precedents of pre-Tudor and pre-Stuart times in asserting their claims to parliamentary supremacy. Sometimes, however, the borrowing from a more remote past is less conscious, and a brief glance at Russian legal history will therefore be necessary if we are to see which of its elements have been included, consciously or unconsciously, in the present Soviet legal system.

Perhaps the most significant event in Russian history, at any rate so far as legal development was affected, was the Tartar conquest. The period of the Mongol Yoke, as it is often termed, lasted from 1240 to 1480. At the time of the Tartar conquest, Kievan Rus, the old Russia with Kiev as its capital, had a system of law comparable to the legal systems of the contemporary states of Western Europe. It had its primitive legal code, the *Russkaya Pravda,* which first appeared about 1018 and of which there were several later editions. The contents of the *Russkaya Pravda* are similar in style to the contemporary Anglo-Saxon dooms and to continental restatements of customary law, such as the *lex Saxonum* (A.D. 803). Thus the *Russkaya Pravda* laid down penalties such as forty *grivna* for an unavenged murder, or for cutting off another's arm, and three *grivna* for cutting off a finger or stealing a horse. These penalties were payable to the victim, but later on an additional fine became payable to the prince. Rules about the exaction of vengeance were laid down in the first article of the *Russkaya Pravda.* The position was quite like that in Anglo-Saxon England, where the blood-feud still existed, although regulated by law, and where there were detailed lists of penalties for various offences, the penalties (termed *wer* or *bot*) being payable to the injured party (e.g. twenty shillings for the loss of a great toe under the laws of King Alfred) together with a fine (*wite*) to the King or to some other public authority. And, as in Anglo-Saxon England, so in Kievan Rus, trial was often by ordeal, and some cases went to a kind of jury. Intestate succession seems to have been based on a system of descent or relationship traced through males, similar to the agnatic system of Roman law, and wills of property were recognized. (A treaty between the Russian Prince Oleg and the Byzantine Emperor Leo the Wise in A.D. 911 provided *inter alia* that the property of Byzantines dying in Russia and of Russians dying in the Byzantine Empire was to be dealt with according to the laws governing testate and intestate succession in the deceased's country of origin.) The rules of the *Russkaya Pravda* concerning commercial activities suggest a greater level of sophistication than much of the rest; they were doubtless due to commercial intercourse with the Byzantine Empire, and many of them appear familiar to those acquainted with Roman law, for example a rule that when a person has been injured by a slave, the owner of the slave must either compensate him or surrender the slave to him, and a rule that the owner of a slave who permits the slave to engage in commerce is liable for the slave's debts.

There is therefore nothing specially remarkable or surprising about Russian law in the eleventh century; indeed, it has often been said that in the eleventh century Russia was more of a European state than ever before or since. What is surprising and does call for explanation is that

Russian law thereafter made very little progress, and was still in much the same condition at the end of the sixteenth century. There had been no general reception of Roman law, as over much of Western and Central Europe, and there was no expanding body of principles derived from local custom and developed by the courts, comparable to the English common law.

The main reason why Russian law failed to develop and grow for several centuries was the Mongol Yoke. The Mongols or Tartars were interested, almost exclusively, in exacting tribute and service from their Russian subjects: they took little interest in the way they settled their private disputes, and Mongol law had no direct influence whatever on Russian private law. The Mongols had their own law which applied among themselves, but they made no attempt to impose this on their Russian subjects, who, as a subject nation, oppressed by people of a different race, religion, and culture, tended to cling to their own institutions with a far greater tenacity than might have been shown by a free people with less sentimental attachment to ancient ways.[1] Moreover, there was no sovereign Russian power with sufficient authority to alter these customary rules; the supreme rulers were the Tartar Khans, and they were not in the least interested in reforming or improving the private law of their Russian subjects. The effect of the Mongol occupation on Russian private law was to crystallize and mummify it.

But on public law, on the manner and form of government, the Mongol occupation had some considerable effect. The Mongols owed absolute and unconditional obedience to their Great Khan, who was an autocratic ruler in the fullest sense of the term; he claimed and used the right of requiring whatever services he needed to be performed to be executed promptly and immediately by any subject, Mongol or Russian: this is the famous principle of universal compulsory service, which took deep root in Russia. In time, the Princes of Muscovy became delegates for the Great Khan as tax-gatherers and administrators, and so some of the powers of the Great Khan were delegated to the Princes of Muscovy, who applied the same principles to those under them; and, by exacting complete obedience from the general population, they were later able to lead them in revolt against the Mongols, finally asserting complete independence from them in 1480, thus establishing the Muscovy Tsardom, kernel of the Russian Empire.

Muscovy Tsardom, with its capital in Moscow, deliberately built on the ruins of the Mongol autocracy. The new local rulers behaved like

[1] Some may see here an analogy with the alleged failure of Hindu law to develop naturally by reason of British rule in India.

the alien governors they had served, without any constitutional limitations. The greatest of the Muscovy Tsars, Ivan the Terrible (1547–84),
declared: 'The rulers of Russia have not been accountable to anyone,
but have been free to reward or chastise their subjects. Russia has been,
and is, ruled in all things by the Tsar, not by nobles and magnates.'
However, Muscovy Tsardom was not only the inheritor of the Mongol
tradition of absolute autocracy; it inherited Byzantine traditions as well,
for, after the fall of Constantinople to the Turks in 1453, it soon became
the popular opinion that the Kingdom of Muscovy had succeeded
Byzantium as the leader of Orthodox Christianity, as Ivan the Great
(1462–1505), who had freed the country from the Tartars, had married
Sophia, the niece and heiress of Constantine Palaeologus, the last of the
Byzantine Emperors, who had perished in the capture of Constantinople. Under Byzantine law, Church and State had been virtually
identified; the Byzantine Emperor was the head of the Church, and
he appointed and dismissed its leading dignitaries. Moscow thus became the 'Third Rome', and this idea of Tsarist Russia as a missionary
state, whose purpose was the protection and expansion of Orthodox
Christianity, soon took deep root. The Tsar, the autocrat, was
chosen by God as the head of this missionary state, and resistance to
his will was therefore a sin as well as a crime, an idea which persisted
until 1917.[1]

Byzantine traditions certainly improved the legal system to some small
extent, but their chief effect was to add a spiritual sanction to the Tartar
temporal tradition of autocracy. The Church supported the State and
accepted the leadership of the Tsar, claiming only the right to express
disapproval. Whereas the Tartar Khans had been tolerant of all religions,
suppression of religious dissent now came to be regarded as a duty of
the State.

The first comprehensive attempt to codify the law came in 1649 with
the publication of the *Ulozheniye*. This was, in a sense, a great achievement, as it went beyond anything that had been attempted before;
but it was a barbarous effort, if compared with the laws then in force
in contemporary Western European states. The provisions of the
Ulozheniye were not arranged on any real systematic basis, and were
badly co-ordinated; the work, consisting of more than 900 articles, was
divided into twenty-five chapters as follows: 1. Sacrilege and Religious

---

[1] The *Svod Zakonov*, the Imperial Russian legal Code, article 1, says: 'The
All-Russian Emperor is an autocratic and unlimited monarch. Obedience to his
supreme power not only from fear but also from conscience is ordained by God
Himself. '

Revolts; 2. Honours due to the Tsar; 3. The Tsar's Household; 4. Forgery and Counterfeiting; 5. Jewellers, Goldsmiths and Moneyers; 6. Passports; 7. Military Service; 8. The Redemption of Prisoners; 9. Customs Duties; 10. Legal Procedure; 11. The Trial of Peasants; 12. The Trial of those in the service of the Patriarchs; 13. Prelates and Monks; 14. Oaths; 15. Trials (this chapter is concerned largely with preventing repeated trials); 16. Land Law; 17. Succession on Death; 18. Land Tax; 19. Peasants; 20. The Trial of Slaves; 21. Brigandage and Robbery; 22. Capital Offences; 23. The Feudal Militia; 24. The Cossacks; 25. Liquor Licensing. The *Ulozheniye* was still of considerable importance, and was regarded as the starting-point of Imperial Russian law, all previous law being termed 'ancient law'.

Nevertheless, it was not the intention to abolish all ancient customs, but rather to provide a general framework within which local customary law might still continue to operate. The jurisdiction of the Church courts was not interfered with, and the ecclesiastical tribunals continued to rely on their traditional sources of law. Thus the Patriarch Nikon, acting through the ecclesiastical court of Novgorod, in the *Case of the widow Marfitza* (1656), which concerned the extent to which a widow's dowry could be made liable for the payment of her late husband's debts, relied on the provisions of the *Ecloga*, promulgated about A.D. 740 by the Byzantine Emperor Leo the Isaurian in an attempt to bring the *Corpus Juris* of Justinian more into line with Christian principles.

The contents of the *Ulozheniye* moreover, were far from being entirely new; the work was an amalgam of rules drawn from the pre-Tartar *Russkaya Pravda*, and earlier partial codifications (such as the *Ulozheniye Zakon* of 1497, which dealt mainly with the jurisdiction of different courts and with criminal and civil procedure, of which a revised version, termed the *Sudebnik* was issued in 1554) from Roman and Byzantine law, and from the Lithuanian Code of 1588. The criminal provisions provided many very cruel punishments, and trials in many cases were to be by ordeal.

In time oaths came to be substituted for ordeals, and much of the procedure was for the purpose of determining which party should be entitled to take the oath which would settle the case. Judges were elected but received no salary, being dependent on fees paid by litigants, a system which inevitably led to much corruption.

The administrative apparatus of the Muscovy Tsars was chaotic in the extreme: there was the Duma, or Council of Nobles, which had a judicial committee for the hearing of important legal cases; under the

Duma there were some forty Special Boards (*Prikazi*), each of which had jurisdiction over some special subject, such as land, serfs, Siberia, cavalry, infantry, foreign trade, armed robbery. There was much over-lapping, and no separation at all of financial, administrative and judicial functions. The Governors of each Province, appointed and paid by the Tsar, were salaried officials, and their jurisdiction often overlapped that of the Special Boards.

Serfdom, which by the sixteenth century had all but died out in Western Europe, was artificially created in Russia at about the same time. There were various laws tying the peasant to the soil: each successive law was stricter than the last, culminating in the law of 1649 which forbade the peasants to leave their landlords' estates under any circumstances whatsoever. The peasants became the bound serfs of a nobility, itself bound to the Tsar. Muscovy Tsardom can be summed up by saying that it created economic feudalism, but without any sound system of feudal law.

Peter the Great (1689–1725), realizing the backwardness of Russia and wanting to catch up with Western Europe, tried to create a Western European system of government and administration. The capital was transferred from Moscow to the new city of St Petersburg. The old Duma was abolished, being replaced by a Ruling Senate (*Pravitels-tvuyushchi Senat*); the Church was separated from the State, the patri-archate was abolished, and the Church became governed by a Holy Synod under a lay official. The forty-odd Special Boards were replaced by twelve 'Colleges', each having a clearly defined jurisdiction. And, most important of all in view of subsequent developments, in 1722 Peter created the Procuracy under a Procurator-General, its function being to supervise the legality of the acts of all other governmental bepartments, and generally to act as the 'eye of the sovereign'.

But the principle of autocracy remained, and floods of decrees and enactments, often contradictory, emanated from the Tsar and his authorities, as there were no general principles, and no systematic study or attempt to distinguish different branches of law. Attempts were made to tidy up the confusion; three commissions were appointed in 1700, 1714 and 1719, with the task of codifying the law, but they all failed. A number of reforms were introduced into the legal system, but none ever overcame the basic defects of lack of trained lawyers and judges and proper study and arrangement of the existing laws. Peter the Great reformed much in Russia, but the judicial system remained in much the same chaos at the end of his reign as at the beginning.

Throughout the eighteenth century numerous other Codification

Commissions were appointed with the object of codifying and reforming the law, but very little came of any of them. One development, however, is important in view of later Soviet attitudes: large-scale industrial undertakings were often started by the Tsar as state concerns, and once established were then either sold or leased to private individuals for exploitation. Large-scale industry in Russia was state-organized from the first, and did not develop from privately owned small-scale industries, as in many other countries. This is important because by 1917 there was a long tradition of state ownership of industry in Russia: and the revolutionaries of 1917, in expropriating the capitalists who exploited these enterprises for their own benefit, were often only restoring to the State what had originally been State property.

The system established by Peter the Great was modified in certain particulars by Catherine the Great (1762–96) but remained the same in its essentials until the Judicial Reform of 1864. There was a great variety of courts, and in particular, there were different courts for different classes of the population, while the punishments inflicted for criminal offences varied according to the social class of the offender. Most of the judges were nominally elected, but by the early nineteenth century many of them were in fact appointees of the Provincial Governors. Trials took place in secret, on the basis of the evidence collected by the police and reduced by them to writing. The trial court in a criminal case would not see the accused, and its functions were limited to ensuring that certain formal evidential requirements were complied with; the best evidence was the confession of the accused, but the evidence of two eye-witnesses was sufficient. In case of a conflict of evidence the testimony of a man was preferred to that of a woman, that of a nobleman to that of a commoner, that of an educated man to that of an uneducated man, and that of a priest to that of a layman. Despite the fact that the procedure was almost entirely written, many of the judges were illiterate, and the law itself provided that where all the judges of a court were illiterate the decision was to be written down by the court secretary. Corruption was widespread and taken for granted, and court proceedings could be dragged out indefinitely. The administration of justice was regarded simply as a matter of administration, and interference from the executive was common. Professor Spasovich, speaking to the St Petersburg Bar in 1876 about the period before the Judicial Reform of 1864, said:

If one had asked us at that time: what is a court? where is it? we would have been put into an embarrassing position and would not have known what to say. A real law court did not exist, but only an almighty and all-powerful police. . . . The settlement of the case of the accused began and ended with the police. In the meantime, something resembling court proceedings took place only *pro forma*, which consisted in the police records concerning the accused being put on the court table covered with a red or green cloth around which men in gold-embroidered uniforms were seated. These men, without having questioned or seen the accused, would deliberate among themselves about something, decide something, and then send the records back to the police again. It was a court only in name. . . .[1]

The appellate jurisdictions were little better. Sometimes they were so dilatory in rendering decisions that officers of the gendarmerie would be sent to them with instructions not to leave until all appeals pending had been decided. On one occasion it is related that a gendarme arrived at a provincial court of appeal with such instructions, and the president of the court immediately sent for the files of all pending appeals. He distributed the files alternately to the right and left sides of his desk, saying as he did 'Upheld' or 'Reversed' until all the files had been gone through in this way. The gendarme then left to report that all cases pending in the court had now been decided.

However, the Napoleonic Wars brought Russia into closer contact with Western Europe; Napoleon's armies had reached Moscow, and later the Tsar's armies reached Vienna and Paris. By the eighteen-thirties demands for westernization were increasing, and the decade is notable for some achievements in the legal sphere.

All legislation promulgated since the *Ulozheniye* of 1649 was collected and published in 1830 under the title of *Polnoye Sobraniye Zakonov Rossiiskoi Imperii* (Complete Collection of the Laws of the Russian Empire), containing all enactments, starting with the *Ulozheniye* of 1649, up to December 1825; there were 30,920 of them, and they were set out in chronological order in forty-six large volumes;[2] from this material, those laws which were still in force were arranged and classified according to subject-matter in the *Svod Zakonov Rossiiskoi Imperii* (Code of Laws of the Russian Empire), which was published in fifteen volumes containing 42,000 articles in 1833, and confirmed by Tsar Nicholas I. These achievements were due largely to the labours of the

[1] Kucherov, *Courts, Lawyers and Trials under the last three Tsars*, p. 9.
[2] Forty volumes of enactments and six of indices, schedules, tariffs, scales, plans, etc. A second series, in fifty volumes, published later, contained all the enactments promulgated between 1825 and 1881.

great Russian statesman and jurist Speranski. Despite Speranski's own liberal leanings, the *Svod Zakonov* contained little that could be regarded as liberal or progressive, the Tsar having made it clear that the purpose of codification was not to introduce new laws but to put the old laws on a more secure foundation. Only the tenth volume, which dealt with private law, showed some foreign influence, that of the Code Napoleon, and this affected classification more than the actual substance of the rules.[1] The eleventh volume dealt with commercial law, and it was therefore volumes ten and eleven that were of most interest to comparative lawyers outside Russia, and from which foreign views about Imperial Russian law were largely derived. Most of the remaining volumes were concerned with what we should call administrative law, which was remarkable for its bulk and complexity, but was unlikely to excite much interest abroad.

By the end of the eighteen-thirties some members of the Russian intelligentsia were to be found studying in the great Law Faculties of Western Europe, and some of them published books on legal matters on their return. There was still no bar in the strict sense of the term, for paid advocates were not allowed in court, but there were the makings of one, for law was now beginning to be studied systematically, and in view of the increased contact with the west by members of the intelligentsia it was clear that the old system of judicature could not long survive.

The Judicial Reforms of 1864 were preceded by the emancipation of the serfs in 1861. The land formerly worked by the serfs was transferred to the *mir*, the local communal organization of the peasants, and the *mir* distributed this land at intervals to the various households in the community. The *mir* itself was responsible for collecting the heavy taxes imposed on the former serfs to enable compensation to be paid to the landlords, who retained a portion of the land themselves, and who henceforth were obliged to work it by employing hired labourers or landless peasants. Some scholars see the Soviet collective farm as a development of the *mir* and others deny any connection, but at least it may be said that the absence of any strong and long-standing tradition of peasant ownership of the land in many parts of Russia meant that collectivization of the land by the Soviet government, although it met with considerable peasant opposition, was not such a breach with previous tradition as such a step would be in a country like France.

[1] The *Svod Zakonov* was revised from time to time to incorporate new laws. The last edition was in 1893, and was in sixteen volumes. It was reprinted with some alterations in 1914.

c

The main features of the Judicial Reforms of 1864 were:

1. The institution of a regular system of courts, with rights of appeal, staffed by judges independent of the executive and irremovable except for proved misconduct or inefficiency.

2. The abolition of the old class courts, except that the *volost* courts for the peasants were retained.

3. The institution of Justices of the Peace on the English model to deal with minor offences; they were nominated by the newly established local authorities (*Zemstvo*).

4. All trials were to be held in public.

5. Proceedings were to be oral, written procedure being reduced to a minimum. (This reform also was inspired by English practice.)

6. Trial was to be by jury in all serious criminal cases (again, as in England).

7. Two Courts of Cassation (review) were established in the Senate, one for criminal and one for civil cases, above the courts of appeal. (These were modelled on the French *Cour de Cassation*.)

8. A professional Bar was established, and all litigants and accused persons became entitled to be represented by a professional lawyer.

9. Much of the French system of criminal procedure was adopted, especially with regard to pre-trial procedure. (Some of this has survived: Soviet criminal procedure still bears many resemblances to the French system.)

The reforms of the eighteen-sixties could have given Russia a decent and stable system of judicature, because the personnel necessary for its functioning now existed in the foreign-educated intellectuals who had studied in the great law schools of the continent, and the graduates of the Law Faculties which had now been established in the Russian Universities. Their quality was very high; Russia produced a great number of distinguished advocates, judges and jurists during the latter part of the nineteenth century. Almost without exception they endeavoured to apply the law fairly and impartially, in the spirit of Western European justice. Perhaps it is an indirect tribute to them that the years from 1864 to the end of the century saw, not an expansion and extension of the new system, but its continual restriction; more and more limitations and exceptions to its basic principles were introduced.

Even in the original form, there were still some objectionable features, which liberal elements hoped would later be abolished. For example, civil servants and priests accused of certain offences were tried, not by the ordinary criminal courts with trial by jury, but by 'courts with class representatives'. Such a court was constituted by a bench of four official judges and three class representatives, one each from the nobility, the town bourgeoisie, and the peasantry; the bench as a whole decided all questions of law, fact and sentence. Later on 'courts with class representatives', instead of being abolished, came to hear other criminal cases, as trial by jury was withdrawn in respect of an ever-increasing number of offences; the independence of the judges was destroyed as the Minister of Justice was given power to dismiss judges at will; the Minister of Justice and Provincial Governors were also given powers to order trials *in camera* in an ever-increasing number of specified cases. In more and more cases, civilians became triable by courts-martial, and smaller criminal cases could be transferred from the ordinary courts to various administrative authorities. The powers of the justices of the peace and those of the *zemstvo* were restricted. Administrative exile could be imposed by administrative authorities on persons who were suspected of treasonable or seditious activities, but who could not be brought to trial for lack of proof. This procedure was used against the Bolsheviks.

By 1900 the Judicial Reforms still prevailed in principle, but in fact their provisions were largely eroded by the large mass of exceptions. There was no trial by jury in any case where an offence appeared to have been motivated by political considerations, after the acquittal by a jury of Vera Zasulich in 1878 on a charge of having attempted to murder the Governor of St Petersburg. Political prosecutions were brought instead before 'courts with class representatives' or courts-martial.

However, even in non-political cases the authorities attempted to use the proceedings for political purposes, and an account will now be given of the *Beilis Case* (1913) for the purpose of showing the difficulties faced by honest officials and lawyers when political considerations intervened. The *Beilis Case* was perhaps the worst example of an official attempt to pervert the course of justice, but it was far from being an isolated exception.

The body of a boy aged thirteen, Andrei Yushchinski, was discovered on the outskirts of Kiev on 20 March 1911. There were seventeen wounds and pricks on the body, which had lost two-thirds of its blood, but there were no traces of blood near the body, which suggested that the murder had been committed elsewhere and the body dumped where it was found. The investigator charged with the preliminary investigation, Fenenko, at first formed the opinion that the boy had been killed by members of his mother's family in order to obtain pro-perty bequeathed him by his father (the boy was illegitimate), though he later came to the correct conclusion that he had been murdered by a gang of criminals of whose activities he had become aware and who feared denunciation. However, the Minister of Justice, Shcheglovitov, took an interest in the affair, and Fenenko was ordered to arrest Beilis, a Jew employed at a Jewish-owned factory near the place where the body had been discovered. At first he refused, on the ground that there was no evidence against Beilis, but on it being made clear that his resignation would be demanded if he continued his refusal, he complied, believing that Beilis would soon be released for lack of evidence. This did not occur, and when Fenenko terminated the preliminary investigation in January 1912, an indictment against Beilis was confirmed. By this time, however, clear evidence of the guilt of the real culprits had been published in the newspapers; Fenenko's evident lack of enthusiasm for the proceedings resulted in his being given two months' special leave, and the case was sent back for new preliminary investigation by an investigator appointed directly by the Minister of Justice. A new indictment was prepared which charged Beilis with having killed the boy 'with premeditation after previous agreement with persons unknown motivated by religious fanaticism for ritual purposes'. The court accepted the indictment by a 3–2 majority, the president being among the dissenting minority.[1] It appears that the majority were less concerned with the fact that there was little evidence against Beilis than with the fact that he had been in prison for nearly two years already and they felt that he ought therefore to be tried.

The direct evidence against Beilis was that of drunkards and criminals, but the main concern of the prosecution, whose case was that the boy had been murdered by Jews who needed the blood of a Christian child for purposes of religious ritual, was to find some kind of evidence to support this absurd mediaeval legend (belief in which had in fact been denounced by Tsar Alexander I in a *ukaz* of 6 March 1817). Despite orders to all the prosecutors of Russia to find and forward evidence to the Ministry of Justice, the Minister of Justice found to his consternation that not a single Orthodox priest or scholar would come forward to testify as to his belief that Jews in their religious rituals used the blood of Christian children, and he was reduced to calling a Roman Catholic priest,[2] Pranaitis, who had taught Hebrew in St Petersburg but who had been sent to Turkestan by his ecclesiastical superiors

[1] Acceptance of the indictment means that the court considers that there is sufficient *prima facie* evidence against the accused to justify a trial: compare the Soviet procedure at p. 119 *post*.
[2] This was a severe blow, owing to the unpopularity of Roman Catholicism in Russia. A common Orthodox religious device shows the Pope, the Devil and the Turk united in an attempt to wreck the ship of Orthodoxy.

as a punishment for bad behaviour. The trial, which lasted for a month in the autumn of 1913, revolved round the question of ritual murder, and the evidence of Pranaitis was crucial.

Pranaitis could of course produce nothing from the Torah or the Talmud to support his charges, but he relied on the Zohar, a mystical work which enjoyed a certain vogue among the Jews during the late Middle Ages but which is now quite unknown to the vast majority of them, and few even of those who are acquainted with its contents would accept them without reservation. It certainly does not advocate the ritual murder of Christian children; but by using its methods of interpreting scripture,[1] the latter can be made to say whatever is required. Yet when Beilis' chief counsel, Gruzenberg, himself a Jew, attempted to reply, he was interrupted by the presiding judge who reminded him that it was not the Jewish religion but Beilis who was on trial. Nevertheless Beilis was acquitted by the jury despite a far from impartial summing-up by the presiding judge.

But this was not the end of the affair. Vipper, the prosecutor, was promoted, and Gruzenberg was disciplined for having referred to the prosecution witnesses as 'dishonest'. Vera Cheberyak, one of the criminal gang which appeared from the evidence to be responsible for the murder, brought a libel action against the writer of a letter to a newspaper which accused her of the murder and lost it, Fenenko giving evidence for the defendant and stating that he had no doubt about her guilt. Vindictive action was taken by the authorities against various people who had assisted in the defence of Beilis by collecting the evidence against Vera Cheberyak. One was prosecuted for having destroyed papers relating to a tax payment of sixteen kopecks, though he was acquitted, his wife having found the papers in an old trunk at the last moment. Another was less lucky; he got a year's imprisonment for having remained seated when a band playing in a park struck up the national anthem.

[1] Its methods are 1. *gematria*, based on the numerical values of the letters of the Hebrew alphabet. A word having a given value may be regarded as equivalent to or explained by another having the same value, e.g. *achad*, unity, is the same as or is explained by *ahebah*, love, for they both have the same numerical value, thirteen: 2. *notaricon*, according to which a word formed from the initial letters of the words of a sentence explains that sentence, e.g. the initial letters of the words 'Who shall go up for us to heaven'? (Deuteronomy xxx. 12) in Hebrew give the Hebrew word for circumcision; circumcision is therefore a way to heaven: 3. *temura*, an elaborate system of codes in which each letter stands for another letter. It is clear that if such exegetical methods are employed virtually anything may be proved from scripture.

The General Assembly of the St Petersburg Bar protested against the conduct of the prosecution in the Beilis case, and twenty-five lawyers[1] who had subscribed to this protest were charged with having disseminated abusive writings offensive to highly placed official persons, and sentenced to short terms of imprisonment; one of these lawyers was Kerenski, later the head of the Provisional Government.

The *Beilis Case* is cited here because it illustrates the tensions during the last years of Tsardom which often made the impartial administration of justice impossible.[2] The period between 1900 and 1917 was one when blind reaction alternated rapidly with desperate attempts to patch up a machine which was clearly breaking down: and it broke down beyond repair in 1917.

This brief historical introduction has been given because it is important to remember that in considering Soviet law in relation to the Russian legal heritage, we must take into account, not merely the system as it was in the last days of Tsardom, or even as it was immediately after the Great Reforms, but rather the effects of the whole historical development on the Russian people.

Though scholars dispute the extent to which pre-revolutionary legal traditions have influenced the Soviet legal system, the following points should be borne in mind:

1. The Soviet Government, like former Russian Governments, is still confronted with the problems that arise from the enormous size of the country, with its different ethnic and linguistic groups, and in its earlier years it had to cope with the general backwardness, illiteracy and poverty of a considerable portion of the population.

2. Russian political life has always admitted an organized 'power behind the throne'. The relationship between the Government of the USSR and the Communist Party of the Soviet Union, which sometimes puzzles western students, is not vastly different from that which prevailed between the Tsarist Government and the Orthodox Church in former times, and so is in accordance with Russian tradition.

---

[1] Over two hundred members had attended the meeting, but eighty-six were selected for trial, and only twenty-five ultimately prosecuted.

[2] Some may be interested in the later fate of some of the *dramatis personae*. Vera Cheberyak was shot by Soviet troops without trial immediately after the occupation of Kiev by the Red Army. Vipper was tried by the Moscow Revolutionary Tribunal in September 1919 and sent to a concentration camp. Gruzenburg became a member of the Ruling Senate (the highest court of appeal) under the Provisional Government; after the October Revolution he left Russia and died in France in 1940; a few hours before his death he received a blood transfusion from a Christian friend and commented 'Now, how can one assert that Jews do not use Christian blood?'

3. As a result, political dissenters in modern times suffer much of the obloquy and distrust formerly visited on religious dissenters. Free discussion of religious or political differences, especially when these are fundamental, has always been regarded as extremely dangerous in Russia.

4. On the other hand, the old tradition of equating criminal offences with sins has made for a highly subjectivist approach to criminal law: the whole man and his antecedents are being judged, not the particular infraction of the Criminal Code for which he has been indicted. This attitude, highly advantageous for the accused person who may be able to plead poverty or some other mitigating circumstance, operated harshly, in the early years of the Soviet régime, on parties whose 'class origin' rendered them suspect.

5. In Tsarist times, the 'spirit of legality' or the 'rule of law' was notoriously lacking, and there was little principle behind the vast mass of Codes, statutes, orders, and other enactments, which, moreover, were sometimes contradictory and were often not observed in practice, as there was no regular repeal of obsolete enactments. There was thus comparatively little respect for the law, for it could hardly command any. To some extent, this attitude of indifference to the law still survives, and inculcating a respect for 'revolutionary legality' (i.e. for the new Soviet laws) has been a major problem in the USSR. There was no traditional respect for the law such as any Western European government can take for granted.

6. The idea of 'equality before the law' scarcely existed in Tsarist Russia. Traditionally there had been different courts for different classes of the population, with different procedures and penalties. Even after the Judicial Reform of 1864, which was largely inspired by foreign models, the *volost* courts for the peasants remained, and in practice the nobility and the clergy were exempt from the competence of the ordinary courts. Moreover, the four classes; nobles, clergy, merchants, and peasants, had their own special rights and duties. This had an enormous effect on Russian Marxist thought and on Soviet legal development, for the industrial workers did not fit into the traditional classification, so that it appeared that the law made no direct provision for them. This was not quite true because there was some Industrial or Labour Law in force, at any rate after about 1880, but it did not fit in very well with traditional concepts. Moreover, the word *grazhdanski* (cp. German *bürgerlich*) can be translated either 'bourgeois' or 'civil' and this led to the disrepute of 'civil' law in the early days of the Soviet régime, as the term suggested 'bourgeois law' or the law of the former burgher class. Consequently,

early Soviet legislation tended to be penal in character, civil law being neglected and despised. Another factor which doubtless contributed both to the general lack of respect for the law and to the idea that the law was necessarily 'class law' directed against the mass of the people was the general rule (there were some exceptions) in Tsarist times that, where there was a direct conflict of evidence given in court, the more educated witness had to be believed.

7. The tradition of universal compulsory service for the State originated during the period of Mongol domination and was continued by the Muscovy and Petersburg Tsars for their own purposes. The extent to which the modern Soviet citizen is 'regimented' has been somewhat exaggerated in the West, but, even in so far as it is true, it is part of the Russian tradition and not a specific feature of the Soviet system.

8. Offences, or alleged offences, against the security of the State, have always come under the supervision of a special government department in Russia: Soviet practice does not differ radically in this matter from former Russian traditions. Equally, the jurisdiction of courts-martial over civilians in certain matters affecting the armed forces is not an innovation of the Soviet régime.

9. The Procuracy, about which more will be said later,[1] deserves note in this connection. While this institution exists in most continental countries (not to mention the procurator-fiscal in Scotland) and did in Tsarist Russia, the Soviet Procuracy has very distinct features when compared, say, with the French Procuracy. Nor is the Soviet Procurator the equivalent of the Russian Procurator of the early twentieth century: he is the lineal descendant of the Procurators of Peter the Great.

THE SOVIET LEGAL SYSTEM 1917–1953

The history of the Soviet Legal System falls conveniently into four periods: 1. War Communism, from 1917 to 1920; 2. the New Economic Policy, from 1921 to 1927; 3. Stalinism, from 1928 to 1953; this period, now commonly termed in the Soviet Union 'the period of the cult of personality', is divided by most Soviet writers into two sub-periods, the first, from 1928 to 1936, covering the first two Five Year Plans, being termed 'the period of the construction of socialism'; and the second, from 1936 to the death of Stalin in March 1953, 'the period of the consolidation of socialism', or the period of stability; 4. the period since the death of Stalin, commonly termed in the Soviet Union the period of the construction of communism.

[1] See p. 132 post.

THE PERIOD OF WAR COMMUNISM

The Imperial Russian Government fell as a result of the 'February Revolution' of February 1917, and was replaced by the Provisional Government of Prince Lvov and Kerenski. The Provisional Government's powers were much weakened by the existence of local Soviets (councils) of workers' and soldiers' deputies in many areas and their delegates in the capital; these often exercised *de facto* control of the situation, and by the October Revolution of 25 October/7 November 1917,[1] under the slogan, 'All power to the Soviets' they swept away the Provisional Government. But although the Bolshevik Party (at first in an uneasy alliance with the Social-Revolutionary Party) had seized power in Petrograd (St Petersburg) it was one thing to take control in the capital and another to secure power throughout the country.

Risings took place and before long the new Soviet Government of Russia became involved in a full-scale civil war; the opponents of the new régime, the Whites, were often aided by foreign Governments, for many foreign states were only too keen to see the new Soviet Government of Russia overthrown. It may be noted, for the fact is sometimes ignored, that although many persons of loyalist and patriotic sentiments served in the White armies, none of these armies had the restoration of Tsardom on its political agenda. The Civil War and the War of Intervention lasted until the end of 1920, and many of the measures taken by the communist authorities during this period were dictated as much by military necessity as by political conviction. Frequently, however, military necessity and political conviction coincided: a country at war has to obtain direct control over the production and use of commodities, to ensure supplies, and it often has to do this by means that would be resented in ordinary peace-time conditions. Nevertheless the public control of national resources was an important item in the Bolshevik political programme, and the nationalization measures introduced by the Soviet Government during the earliest period of the Soviet régime could be represented to its supporters at home and abroad as important measures for the establishment of a communist state. The new Soviet Republic was most anxious to secure the support of the

[1] Where two dates are given, as here, the first is the date according to the Julian Calendar formerly in use in Russia, the second is the date according to the Gregorian Calendar generally used elsewhere. The Gregorian Calendar was adopted in Russia by a decree of 26 January/8 February 1918, which provided that the day after 31 January (according to the Julian Calendar) should be 14 February. It is for this reason that the anniversary of the 'October Revolution' is celebrated each year in the USSR on 7 November.

working classes in other countries, and some of its measures had a propagandist significance rather than a strictly practical one, for the Government often lacked the means and resources to enforce its own measures. The period was one of great confusion, of the breakdown of industry and commerce, and regular communications between the capital and the rest of the country were often lacking.

a. Constitutional Provisions

The Congress of Soviets, consisting of representatives of local workers' and soldiers' Soviets, became, as a result of the Revolution, the supreme organ of state power, and between its meetings its powers were vested in a Central Executive Committee of 200 members. The actual government, consisting of the Council of People's Commissars, was responsible to this Central Executive Committee. However, there was little distinction in law or practice between legislative enactments, administrative regulations, individual decisions, and policy declarations, and whether a particular law or decree emanated from the Congress of Soviets, the Central Executive Committee, the Council of People's Commissars, or one of the eighteen individual People's Commissars, seems to have been purely a matter of chance; however, as the doctrine of the separation of powers, under which legislative, executive and judicial powers should be sharply distinguished, was expressly rejected, this was not a serious matter to the new Government. Moreover, relations between the Government and the Communist Party were very close; many laws and decrees were signed by representatives of both party and government.

On 10 July 1918 the All-Russian Congress of Soviets adopted the first post-revolution Constitution, the Constitution of the Russian Socialist Federative Soviet Republic.

This Constitution, consisting of 90 articles, was divided into six parts: 1. the Declaration of the Rights of the Labouring and Exploited People (which had already been adopted by the All-Russian Central Executive Committee in January 1918); 2. General Constitutional Provisions; 3. The Organization of the Soviet State; 4. Active and Passive Electoral Rights; 5. Budgetary Provisions; 6. Coat of Arms and Flag.

The first part was largely of a propagandist nature; the second part confirmed the position of the Congress of Soviets, the All-Russian Central Executive Committee, and the Council of People's Commissars as outlined above. By an amendment of December 1919 it was laid down that the All-Russian Central Executive Committee should meet every two months, and that in the intervals between its sessions its main powers were to be exercised by a Praesidium. The powers of the Praesidium of the All-Russian Central Executive Committee were further enlarged by a constitutional amendment of 29 December 1920, which also extended the rights of the Council of People's Commissars, but which restricted the right of individual People's Commissariats to issue orders and decrees; in effect, they were restricted to matters which fell strictly within their competence.

As far as electoral rights were concerned, the Constitution brought to Russia principles such as the right of all persons to vote and be elected to the Soviets irrespective of race or ethnic origin, sex, education, or religious belief. Some categories of the population, however, were disfranchised, namely: persons who employed hired labour for the purpose of profit-making, persons who lived on unearned income, private merchants and commercial agents, monks and ministers of religion, former members of the Tsarist police, gendarmerie and secret police, and members of the family of the former ruling dynasty. Moreover the Constitution provided for weighting in favour of the urban working class; representatives to the Congress of Soviets were elected by town Soviets on the basis of one delegate per 25,000 electors, and by provincial (*gubernia*) Soviets on the basis of one delegate per 125,000 inhabitants.[1] Only elections to town and village Soviets were direct; the Village Soviets sent representatives to *gubernia* Soviets. This system of indirect election (by local and provincial Soviets) and of weighting between different classes of the population seems invidious, but it had been traditional in Russia, and was far more egalitarian than any electoral system which had ever prevailed in Russia before; under the Empire, the Duma (Lower House) consisted of representatives chosen by electoral colleges in each province (*gubernia*); each electoral college consisted of three electoral assemblies, the first of landowners, the larger landowners attending in person, the smaller landowners being represented by elected delegates; the second, of urban taxpayers, representation being weighted in favour of the wealthier ones; the third, of peasants elected by *volost* assemblies. The whole system was weighted in favour of the wealthier town-dwellers and the large landed proprietors, and also in favour of the Russian population as distinct from the subject nationalities.[2]

As regards the non-Russian nationalities, the Constitution provided

[1] The significance of the distinction between 'electors' and 'inhabitants' is not obvious, but it would slightly reduce the effect of the weighting.

[2] 'Nationality' in Russian usage refers not to state citizenship but to membership of an officially recognized ethnic group.

that in regions with a specific mode of life and specific national composition the Soviets could form autonomous regional units joining the federation. It also declared illegal the granting of privileges to citizens by virtue of nationality or race, together with any restriction of rights of national minorities.

Higher local authorities were the *gubernia* congresses of Soviets which had the power to annul decisions passed by lower Soviets within its area.

b. The Land

On the day following their seizure of power the Congress of Soviets enacted the Decree on the Land of 26 October/8 November 1917. The Decree provided that all large estates and their stocks were expropriated, but that the position of ordinary peasant holdings (i.e. the holdings of peasants who worked the land with their own families and did not employ outside hired labour) was not affected. The land expropriated was to be disposed of by local Soviets in accordance with the terms of the 'Peasants' Instruction' (*Nakaz*) of 19 August 1917; this document formulated the demands of the Social-Revolutionary Party, largely a peasant party, the left-wing elements of which had collaborated with the Bolshevik Party in making the Revolution. The Peasants' Instruction had demanded the expropriation, not only of the larger estates, but also of all farms worked with hired labour, the expropriated lands to be distributed to landless peasants and to established peasant communities (*obshchina*) for periodical distribution according to need and traditional peasant custom. In fact in many areas it was not only the large estates which were expropriated. The peasant was to retain as his own any land held by him before the distribution.

The new order was confirmed by the Land Law of 19 February 1918, which elaborated the principles of the earlier Decree. A distinction was drawn between ownership of land, which was abolished unconditionally and without compensation, and the right of land user which, where agricultural land was concerned, vested in those actually engaged in working the land. The right of ownership in houses (as distinct from ownership of the land itself) was not expressly confirmed, but seems to have been recognized by implication, for there was certainly no intention of expropriating owner-occupiers. The Land Law of 19 February 1918 was passed while the left-wing elements of the Social-Revolutionary Party were still in coalition with the Bolsheviks, and to a large extent fulfilled the programme of the Social-Revolutionary Party.

c. Industry and Commerce

As the whole Bolshevik position was based on opposition to capitalist control of the means of production, it is not surprising that within three weeks of taking power the new government passed the Decree on Workers' Control of 16/29 November 1917. This enactment did not directly expropriate the private capitalist, but in the administration of his factory he was obliged to carry out the orders of the local representatives of Workers' Control (usually in fact shop stewards in the factory) subject only to a period of three days' grace in order to appeal to a higher authority of Workers' Control, that is, to the economic affairs department of the local Soviet. But few owners were prepared to continue under such conditions, and there followed numerous decrees expropriating either individual factories or entire businesses; such factories and businesses became state property and passed into the control of the Supreme Economic Council, which was a government department and regarded as a People's Commissariat, although it had a different name. In expropriated enterprises the existing staffs were kept on, now in the position of civil servants. The banks were nationalized by a decree of 14/27 December 1917, and banking was declared a state monopoly. However, expropriation and nationalization during 1918 seems to have been governed as much by the needs of the civil war (including the need to honour the ration-books) as by political ideology, for the match, candle, rice, coffee and pepper trades were nationalized on 7 March 1918, to be followed by sugar on 2 May, but the oil industry only on 20 July. Foreign trade became a state monopoly on 23 April 1918. Whether 'Workers' Control' was originally seen as a transitional stage to full nationalization, as is usually argued by Soviet writers, or whether its failure necessitated full nationalization is a point much debated by scholars.

The Tsarist National Debt was repudiated on 16/29 December 1917, though compensation was provided for those whose holdings did not exceed 10,000 roubles; however, inflation soon rendered the compensation illusory.

d. Ordinary Civil Law

Private property in urban buildings (other than industrial buildings) was declared to be abolished on 20 August 1918, though some exceptions were allowed. In towns with more than 10,000 inhabitants the houses passed to the local Soviet where their value exceeded a minimum fixed by the local Soviet itself. The enactment seems to have been intended not so much to deprive the owner-occupier of his dwelling as to pass entitlement to rent from private landlords to the local Soviets, for in small towns a much larger proportion of the houses were owner-occupied; in large towns, most were owned by private landlords. In fact many owner-occupied houses were taken over by the local Soviets. There were some limited provisions for compensation to owners and mortgagees up to 10,000 roubles, but in view of the inflation the right to rent under older agreements was becoming virtually meaningless and the inflation soon swallowed up the value of the compensation payable.

How ordinary civil cases were disposed of by the courts will be considered later, but in two fields comprehensive Codes were enacted, the Family Code of 17 October 1918, and the Labour Code of 28 November 1918. (Family Law and Labour Law are regarded by Soviet lawyers as separate branches of law distinct from Civil Law.)

The Family Code of 1918 brought Family Law into line with ideas generally accepted by liberal thinkers. Imperial Russian family law was based largely on patriarchal conceptions, with the wife subjected in many matters to her husband, and with marriage and divorce governed by the rules of the religious denomination of the parties.[1] Under the Code of 1918 divorce was a simple and automatic matter if demanded by both parties, but a judicial decree was required when it was demanded by one party only. Marriage had no effect on property relations, and the equality of the sexes was guaranteed. Neither parent had any superiority with regard to the custody and upbringing of children, and disputes between the parents were to be decided by the court.

The Labour Code of 1918 dealt in detail with the contract of greatest importance to the ordinary city worker, namely the contract of employment; it regulated such matters as minimum wages, hours of employment, holidays, as well as fines and labour discipline. To some extent the Labour Code gave effect to the egalitarian principles that were popular at that period, but the ideal of complete equality in wages was never achieved.

e. The Judicial System

The First Decree on the Courts, of 22 November/5 December 1917, abolished the general court system of the Tsarist régime together with the commercial courts of Petrograd, Moscow and Odessa, and sus-

---

[1] The ecclesiastical court of the Russian Orthodox Church, the church of the great majority of the population, granted divorces in certain cases such as adultery, but the procedure was slow and costly, as the readers of Tolstoy's *Anna Karenina* may remember. For Roman Catholics there was, of course, no possibility of divorce.

pended the activities of the courts of the justices of the peace which were still functioning in many areas. It declared that a new system of courts would be introduced subsequently, and in the place of the courts of the justices of the peace it substituted a new court, composed of one full-time professional judge, sitting with two lay assessors, to hear civil cases where not more than 3,000 roubles was in issue, and criminal cases where the maximum punishment did not exceed two years' imprisonment. Some difficulty was found in setting up these courts immediately, but they were operating in over two-thirds of the area controlled by the new government by July 1918. Local Soviets in some areas had already established revolutionary tribunals, and these were formally sanctioned by the First Decree on the Courts, though for dealing with counter-revolutionary cases only. At this period civil cases were few and unimportant; the first civil case which came before the new court in Moscow, which opened its doors on 16/29 December 1917, concerned the ownership of a samovar. It was felt that for many types of civil dispute, state intervention would not be necessary, and the First Decree on the Courts stated that rules concerning arbitration would be issued shortly; these followed on 16 February 1918. The First Decree on the Courts also abolished the old professional bar, and the system of procurators and court investigators, but the clerical personnel of the old agencies were instructed to remain at their posts under the supervision of special commissars who were to take possession of their files.

The First Decree on the Courts instructed the courts to use as a guide the laws of former régimes to the extent that they had not been revoked by the Revolution and were not contrary to revolutionary conscience.

The Second Decree on the Courts, of 15 February 1918, made provision for District People's Courts for the purpose of trying those more serious civil and criminal cases which were outside the competence of the new courts established by the First Decree on the Courts, and also for the purpose of hearing cases which had been pending in the old courts when they were abolished. In order to decide these latter cases properly, it was necessary to have people acquainted with the law of the old régime as judges, and the Second Decree on the Courts expressly provided that judges of the old courts might be nominated to staff the District People's Courts. Many of them were so appointed, and this led to complaints from militant communists in various areas. The Second Decree provided for a system of appeals, but the appellate courts in fact were never set up. In view of the fact that this Second Decree made certain concessions to the old régime, it should be noted that the People's Commissar for Justice from the middle of December 1917 to 4 March

1918 was Steinberg, who was not a communist but a member of the left wing of the Social-Revolutionary Party, which at that time was participating in a coalition government with the Bolsheviks. The Second Decree instructed the District People's Courts to be guided by the civil and criminal laws hitherto existing, to the extent that they had not been revoked by Decrees of the Central Executive Committee and the Council of People's Commissars and did not conflict with socialist justice; but any departure from pre-revolutionary law was to be accompanied by a reasoned opinion. As far as criminal law was concerned, it seems that, although in the main the old substantive law was applied, the District Courts did not abide by the rules concerning punishment laid down in the Imperial Criminal Code; offences against property were treated very leniently, but illegal distillers, who were commonly speculators using much-needed grain for making alcohol, received sentences more severe than the comparatively mild penalties provided for violating the Imperial Excise Tax laws. The District Courts were authorized to apply the Imperial Codes of Civil and Criminal Procedure, but were to reject arguments based on purely procedural points, and were free to admit or reject any evidence they considered relevant.

The Third Decree on the Courts, of 20 July 1918, enlarged the jurisdiction of the People's Courts and thereby diminished that of the District Courts; the People's Courts were now given jurisdiction in civil cases up to 10,000 roubles and criminal cases which either 'law (i.e. the old Imperial law) or 'socialist conscience' regarded as punishable by up to five years' imprisonment. The District Courts' criminal jurisdiction was stated to include cases of attempted murder, rape, robbery, banditry, counterfeiting, bribery and speculation (black marketeering); the last two cases had previously been within the exclusive jurisdiction of the Revolutionary Tribunals.

Further changes were made by the Law on the People's Courts of 30 November 1918. This enactment made the People's Courts the sole courts in Russia with the exception of the Revolutionary Tribunals, which dealt with cases of counter-revolutionary activity and sabotage, and the District Courts were ordered to cease their activities by 1 February 1919 at the latest. The most important feature of this law is that it expressly forbade any reference to laws enacted before the Revolution; the judges were to apply the laws of the new government, and the socialist concept of justice. Another original feature of this law was that the legal profession was made part of the salaried civil service. 'Colleges of defenders, accusers and representatives of parties in civil suits' were established, the salaries being the same as those of the professional judges in the courts. Parties, however, were free to be represented by close relatives. Investigating agencies were attached to the courts to investigate serious criminal charges with which the local police could not cope. Civil cases and less serious criminal cases came before a court composed of one professional judge and two lay assessors, the more serious criminal cases before one professional judge and six lay assessors; it will be remembered that serious cases under the Empire had, in principle, been tried by jury. All interlocutory proceedings came before a single professional judge, as did divorce cases and uncontested civil suits.

The People's Court Act, of 21 October 1920, as amplified by a Decree of 10 March 1921, instituted a system of review of decisions by setting up a department of court control in the People's Commissariat of Justice, to ensure the correct and uniform application of the legislation of the RSFSR. The department was given authority to issue guiding instructions to the courts and to declare a judgment void if it was contrary to the law, even though it had already gone into effect. This in effect ended the period of experimentation and local autonomy.

The main features of these early years seem to have been a considerable distrust of legal formalism, and of lawyers who were believed to be wedded to this formalism, and a belief that law, legal procedure and the settlement of disputes could be a simple matter provided only that the courts were manned by persons with the correct political orientation and imbued with the spirit of socialist justice. Traces of this naïve Utopianism still exist: it is of course not only in the USSR that the lawyer is felt to be a pedant, and distrust of lawyers exists in many countries. Moreover, law was, in accordance with Marxist teachings, class law, and therefore suspect.

The system of salaried lawyers soon broke down, and the colleges were reorganized, with special scales of fees laid down.

THE PERIOD OF NEP

By 1921 the Civil War as virtually over and foreign intervention had ceased: but the country was in chaos. Agricultural production was less than half what it had been in 1916, and the government frequently found it difficult to honour the ration-books. Industry had come almost to a standstill, for most industrial concerns had been taken over by the central or local authorities, which often had no personnel capable of managing them; the managerial staff had been depleted by the civil war, persecutions and emigration, and many of the workmen had been drafted into the army or had returned to the villages where conditions were sometimes not as bad as they were in the towns.

D

It was necessary therefore to restore the economy of the country, and this called for a temporary retreat from orthodox Marxist principles. The main purpose of the New Economic Policy, introduced in 1921, was to allow a temporary restoration of capitalism, subject to strict control by the State. The period of the NEP lasted from 1921 to 1928, and the chief beneficiaries of the period were the NEPmen, small private capitalists engaged in production or in the retail trade, and the *kulaks* (literally 'fists'), the richer (and to the village poor, the more grasping) peasants who were again allowed to employ hired labour, subject to certain restrictions. But private production and trade required proper legal protection in order to flourish, and the period of the NEP was therefore a period of codification of the law.

a. Constitutional Provisions

The RSFSR, which had had close military and economic links with other Soviet Republics set up in certain non-Russian areas of the former Russian Empire, notably in the Ukraine, White Russia (*Byelorossia*) and in Transcaucasia, combined with these other Republics to form the Union of Soviet Socialist Republics, which came into formal existence on 30 December 1922.

On 31 January 1924 the first Constitution of the USSR was adopted. Its distinguishing feature was the provision made for securing consideration of the wishes of representatives of the smaller Republics and of individual ethnic groups. Supreme power was vested in the Congress of Soviets which met annually; its members were chosen by town Soviets on the basis of one delegate for every 25,000 electors, and by *gubernia* Soviets on the basis of one delegate for every 125,000 inhabitants. Between sessions of the Congress of Soviets supreme power was vested in the Central Executive Committee, which consisted of two chambers, the Soviet of the Union and the Soviet of Nationalities. Members of both chambers were chosen by the Congress of Soviets, but on different principles; representatives to the Soviet of the Union were chosen from representatives of the constituent Union Republics in proportion to the population of each Republic, whereas the Soviet of the Nationalities was formed on the basis of five representatives from each Union Republic and each Autonomous Republic and one representative each from each Autonomous Region. Each chamber of the Central Executive Committee elected a Praesidium of five members, and these ten persons, together with another seven (later nine) elected at a joint session of both chambers, formed the Praesidium of the Central Executive Committee which had full legislative, executive and administrative power subject only to its accountability to the full Central Executive Committee. The Praesidium appointed the members of the Council of People's Commissars which was the ordinary executive and administrative body, and which also had legislative powers in matters not affecting the principles on which the political and economic life of the country was based; but the Council of People's Commissars could not introduce radical changes into the working of the State apparatus, as this was reserved for the Central Executive Committee. The right to amend the Constitution was vested in the Congress of Soviets.

Direct participation by the electors was confined to the election of town and village Soviets, and NEPmen and *kulaks* were disfranchised and could not be elected.

b. The Land

The worst failures of the period of war communism were in connection with agriculture. The Soviet authorities were obliged to appropriate the peasants' surplus forcibly in order to honour the town-dwellers' ration-books, but this resulted in the peasants largely reverting to subsistence farming, and terrible famines ensued, relieved in part by considerable American aid. Some early attempts at collectivization of the land had been made, but the principles on which the collectives were run and the results actually obtained did nothing to inspire peasant confidence.

In order to persuade the peasant to cultivate his land properly it was necessary to allow a free market in grain, and also to ensure that there were commodities available for him to purchase with the money so obtained.

Agricultural co-operatives were allowed by an enactment of 16 August 1921; this gave them legal personality once certain registration requirements had been fulfilled, with comparative freedom to manage their own affairs, and priority with regard to obtaining credit, materials and orders from the State.

The Land Code of 30 October 1922 retained the principle of land nationalization but gave the peasant a right to use the land, either as an individual or by joining a peasant community or by some other form of co-operative farming. A peasant desiring to work land could be allotted a share of the land fund of a village, but the buying, selling and testamentary disposition of agricultural land so allotted was prohibited. Leases up to three years might be made, however, and employed labour could be hired, provided that all the members of the employer's family physically capable of working on the land so allotted, in fact did so; allotted land was not to be used for the enrichment of a family that did not work it itself. Large-scale agricultural enterprises (*sovkhozy*, State farms) however continued to be run by the State.

The traditional village peasant community (*mir*) was encouraged on a sound legal basis, and was given the right to vote in favour of a transition to collective farming, the right of dissenters to secede being preserved.

c. Industry and Commerce

Although the State retained control over the 'commanding heights' of the economy, small private capitalists employing not more than twenty people were to be encouraged; but the new capitalists or NEPmen were to be kept strictly out of the political sphere. The law of the NEP period therefore shows a double character; freedom for small capitalists in the economic sphere, combined with the tightening of political control. Some of the smaller enterprises nationalized earlier were returned to their former owners, and other nationalized enterprises were let on six-year leases to private capitalists. As far as industry was concerned, by September 1922, of some eight thousand industrial concerns, about half were either in the hands of the former owners, or run privately under leases. But they were the smaller ones; the private sector employed some 70,000 persons and accounted for some 5 per cent of total industrial production (mostly consumer goods) whereas the public sector of industry employed 1,300,000 people. The NEPman was more important in commerce than in industry, however.

The restoration of private enterprise, however limited, required a system of civil law within which it could operate. Codes of Civil Law and of Civil Procedure were enacted in 1922 and 1923 respectively; and it was expressly provided that enterprises could be nationalized only by decree of the Central Executive Committee, and that only the courts could declare contracts void: these provisions were required in order to protect the NEPman from arbitrary action by local Soviets, many of whose members were hostile to the NEP.

The Labour Code of 9 November 1922 reverted to the idea of negotiated contracts of employment, particularly collective agreements negotiated by employers and trade unions. The 'Workers' Control' of the earlier period had gone. The Labour Code contained principles normally accepted by trade unions in other countries, and had provisions for compulsory arbitration in the event of differences regarding interpretation of contracts or collective agreements already concluded, and a trade union was entitled to annul a collective agreement at any time. But although there were conciliation procedures where there were

differences on a new agreement, there was no power to force an agreement on managements or unions.

d. Ordinary Civil Law

Particular interest is attached to the Civil Code of 1922 as the first
codification of civil law by an avowedly socialist government. Yet its
contents are disappointing; there is little in the Code which would
surprise or seem novel to anyone familiar with the continental civil
codes, except the fact that it is considerably shorter. Even this may be
partly accounted for by the fact that it does not deal with family law,
labour law, or land law, these being the subject-matter of separate Codes.
It is confined to property law, contract, tort and succession, and it deals
with these matters in a traditional continental way; in fact, much of the
text was taken from a Draft Civil Code which had been submitted to the
Imperial Russian Duma in 1913, but which had not been proceeded with
owing to the outbreak of war the following year, and this Draft had been
much influenced by the continental civil codes. The Civil Code was
commonly said to be 'capitalist law in a socialist state'.

However, although the Code was intended to give a measure of
security to the new capitalist, or NEPman, it was feared that the NEPmen
might, by legal devices, obtain greater control and power than they
were intended to have, and so one article of the Code, the first, contained a general provision of a wide and unusual nature: 'Civil rights
are protected by law except in those cases when they are exercised in a
manner contrary to their social and economic purpose.' This wide
provision was intended to enable the courts to declare void transactions
between private businessmen if these transactions seemed prejudicial
to the State, even though on general grounds such agreements would
have been enforceable as contracts, and equally, it would allow the
courts to refuse to recognize private property rights in cases where such
recognition would be contrary to the policy of the State. Thus article 1
represented the 'socialist element' in what was otherwise a more or less
typical continental Civil Code. Article 1 was at first fairly widely applied
by lower courts, but the appellate courts saw that so long as it was
government policy to encourage private enterprise in industry and trade
the rights of the private businessman must be protected, and in fact
article 1 was not widely applied by the higher courts except in cases of
obvious abuses, as where a factory owner let the factory remain idle in
order to avoid the payment of taxes; Russia in the nineteen-twenties
could not afford to allow productive resources to remain idle, even
though they might nominally be in the ownership of private individuals.

The Code contained a provision similar to those in other systems about contracts concluded under duress, but was wider, in that any contract entered into by a person under duress to his evident detriment, could be annulled by a court, not only on the application of the party concerned, but also on the application of appropriate state authorities or social organizations.

The provisions of the law of Tort modified those of the French Code; they raised a presumption in favour of the victim, which the person or organization causing harm had to rebut. Employees, on the other hand, were required to prove that their employer was at fault, and this meant that the worker had a poorer remedy at first against the State, but this was later corrected.[1]

Perhaps it was the Family Code of 1926 (which replaced the Code of 1918 as re-enacted in 1921) which, from the point of view of the contemporary bourgeois world, was the most novel and even scandalous, for it was this Code which introduced the system of so-called 'postcard divorce'. Parties wishing a divorce could notify their desire to the Registry of Civil Status (corresponding roughly to our Registries of Births, Marriages and Deaths), but if only one party notified the Registry, the Registry would simply inform the other spouse by postcard that the marriage was dissolved; there was no need for judicial procedure at all. But there were other important changes. For one thing, the earlier Family Codes had established a régime of complete separation of property between husband and wife, so that everything bought with the husband's earnings belonged to him. The Family Code of 1926 established a system of community of property between husband and wife (technically this amounted to what continental lawyers term a 'community of acquests'); anything owned by a spouse before marriage remained that spouse's individual property, but all property acquired after marriage was held by them in common. The Code did not specify that it was to be held in common in equal shares, but provided that the share belonging to either husband or wife, should, in the event of dispute, be determined by the court. This provision was important in the case of the urban population and the rural intelligentsia, but as far as peasant families were concerned the old rules relating to the peasant household (*dvor*) remained.

Moreover, *de facto* marriages were treated on the same basis as registered marriages. The question whether two people were married thus became a question of fact rather than a question of law, and where a deserted woman was claiming a share in property acquired by a man

[1] See p. 167 *post*.

during the period of cohabitation her claim would not be defeated *in limine* merely by showing that there was no registered marriage, nor even by showing that the man had a registered marriage subsisting with another woman; in the latter case the court, after having established the date at which cohabitation with the petitioner began, could declare the registered marriage void as from that date, and could therefore treat the petitioner as the *de facto* wife.

After a divorce, either party might be able to claim maintenance from the other for a limited period, and disputes about custody of children were taken from the courts and transferred to specially created guardianship authorities. Both parents had equal rights as regards children, but it was expressly stated that these rights were to be exercised in the interests of the children. The Code also contained provisions for the maintenance by their adult children of parents who were unemployed or unable to work and in need; at this time there was still a considerable amount of unemployment in the USSR and the social security services were not as comprehensive as they are now.

e. The Criminal Law

A Criminal Code was promulgated in the RSFSR in 1922. However, after the formation of the USSR the new Constitution gave the Union competence to promulgate Basic Principles of criminal law (as distinct from detailed codes, which remained within the competence of the constituent Union Republics) and such Basic Principles were promulgated on an All-Union basis on 31 October 1924. In order to bring its legislation into line with the Basic Principles the RSFSR adopted a new Criminal Code in 1926.

The Criminal Codes were, in general, not unlike those usually found in continental countries, but counter-revolutionary offences were severely dealt with, and every act or omission directed against the Soviet régime was to be treated as an offence. From the point of view of western lawyers the most serious defect in these Codes was that they violated the principle of *nulla poena sine lege* by introducing the principle of analogy (perhaps 'reintroducing' would be more accurate, for the principle of analogy was eliminated from Imperial Russian Criminal Law only in 1903).

Article 16 of the Criminal Code of 1926 said 'If any socially dangerous act has not been directly provided for by the present Code, the basis and extent of liability for it is determined by applying to it those articles of the Code which deal with the offences most similar in nature'. Sometimes this provision was used to enable an offence to be dealt with as one more serious than would have otherwise been the case; for example thefts in hotels and railway stations were, under the Code, by reason of the greater facilities offered, punished more severely than ordinary thefts; it was therefore held that a theft in a factory canteen could be dealt with 'by analogy' as a theft in a hotel. During the Second World War, provisions relating to robbery by armed gangs were applied 'by analogy' to enable severe sentences to be imposed on members of groups who stole from flats left unguarded by reason of men being called up for military service or children being evacuated to safe areas. Sometimes, however, article 16 was used for cases where there was no offence under the letter of the law; maintaining a store of bayonets, however likely to arouse suspicion of evil intention, was nowhere stated to be an offence, but it was treated 'by analogy' with storing dynamite, which was a specific offence. In such cases the prosecutor had to find an offence similar in kind and importance to the one committed.[1]

These provisions are only in part explicable on the grounds that the Codes were prepared at great speed, and that skilled legal draftsmen were in short supply, though both these facts are true; they seem to reflect a fixed idea on the part of the Soviet authorities that skilled lawyers would be at the service of *kulaks* and NEPmen anxious to undermine Soviet authority, and would take full advantage of any *lacunae* or ambiguities. In deciding whether an act was punishable, therefore, a judge might still have to use his 'revolutionary consciousness'.

Another defect, from the western point of view, was that the Codes created at least one retrospective offence: capital punishment was provided for those who, as leading officials of the Tsarist Government, or as *agents provocateurs* of the Tsarist secret police, had authorized or participated in oppressive measures against the revolutionary movement. This might be 'proletarian justice' but it could hardly be justice of any other kind, for the persons penalized had merely been carrying out their official duties under the old régime.

Moreover, where counter-revolutionary offences were charged, the courts held that a charge of active counter-revolution (treason), which carried the death penalty, would lie, even though the acts committed came squarely within the definition of some lesser counter-revolutionary offence carrying only imprisonment.

In the trial of the leaders of the Roman Catholic Church in Russia,

---

[1] In 1936 there was a case in which a man complained to the procurator that his wife had eloped with another man. In order to bring a criminal charge the procurator had to find an 'analogous' offence, and he relied on an article in the Criminal Code which penalized 'hunting without an appropriate permit'.

in March 1923, one of the accused was in law undoubtedly guilty of active counter-revolution (treason) for he had appealed to Poland for assistance. But the other defendants, against whom no more could be proved than that they had instigated demonstrations against individual measures of the Soviet Government (the Disestablishment Laws) or demonstrations against the Soviet régime as such, both of which offences were under the Code punishable by imprisonment, were also condemned to death for active counter-revolution. The sentences, however, were not carried out.

In the case of non-political offences, the penalties imposed were often mild in comparison with the penalties provided by contemporary continental (or present Soviet) codes, but even here there were preventative measures which could be employed against persons who constituted a social danger. Where a person was regarded as a social danger by reason of his criminal past or his continued association with habitual criminals, even though he should be acquitted of the specific offence charged against him for lack of evidence, he could be banished from a given locality for a period of up to five years. This provision was, however, dropped in 1927; thereafter banishment could be imposed only after conviction of a specific offence.[1]

Usury was a specific offence, and, as the law contained no rules about permitted rates of interest, much would be in the discretion of the court in a particular case; the article prohibiting usury was aimed primarily at *kulaks* who might see in it a means of exploiting the difficulties of poorer neighbours for their own advantage. A loan of money at interest concluded between parties at arm's length was not regarded as 'usury'.

f. The Judicial System

The judicial system was reformed in 1922. The People's Courts were retained for the less serious criminal cases and the smaller civil cases, but *gubernia* courts were established in each province (*gubernia*) for the trial of more serious criminal cases and the more important or more complicated civil cases. The Revolutionary Tribunals were abolished, and jurisdiction over counter-revolutionary offences passed to the *gubernia* courts.

Above the *gubernia* courts were the Supreme Courts of the Union

---

[1] Banishment (*vysylka*) must be distinguished from exile (*ssylka*). A person who is banished is prohibited from residing in a certain place or places (usually the largest towns in the country). A person who is exiled is required to take up residence in a specified area, commonly in some part of Siberia. In neither case is there any further restriction on personal liberty beyond certain formalities such as reporting regularly to the police.

Republics, with the Supreme Court of the USSR as the apex of the system. Thus there was a four-tier system, with one appeal lying as of right to a higher court. The appeal could be brought by either party, so the prosecutor could appeal against an acquittal. But after the right of appeal had been exhausted and the sentence or judgment had come into force, there were possibilities for cases to be reopened by way of revision (*nadzor*). The parties, however, could not require revision as of right; the right to demand that a case be revised rested in the procurator (public prosecutor), though the higher courts could also themselves take the initiative in ordering a revision. The procurator, although prosecuting in court, was under a duty to ask for revision in any case if he thought the judgment or sentence wrong in law; in a criminal case he might ask for a decision to be reviewed on the ground that the court had imposed a sentence greater that that authorized by law, just as he might on the ground that the court had convicted the accused under an inappropriate article of the criminal code.

THE SOVIET LEGAL SYSTEM UNDER STALIN

By 1927, ten years after the Russian Revolution, the Soviet Union had a legal system which was comparable in many ways to the legal systems of other European states. There were, indeed, certain fundamental differences: article 1 of the Civil Code gave the courts wide powers of discretion to ignore civil rights if these were exercised in a manner contrary to what was conceived to be their proper purpose; article 16 of the Criminal Code allowed the punishment of acts not specifically forbidden by law but 'analogous' to some act that was forbidden by law: and the security service now termed the OGPU (All-Union state political board) had extensive powers to banish and exile without trial in cases where counter-revolutionary activities were suspected. Nevertheless on paper the system appeared on the whole to be a traditional European legal system. In practice its defects arose not so much from its express forms as from the fact that it was operated to a large extent by people with very inadequate training. Judges, procurators, police, defence counsel, notaries and officials had to be recruited and people with legal training were in short supply. Legal training had not been one of the first priorities of the revolutionaries, many lawyers trained under the old régime had perished during the Civil War or emigrated, and the level of legal ability in all spheres was rather low. Many of the defects in the system, as it worked in practice, were due to the low level of competence of those who worked it.

However, as the Revolution of 1917 itself was succeeded by a period

of chaos and emergency legislation, termed the period of war communism, to be followed by the period of NEP and relative stability, so
history was to repeat itself, for the period 1927/8 saw what has been
termed 'the second revolution' or 'the revolution from above'.

This involved the abandonment of the New Economic Policy, the
introduction of large-scale collectivization of agriculture, large-scale
industrialization of the country, and, in particular, a system of economic
planning.

The first Five Year Plan for industrialization of the country in fact
achieved its objects in four years, and so covered the period 1928 to
1931; the Second Five Year Plan covered the years 1932 to 1936. The
period of the two plans, that is, the period 1928 to 1936, sometimes
termed by Soviet writers 'the period of the construction of socialism',
meant a systematic consolidation of industry and trade in the hands
of the State, or to be more accurate, in the hands of State-controlled
corporations, termed 'socialist organizations'. This 'second revolution'
was accomplished largely outside the framework of the law, by means of
administrative action, and the courts were kept out of the whole business. Much could be achieved without any breach of the law at all, for
most of the leases of factories, shops, etc., that had been granted by the
State or by local authorities to the new businessmen, the NEPmen, had
been for a term of six years, and they were simply not renewed when
the term of the lease expired. In other cases the NEPmen were bought
out, or subjected to various pressures, sometimes legal, as by increased
taxation, and sometimes illegal, to give up their businesses. Administrative regulations prohibited trade in more and more commodities, and
finally in 1932 private trade, with a few insignificant exceptions, was
abolished, as was private industrial production.

The other main feature of the period 1927–36 was the collectivization
of agriculture. Here the authorities acted with comparatively little
regard for the law.[1] The peasants were forced into the collective farms,
which were nominally voluntary associations. Those who refused to
join, however, were liable to be persecuted as '*kulaks*' and large numbers
of *kulaks* were sent to labour camps for their opposition to the measures

---

[1] The OGPU was expressly authorized by a decree of August 1932, at a time
when forced collectivization had led to famine conditions in some areas, to send
'speculators' to concentration camps for a period of from five to ten years. Since
persons with grain to sell would normally be *kulaks* or middlemen acting for
them, this provision is to be seen as part of the campaign against the *kulaks*.
This decree, incidentally, is one of the very few which expressly use the term
'concentration camp' instead of the more usual euphemism 'corrective labour
camp'.

for the collectivization of agriculture; these included the repeal of the laws which had permitted the leasing of agricultural land and the hiring of farm labour. But expulsion of *kulaks* was carried on irrespective of any offence on their part. By 1936 agriculture had been almost entirely collectivized, and individual peasant farming remained only in a few backward or sparsely inhabited regions.[1]

Just as it had during the period of war communism, the taking over of industry caused considerable chaos, for the authorities were concerned with developing the industrial power of the country as quickly as possible, and many consumer commodities of minor importance, such as pins and needles and sweets, which had been made and sold by small private dealers, became unobtainable. Lack of peasant co-operation in the collective farms often led to serious food shortages and famines in the towns, and there was considerable unrest below the surface. But this time the authorities were well prepared.

The OGPU was given ever wider powers to deal with opposition to the régime, and it did not hesitate to use them. By 1933 it was like an army, with uniformed detachments, artillery and tanks, as well as plain-clothes formations. In that year its power to carry out summary executions, as well as to deport people to labour camps, already exercised in fact, was put beyond all legal doubt. The labour camps under its control played a significant part in the development of the country in such work as draining swamps and building canals.

In 1934 it was again reformed, and combined with the People's Commissariat for the Interior to which it was nominally subject but which in fact it controlled, and the new organization was known simply as the NKVD, People's Commissariat for Internal Affairs; it had other duties, but the security function was by far the most important.[2]

Of this period it may be said that the courts worked quite well with regard to such cases as they were allowed to hear, but the policy of government was to see that all important matters were kept well away

---

[1] From a purely formal point of view there may have been no illegality, in view of the wide powers assumed by the Government, but from any other point of view the proceedings could hardly be seen as 'lawful' in view of the fact that the term '*kulak*' was never defined. The liquidation of the *kulaks* as a class (though not necessarily as individuals) and the expropriation of their property may perhaps be compared with the dissolution and expropriation of the monasteries under Henry VIII in that a segment of society was deliberately and for political reasons broken up by means that were formally 'legal' though with ruthless disregard of previous rights.

[2] It became the MVD (Ministry of Internal Affairs) in 1946 when all the People's Commissariats were designated Ministries.

from the courts. Moreover, despite the campaign against the *kulaks*, the courts were discouraged from invoking the provisions of article 1 of the Civil Code, so as to give arbitrary decisions in cases involving *kulaks*. Moscow District Court, in a circular letter of 25 January 1930, instructed People's Courts within its area that article 1 should be used to defeat claims by *kulaks* against public corporations and to deny claims by *kulaks* under the law of inheritance or under deeds of gift. It received a sharp rebuke from the Supreme Court of the RSFSR which, by a direction of 18 February 1930, ordered the circular letter to be withdrawn, on the ground that it corresponded neither with the law nor with government policy, and amounted to a usurpation of legislative power. The NKVD dealt with cases of sabotage, treason and other counter-revolutionary offences, and the civil courts lost a good deal of business simply by reason of the fact that private trade and industry no longer existed, so commercial cases no longer came before them. Instead, to deal with cases between public corporations in industry and commerce, where disputes of a commercial character arose, e.g. complaints that goods delivered were not of the contract specifications, a new series of tribunals, the state arbitration tribunals, were set up in 1931. They acted partly according to the rules of the Civil Code governing matters such as contract, sale of goods, hire and so on, but largely according to what were considered to be the needs of the moment, so that to a considerable extent economic expediency replaced law in the realm of the state-controlled economy.

The existing system of courts remained in operation, and dealt with routine cases, but became much less important than it had been before. Administrative agencies were taking over many of the traditional functions of the courts; disputes between workers and managements went to special conciliation commissions, special agencies decided on rights to social insurance benefits and compensation, and many thought that the traditional forms and categories of law would soon be replaced by simple administration. People were saying that in ten years' time the ordinary courts would have ceased to exist, law students asked if it were necessary to continue their studies, and some judges even closed their courts without authority and took other jobs.

However, this attitude did not last long. Stalin was adopting the contradictory position that he long displayed, that of calling for stability of the law and respect for the law, and at the same time constantly ordering his subordinates to take actions which could not be justified in law. An important turning point was 1936, the year of stabilization and of the new Stalin Constitution.

The Constitution of 1936, which is often termed the Stalin Constitution, was to a large extent a consolidating measure. A bi-cameral legislature, the Supreme Soviet, replaced the Central Executive Committee and the Congress of Soviets. The Constitution ironed out a number of anomalies, in particular with regard to the abolition of various disabilities which had been imposed on certain sections of the population, such as priests, former bourgeois and former high-ranking Tsarist civil servants and policemen. Though to some extent its importance was of a psychological or propagandist nature, it did nevertheless help to instil the notion that legality was important, and that the era of purely arbitrary action by the state authorities was over. Many people outside the USSR, and probably many inside as well, thought that the Constitution heralded the dawn of a new era of greater liberalization and respect for traditional legal values and concepts. Stalin said 'We need stability of laws now more than ever' and the idea that the law would soon wither away and the courts soon be closed was castigated in no uncertain terms.

The Constitution contains a chapter, 10, on the 'Fundamental Rights and Duties of Citizens', which enumerated a number of rights which are normally taken for granted in free societies, such as Freedom of Speech, Freedom of the Press, Freedom of Assembly, and Freedom of Demonstrating. What these rights meant in practice was another matter which will be considered in detail at a later stage,[1] but here it can be noted that the Constitution itself said that these rights were 'for the purpose of strengthening the socialist system' and it was never intended that they should be used for criticizing or attacking the socialist basis of the Soviet economic system: however, even accepting this limitation, freedom of speech in fact came to mean very little.

Another point is that no effective guarantees for the exercise of these rights were given. The existing civil and criminal codes remained in force, though, with the abandonment of the New Economic Policy many of the provisions of the Civil Code were no longer applicable, and provisions of the Criminal Code in many cases became irrelevant (even when not expressly repealed) because new enactments, imposing much more severe penalties, had replaced them. Persons stealing property being transported by rail or river became liable to the death penalty, using force or threats against collective farms or collective farmers could entail deprivation of liberty from five to ten years if committed by *kulaks* or other anti-social elements, and there were many other laws of the period from 1929 to 1935 under which draconian penalties could

[1] See p. 97 *post.*

be and were imposed. After 1935 there was some return to normality; for example, article 7 of the Criminal Code of 1926, under which people might be penalized on the ground of social danger because of their connection with a criminal environment or because of their past activity, was repealed in 1938. The Constitution, although it was stated to be a 'Fundamental Law', was rather in the nature of a programme or statement of intention or principle than a set of precise legal rules which could be applied by the courts. The Constitution therefore had almost no direct effect on the ordinary work of the civil and criminal courts.

Indirectly, however, the new Constitution, seen as part of a general policy in favour of stability and predictability of law, did lead to a decline in the frequency of the application of article 1 of the Civil Code, and article 16 of the Criminal Code. The judges in the courts were acquiring greater legal knowledge and experience, law was regarded as a more important factor than hitherto, and so the need to rely on the 'revolutionary consciousness' of the judge arose less frequently. The Supreme Court of the USSR became active in reversing convictions in cases where there was no clear evidence of the accused's intention to commit a crime, and the doctrine of 'eventual intention'[1] affirmed by the Supreme Court in 1928 was expressly rejected by it in December 1938; under this doctrine, which applied particularly in the case of counter-revolutionary crimes such as sabotage, although the Criminal Code might require 'intention' as an element of the offence it was sufficient if the accused realized that his act might have the consequences, such as harm to the State, which the relevant article of the Code was concerned to prevent. In the terminology of English law, recklessness was equivalent to intention.

Moreover by the end of the nineteen-thirties it came to be recognized that the state arbitration tribunals, which decided disputes between public corporations, should be guided by law and not merely by expediency in deciding disputes. This should be seen as part of the drive for putting public corporations on a strict accountancy basis: each public corporation was allocated a certain amount of capital and was expected to comply with the instructions or directives of the planning authorities: but, within this framework, it had to conclude contracts with other public corporations for the supply of materials, and for the sale of its products, and its balance sheet and profit and loss account would show its success and efficiency in conducting its operations. Clearly, a public corporation might suffer losses not by reason of its own inefficiency or fault, but, for example, because its suppliers failed to supply it with the necessary raw

[1] Known as *dolus eventualis* to continental criminal lawyers.

materials on time. There would therefore be a breach of contract, and it would be able to recover damages for the breach of contract from the corporation at fault, so that its own financial position would not be affected by the action of other corporations for which it was not responsible. The state arbitration tribunals which heard these cases, mostly cases arising from breach of contract, had at first operated very much on the principle of economic expediency without bothering very much about the details of the law of contract as set out in the Civil Code; for the Civil Code was still thought to represent 'bourgeois law' to a large extent, and its principles were therefore not suitable for application to disputes between 'socialist organizations', which was the term commonly used for what we would call public corporations; but this attitude was now changing.

Respect for law, and legal stability, came to be manifested in a number of other ways; law teaching was reformed on more traditional lines, lawyers trained under the Tsarist régime found themselves more in demand as consultants to public corporations and government departments, cases of arbitrary action by local authorities or minor officials were condemned, and attempts were made to consolidate the numerous enactments of the Soviet government into a more ordered scheme and to repeal those whose usefulness had been outlived. In the sphere of family law divorce was made more difficult by the imposition of higher fees in 1936, and by the requirement of a formal judicial process in 1944. Succession duties were reduced, and powers of testation enlarged.

Yet there were very definite limits to this restoration of legality: it certainly did not apply in all spheres, nor did it bring about any increase in the freedom of the individual, for in some ways the later Stalinist period was one of the most oppressive that has ever been known in Russia.

There are, from the point of view of the legal system, two sides to this: first, the enactment of oppressive legislation. Even before the passing of the Stalin constitution, an enactment of 1934 had provided a special summary form of procedure to be used in the case of persons charged with certain capital counter-revolutionary offences; under this enactment the accused might be tried in his absence, and if convicted had no right of appeal or even a right to ask for mercy, and if the death sentence was imposed it was to be carried out immediately after judgment. The form of procedure made it virtually impossible for the accused to rebut any evidence produced against him by the OGPU, or the NKVD as it became in 1934, for the accused was not entitled as of right to have a lawyer to represent him; this lay within the discretion of the court trying him. Such a proceeding of course violates all the traditionally accepted canons of criminal procedure, for the accused could be, and often was, completely deprived of any possibility of defending himself against the charges brought against him. Nevertheless, as the procedure was provided for by statute, it could not be said to be actually illegal, however unjust it might be. Similarly a law of 1937 by implication authorized the NKVD to use torture in the examination of persons suspected of counter-revolutionary offences, again a monstrous provision contrary to all modern civilized standards.[1] That the NKVD did on occasion use torture to obtain confessions was widely known before 1937, though strictly speaking before that date this was illegal, whereas after the enactment of 1937 it became legal. One might even cite this enactment as evidence of a growing concern for legality, but in fact there is the other side to the matter; where Stalin or his immediate subordinates saw any threat to the security of the country or of the régime or of their own positions, legality became irrelevant.

The NKVD was so powerful that no-one could attempt to bring its members to justice even for admitted illegalities; any attempt to do so would probably have been regarded as counter-revolutionary. It is true that, so far as is known, few heads of the state security force (Cheka, GPU, OGPU, NKVD, MVD, as it was called at different times) have died in their beds, for they themselves have usually become victims of the organization; but their removal has not been due to any respect for 'legality' but for purely political reasons.

Some students of Soviet affairs consider that the labour camps under the control of the security forces played an important part in the economy at this time, for they carried out important reclamation works in Central Asia, and in the extreme north of the country, and in other places where climatic and other conditions were such that it would have been almost impossible to attract voluntary labour. It may be that to some extent Stalin considered that it was necessary to maintain an atmosphere of terror and purges not only for political reasons, to safeguard his system and policy, but also for economic reasons, to obtain large quantities of convict labour for the development of these areas in the extreme north, and in central Asia. However that may be, we know that the years of the middle thirties were the years of the great purges in Russia; a few leading figures were tried in open court, but much

---

[1] What the law actually said was that in such cases 'all methods of investigation are permissible': this was taken to mean that the safeguards provided by the Code of Criminal Procedure did not apply.

E

larger numbers were tried before the so-called 'special boards' of the NKVD; these tribunals had power to deport to a labour colony for five years with the right to add further periods of five years indefinitely when the sentence expired. Numerous others were tried under the provisions of the law of 1934 mentioned above, and others were 'shot whilst trying to escape', a euphemism that covered a variety of unpleasant fates suffered at the hands of the NKVD.

The Stalinist system, already dictatorial, needed far less alteration to meet the needs of the war than did the legal systems of the countries of Western Europe, for in a sense the Soviet system was already organized on an emergency footing. An enactment of 1940 however, passed while the USSR was still at peace, tied workers to their jobs: a worker could not leave his place of employment without the consent of the management of the enterprise employing him, subject to certain qualifications. Equally lateness in arriving for work exposed the offender to the penalties of the criminal law.

Harold Berman reports a case[1] which illustrates the duality of the system on the eve of Hitler's attack on the USSR. In 1940 Buligin, a professor of engineering, drew up plans for a construction project in Kazan. His plans were altered by higher authority without his consent, and he had to superintend the execution of the revised plans. The foundations sagged, and Buligin was suspected of sabotage (he had relatives abroad). After prolonged questioning by the NKVD he was charged, not with sabotage, but criminal negligence, and was tried by the Leningrad City Court. The prosecutor avoided all engineering technicalities, and the witnesses were persons anxious to avoid charges of negligence themselves. One point emerged incidentally during the evidence; the People's Commissar for heavy industry had visited the site and had taken it on himself to order additional pumping and drainage, but the court refused to consider the possibility that this had washed away some of the soil, thereby causing the sagging, and Buligin got a six-year sentence. On appeal the Supreme Court of the RSFSR ordered a new trial with a new investigation. This time the investigator was attached to the procuracy, not to the NKVD. The second trial was conducted perfectly fairly, and all the evidence was considered. The expert witnesses were asked pointed questions, and after a trial of three days the court deliberated for six hours and Buligin was acquitted. Buligin himself was confident that once the case was out of the hands of the NKVD justice would be done, and his optimism proved justified; the NKVD was not bound to bring cases to court, and when it did, it

[1] Berman, *Justice in the U.S.S.R.*, p. 58.

expected convictions, and this clearly influenced the court at the first trial. Once the NKVD had lost interest in the case there was no impediment to a fair hearing.

During the war the whole system was tightened up in some ways, especially with regard to rationing, and relaxed in others; for example, the Orthodox Church obtained greater freedom in return for support of the war efforts of the Soviet Government.

In the period immediately after the war, reconstruction of the devastated areas took precedence over legal reforms, and then the onset of the cold war provided justification for keeping the system of restraint in full force. By the early nineteen-fifties, however, acute differences of opinion existed, though, to a considerable extent, these were smothered; then, early in 1953, the newspapers announced the discovery of a conspiracy among a group of Jewish doctors to kill a number of leading members of the government, including Stalin. Such an announcement seemed to Soviet readers to mean that the purges of the nineteen-thirties were to be repeated, and the population thought that a new reign of terror was coming. Then Stalin died, in March 1953, and this was the signal for a release of built-up tensions throughout the system.

FURTHER READING

J. N. Hazard, *Law and Social Change in the U.S.S.R.*, London, 1953.

J. N. Hazard, 'Law and Tradition in the New Russia' (1953), 4 *Oxford Slavonic Papers*, p. 132.

J. N. Hazard, *Settling Disputes in Soviet Society – The Formative Years of Legal Institutions*, New York, 1960.

S. Kucherov, *Courts, Lawyers and Trials under the last three Tsars*, New York, 1953.

W. W. Smithers, 'Russian Civil Law' (1904), 52 *University of Pennsylvania Law Review*, p. 137.

A. Y. Vyshinski, *The Law of the Soviet State*, New York ¸1948.

CHAPTER THREE

The Soviet Legal System since Stalin

Stalin died in March 1953, and in this chapter we shall be concerned with the main changes that have taken place in the Soviet Legal System since that time.

The death of Stalin led to a rather confused struggle for power between three groups with much interlocking membership; the official State apparatus, the MVD with its private army and wide powers of suppression, and the Communist Party. The Government (official State) group and the Party were very conscious of two things: first, that no individual, however highly placed, was safe from the MVD, for the latter often acted on unfounded denunciations, and secondly, that the MVD was hated and feared by the mass of the population, and that therefore any group would receive mass support if it could eliminate the secret police as an active part in their lives. During Stalin's time the MVD had their representatives in most large factories and plants and even the manager of the factory was not allowed to enter their office; the ostensible function of the MVD representative at the factory was to ensure that no employee at the factory evaded the call-up for military service, and to see that the factory did not employ anyone who had failed to respond to the call-up, or who was a deserter from the armed forces, or a foreign spy, but this ostensible function of course gave the MVD an excuse for making enquiries about all the activities of the employees of the factory, and in particular about their loyalty to the régime. After Stalin's death the Government and Party groups combined against Beria, the MVD chief, who was sentenced to death by a special court which met *in camera* in December 1953, though some reports say that in fact Beria had already been shot some months previous to the trial. There may have been other irregularities about Beria's trial too,[1] but in any

---

[1] I was a member of the British Legal Delegation which visited the USSR in September 1954. We met one of the judges who had participated in the Beria

case all the leading figures were determined that the whole repressive system represented by the MVD and its 'special boards' was to go, and the special MVD boards were abolished in September 1953, though the fact was not publicly announced until 1955.

Of itself the abolition of the special MVD boards might not have seemed particularly important, as the existing criminal law remained in force, as did the decrees of 1934 and 1937 authorizing special forms of procedure for the trial of terroristic political acts and other counter-revolutionary offences; the law thus still permitted the trial of the accused in his absence without giving him any adequate opportunity of rebutting the evidence adduced by the prosecution, and required the death sentence to be carried out immediately, thereby precluding any right of appeal or possibility of reprieve being granted. But in fact, what was important was not so much the change in the law as the change in the whole atmosphere after Stalin's death. Whatever the law might be, people felt freer, and they felt free to criticize the oppressive enactments of the Stalinist régime which still remained on the statute-book; and in fact the decrees of 1934 and 1937 were repealed in 1956.

Another important repeal was that of the law of June 1940 governing the movement of labour. Under this enactment employees could not leave their jobs without the permission of the management of the concern for which they worked, apart from special circumstances such as ordinary retirement, maternity, illness or call-up for the armed forces. It must of course be remembered that in 1940 the Second World War had already started, and although the USSR was still a neutral, it was clear that she might become involved at any time. Countries at war commonly control labour, and as a war-time measure the enactment could be justified. However, it remained in force after the end of the war. After Stalin's death its retention was explained by the consideration that, although in all ordinary cases permission to leave was normally given, it was still necessary to maintain the law in force in order to prevent certain highly qualified specialists from leaving their jobs before someone else was available to replace them; but even then it was hardly ever invoked, and it was formally repealed in 1956.

Thus the first few years after Stalin's death were devoted to removing some of the worst features of his régime. Extensive amnesties were

trial, but very little information about it was forthcoming. In reply to the question whether Beria had been allowed defence counsel we got the answer, 'If he had asked for counsel his request would have been considered.' It is clear, however, that Beria was tried under the special procedure provided by the decree of 1934.

granted in 1953, 1955 and 1957; rules were introduced enabling prisoners to be released before the expiry of their sentences (which had often been very long); a number of cases in which people appeared to have been convicted on fabricated evidence were retried and in many cases the persons concerned acquitted, and altogether a more humane attitude was adopted with regard to the administration of justice.

Then the authorities, having dealt with some of the worst abuses of the Stalinist period, began to consider more permanent reforms in the legal system and in the whole system of administration. As far as the general administration of the country was concerned, there was a move towards decentralization; this resulted in an increase in the powers of the Union Republics and of the various organs of local government within the Union Republics, and a decrease in the number of All-Union Ministries in Moscow. Control was gradually being devolved from the centre, and the idea of All-Union criminal and civil codes, on which jurists had been working in Stalin's time, was abandoned, but it was decided that in these branches of law Basic Principles should be laid down by the Supreme Soviet of the USSR, and that these Basic Principles would be in force throughout the country, but that subject to them each Union Republic would have the right to enact its own rules for each branch of law. Any enactment by a Union Republic of rules contrary to the Basic Principles would be void.

In view of the abuses that had taken place in Stalin's time the most immediately important sphere seemed to be that of Criminal Law and Criminal Procedure. The new enactments naturally took some time to prepare, but in December 1959 the Supreme Soviet of the USSR adopted Basic Principles of Criminal Law, and Basic Principles of Criminal Procedure, as well as a new enactment on crimes against the State. In consequence, the Criminal Codes and the Codes of Criminal Procedure of the Union Republics had to be remodelled to bring them into agreement with the new Basic Principles, and this process was completed by 1961, the new Criminal Code and the new Code of Criminal Procedure of the RSFSR appearing in October 1960.

We shall now consider some of the ways in which the present criminal law and criminal procedure, under these enactments, differs from that previously in force.

1. The analogy principle, contained in article 16 of the Criminal Code of 1926, has gone. This is expressly laid down in article 3 of the Basic Principles, which says:

Only a person who is guilty of the commission of a crime, that is, a socially dangerous act committed intentionally or negligently and forbidden by law, incurs criminal liability and is liable to punishment. Criminal punishment is inflicted only by sentence of a court.

The importance of this is that the criminal act must be one 'forbidden by law' and therefore the court is no longer free to sentence a person for an act not expressly forbidden by law, but merely analogous to some act expressly forbidden by law. The significance of the last statement 'criminal punishment is inflicted only by sentence of a court' means that administrative bodies can no longer impose criminal punishments. This does not mean that they can no longer impose sanctions, however; there are still certain petty offences that can be dealt with administratively, and for which fines may be imposed, e.g. on the spot fines for traffic offences, petty hooliganism, or even in some cases up to fifteen days' detention: the significance of this is that these measures, not being technically 'criminal' punishments, do not form part of a person's criminal record (*sudimost*). Moreover, a person cannot be dismissed from his job on the ground that he has been convicted of a criminal offence in such cases.

2. Another rule that has gone, is an amendment to the Criminal Code made in 1934, to the effect that where a Soviet citizen had been convicted of treason, espionage, or certain other offences against the State, members of his family who had assisted him or had even known of his plans, but did not denounce him, could be punished for the same offence, and even, that those members of his family who did not know of them could be exiled to Siberia for five years. Technically, the exile in this case was not a 'criminal punishment' but an 'administrative measure', but despite this rather legalistic point, it was commonly felt to be punishing a person for an offence he had not committed, and was known as 'guilt by association'. The rules for those who assist or fail to denounce counter-revolutionary activities remain, but there is no penalty for members of the family who had no knowledge of the offence, and indeed, if the offender's property is confiscated as part of his punishment, members of his family are entitled to continue living in his house for a period which varies according to circumstances. The house is forfeited to the State, but it must allow the family to remain in it for a certain time.

3. The punishments for a number of offences have been greatly reduced, especially long terms of deprivation of liberty, and the emphasis is on reformation of the criminal rather than on punishment as such, or deterrence of others.

4. Other important changes have been made in the sphere of criminal procedure, and the rights of the defence have been considerably strengthened. Article 21 of the Basic Principles of Criminal Procedure lays down that in all cases the accused is entitled to be defended by defence counsel. Under the previous law there were certain cases in which the accused could not insist on being defended by counsel: these were in the main comparatively minor cases such as petty assaults, where the victim of the offence was prosecuting in person. Now, however, the accused may instruct counsel even in these cases.

Union Republican legislation lays down cases in which the accused must be represented by counsel; these are cases where the accused is under eighteen; cases where he is physically or mentally incapable of defending himself; cases where the death penalty may be imposed or where there is a state or social prosecutor; cases where the accused does not understand the language in which the proceedings are conducted, and cases where there are several accused persons whose interests conflict, except when all of them expressly renounce their right to counsel.

One point on which there has been a great deal of controversy, not only in the USSR, but also in other countries which follow the continental method of criminal procedure, and which has been decided in different ways in different countries, is the right of the accused to have counsel present during the preliminary investigation of the charge. Under the usual continental system, once a person has been charged with an offence, a preliminary investigation is conducted by an investigator (in France the *juge d'instruction*) whose job it is to collect all the evidence he can find about the case, interview witnesses, examine documents, and visit the scene of the crime, and his report is submitted to the court to decide whether there is sufficient evidence to justify putting the accused on trial. There was considerable demand from the legal profession in the USSR for a rule that defence counsel should be allowed to be present during the preliminary investigation, but in fact a compromise rule was adopted: defence counsel is allowed to be present throughout the preliminary investigations only in the case of serious charges against persons under eighteen: in other cases, he can be present only when the accused himself is being questioned by the investigator, or when some witness called by the accused is being questioned, and in these cases only if the investigator in charge of the investigation gives permission. This is not as much as many lawyers had hoped, but at any rate it gives opportunities for experiment and obtaining experience of the effects of allowing counsel to be present during part of the investigation, and may lead later to allowing participation by defence counsel in a more general way.

5. Another important change was in connection with confessions by the accused. In English law there is a distinction between confessions, admissions, and pleas of 'guilty'. Under our system, an accused person can plead 'Guilty' to the charge, and then the judge merely hears such evidence as is necessary to enable him to decide on the appropriate sentence, including of course any plea in mitigation put forward by the defendant. But if the accused pleads 'Not Guilty' the prosecution may put in evidence that before the trial the defendant had made a confession, i.e. a complete confession of guilt, or an admission, i.e. an acknowledgment of some fact material to the charge; for example, on a charge of theft the defendant may admit taking the article, but deny having intended to steal it, saying, perhaps, that he mistook it for his own, or thought that it had been lent to him.

Under the former Soviet system a confession could be made in court, and the court might proceed to sentence the accused, so that superficially this would resemble proceedings under the English system. But the difference lay in the fact that under the English system there is normally a preliminary investigation before the magistrates in public. Counsel for the accused will have heard the witnesses for the prosecution at the preliminary investigation before the magistrates, and so will be able to decide for himself whether any serious defence can be put up: he may feel, when he hears the prosecution witnesses at the preliminary enquiry, that they are not telling the truth and would collapse under cross-examination, or that their stories are contradictory. And similarly the accused will have heard the evidence that is to be given against him at the trial. But under the former Soviet system defence counsel was not present at the preliminary investigation, which was not in public, nor was the accused necessarily present when the evidence of witnesses was taken. It is true that once the preliminary investigation was ended, the accused and his counsel were entitled to see the depositions (the statements of the witnesses) but this is not anything like the same as seeing the witnesses themselves. If pressure had been put on the accused to confess to a faked-up charge, his counsel would have had no opportunity of deciding for himself how strong the evidence was, and if the accused confessed in court, the witnesses would not always be called again, though their statements would often be read out.

The 1926 Code of Criminal Procedure of the RSFSR in principle did not accept a plea of Guilty and did not regard a confession as decisive, but in practice these safeguards had not been observed. The reforms succeeded in removing this abuse. This is the effect of article 17 of the Basic Principles of Criminal Procedure, which does not mean very much unless one understands the background: the article says 'No evidence whatever shall have pre-established value for the court . . .' This means that a confession by the accused, whether made in open court or during the preliminary investigation or while awaiting trial, is not to be regarded as conclusive of the accused's guilt. People confess to crimes for various motives, and this fact is now fully recognized.[1] In Tsarist Russia, and in some other countries, a confession by the accused was regarded as the *Regina Probationum*, the Queen of Evidence, and even in the USSR in Stalin's time it was regarded as decisive in the case of political charges. Vishinski, the leading lawyer of the Stalinist period, laid down that courts could convict solely on the confession of the accused in political cases; in other cases a confession, though of very great weight, should be accompanied by some other evidence against the accused before a conviction was decided on.

6. Another abuse which was common during the Stalinist period (and is not unknown in Western Europe or the United States, but which in England is reduced to negligible proportions by the English rules relating to contempt of court) was 'trial by newspaper'. Accused persons could, before trial, be viciously attacked and described as criminals in officially inspired newspaper articles, and this made an independent approach very difficult even for a well-intentioned judge, for the prosecutor would refer to 'facts proved by the press' and would often add, for good measure 'it is well known that our Soviet press does not lie'. This abuse has not been altogether eradicated, but an attempt to deal with it has been made in article 139 of the Code of Criminal Procedure which provides that the data of a preliminary investigation may be given publicity only with the permission of the investigator or of a procurator, and only to the extent allowed by him. Where necessary the investigator may warn parties and witnesses and other persons concerned of the impermissibility of divulging such data without his permission.

7. Other developments of the post-Stalin era are, that although punishments for minor offences have been greatly reduced, in the last few years a much sterner attitude has been adopted towards the regular professional criminal or the 'especially dangerous recidivist' as the Russians term him, and the death penalty has been introduced for a number of more serious offences of the kind normally committed by the hardened professional criminal. During 1960 it became obvious

[1] See p. 123 *post.*

that while many minor offences were decreasing, there was an increase in really serious crime. This was partly due to the fact that after Stalin's death the courts became much more lenient, serious offenders received shorter sentences, and so were coming out of corrective labour camps earlier and recommencing their offences, and partly to the fact that the shorter sentences were less of a deterrent. In 1961 a decree of 5 May entitled 'On intensifying the struggle with especially dangerous crimes' extended the death penalty to offences such as large-scale theft of state property, large-scale embezzlement of public funds, extensive acceptance of bribes by officials, large-scale black marketeering, attacks on warders in prisons and other places of detention, attempted murder of policemen, forgery of banknotes, as well as murder committed by gangs, and murder committed in the course of rape. The professional criminal has a much harder time now, for one reason because his existence has at last been officially admitted; at one time it was said that there were no professional criminals in the USSR, and as long as that was the official attitude obviously the problem could not be tackled seriously.

For minor offences, such as petty hooliganism and drunkenness, the 'Comrades' Courts' which functioned until the middle of the nineteen-thirties have been revived. They can impose public censures and reprimands, and even small fines. They consist of fellow members of the staff of the place of work of the accused, or other residents in the block of flats where he lives, and deal with various minor anti-social acts; they have relieved the ordinary courts of a good deal of business of a very petty kind. They seem to be quite effective in dealing with a wide variety of minor matters.

An innovation of the post-Stalin period is the creation of a People's Volunteer Militia to act alongside the regular Militia (police force) in keeping order in streets, at public meetings, sporting events and so on. This is an attempt to draw the general public into the area of law enforcement, though the leading members of these Volunteer Militia groups are usually Party members or Komsomol members. Serious cases are handed over to the police for prosecution before the ordinary courts, whereas minor cases are dealt with by reprimands or by transfer to comrades' courts.

8. In order to appreciate something of the extent to which the present legal atmosphere differs from that of Stalin's time, we may consider the trial of the writers Sinyavski and Daniel in February 1966. These writers, under the pseudonyms of Tertz and Arzhak, had published works in the West which were, or which could be considered as, highly

critical of the Soviet régime. They were arrested in September 1965 on a warrant issued by the Procurator-General of the USSR, and news of their arrest became known in the West the following month, though it was not publicly announced in the Soviet Union until January, when a vitriolic attack on them was published in *Izvestia* on 13 January and in *Literaturnaya Gazeta* on 22 January. The preliminary investigation was conducted by the KGB, the state security police. The trial began on 10 February before the Supreme Court of the RSFSR, and the writers were charged under article 70 of the Criminal Code for the dissemination of slanderous material defamatory of the Soviet State and social system.[1] Both denied the charge. In addition to the State prosecutor (the Deputy Procurator-General of the USSR) there were two 'social prosecutors' from the Union of Soviet Writers. Both accused were represented by counsel. Reliable reports of the actual proceedings are not available, as, although the court supposedly sat in public, only persons with 'invitations' issued by Soviet organizations were admitted to the trial, and no such 'invitations' were issued to any Western newspapermen in Moscow. The official Soviet news agency *Tass* gave a detailed account of the prosecution case, and admitted that the two accused 'put up a spirited defence'. They did not deny their authorship of the books alleged to have been published by them in the West but claimed that they were purely literary works and that they had no intention of defaming the Soviet State. According to the *Tass* report, when Sinyavsky was confronted with a passage from his book *Thinking Aloud* which said, 'Drunkenness is the fixed idea of the Russian people. A nation of thieves and drunkards is incapable of creating culture', and asked, 'What can you say about this?' he replied, after a long silence, 'You see, I love the Russian people. You cannot reproach me with any partiality for the West – I was even called a slavophile.' The 'social prosecutors' from the Union of Soviet Writers asserted that the works had no literary merit but were profoundly anti-Soviet.

A report of Sinyavski's speech in his defence was published in Milan. According to this report, the authenticity of which cannot be established beyond doubt, he criticized the position taken by the prosecution, according to which literature is a form of agitation and propaganda and said, 'Now agitation can be only Soviet or anti-Soviet and if it is not Soviet this means it is anti-Soviet. I cannot share this idea.' Later, he rejected the attitude of 'He who is not with us is against us' adopted by the prosecution, saying, 'At certain times, revolution, war,

[1] The full text of article 70 is given on p. 154 *post*.

civil war, this logic can be just, but it is very dangerous in time of peace, above all when it is applied to writing.' Sinyavski was convicted and sentenced to seven years' deprivation of liberty in a corrective labour camp with a strict régime (the maximum that could be awarded for the offence charged), and Daniel was sentenced to five years in such a camp. As the sentence was given by the Supreme Court of the RSFSR there was no possibility of appeal.

After the trial a group of writers in Moscow and a similar group in Leningrad (totalling some forty in all) signed letters of protest addressed to the Soviet Government protesting against the institution of criminal proceedings against the two writers and the manner in which the trial was conducted. The poet Yesenin-Volpin stated a few days after the trial, 'Their guilt was not proved. I personally believe they were not guilty of deliberate anti-Soviet activity', and another poet, Yevtushenko, expressed the view that they should have been brought before their literary peers and not before a court. Other writers, and in particular the officials of the Union of Soviet Writers, expressed support for the findings of the court, though some asked why foreign correspondents had not been admitted to the court-room.

Some of the circumstances of this trial recall the political trials of the Stalin period: for example, the 'trial by newspaper' which was conducted before and during the hearing in court. The article in *Izvestia* of 13 January 1966 directly accused the writers of high treason, and while the trial was in progress *Sovetskaya Rossia* wrote, 'The Soviet people will not allow anyone under the guise of "creative activity" to mock at the most precious achievements of the revolution.' The intolerance of satire and criticism of the Government by writers goes back to Stalinism and to the Tsars.

Yet the differences are perhaps even more striking. In Stalin's time political trials were staged; the victims were often former politicians who had fallen foul of Stalin, and it was considered necessary to accuse them of treason in order to discredit them in the eyes of their followers. In Stalin's time a case like that of Sinyavski and Daniel would have been dealt with by the NKVD without any publicity or any trial in a regular court at all. Secondly, it is noteworthy that for the first time since the nineteen-twenties the accused in a widely publicized political trial have denied the charges and have actively defended themselves. Thirdly, Soviet citizens have dared in public to express their dissatisfaction with the conviction, and to ask why no foreign correspondents were admitted to the trial. Another difference, though not one for which the Soviet authorities are responsible, is that whereas the decisions of Soviet courts during the Stalinist period were servilely applauded by the communist movements in all other countries, in this case there was strong condemnation by the communist press of Great Britain, France, Italy and Sweden. Though the trial and conviction of these writers is to be deplored, the whole circumstances of the trial show how far Soviet justice has come since the days of Stalin – and how far it still has to go.

FURTHER READING

A. K. R. Kiralfy, 'Recent Legal Changes in the USSR' (1957), 9 *Soviet Studies*, p. 1.

A. K. R. Kiralfy, 'The Campaign for Legality in the U.S.S.R.' (1957), 6 *International & Comparative Law Quarterly*, p. 625.

'The Sinyavsky-Daniel Trial' (1966), *Bulletin of the International Commission of Jurists*, No. 26, p. 32.

CHAPTER FOUR

The Foundations of the Soviet Legal System

MARXIST LEGAL THEORY

One aspect of the Soviet Legal System that is almost unique is that the whole system is, or at least purports to be, the expression in legal terms of a very definite philosophy, the philosophy of Marxism. Most legal systems alter and develop as changes in economic and social life occur, but each change is usually viewed as a mere adaptation of the law to meet some different condition; for example, in England the industrial revolution and the factory system of manufacture led to the Factory Acts and to the legislation governing the activities of trade unions, but the changes were regarded merely as an empirical process of 'bringing the law up to date'.

Legal theory or legal philosophy is a much later phenomenon in human history than law, and its exponents usually try to find principles underlying the vast mass of rules that make up a legal system. Very often they attempt to justify the existing system of law on religious, political or moral grounds, or alternatively they suggest the directions in which the law should be changed in order to make the law accommodate itself better to new conditions, or to achieve some socially desired objective. Usually a legal system comes first and legal philosophy comes later. The legal philosophy may of course interact on the law, and it commonly does; but of very few legal systems is it directly claimed that they are an expression of some particular philosophy or religion. We have referred to Mohammedan law as an exception: Mohammedan law has developed mainly by commentary on doctrines contained in the Koran, and to a large extent it claims to be the spirit of Islam as applied to legal relationships. But even in this case Mohammedan law, strictly so called, deals only with part of the field normally covered by law, namely with matters of family law, marriage, divorce and succession on death, and in Moslem countries today there are many

rules of law dealing with matters falling within the sphere of constitutional law, administrative law, criminal law, and especially commercial
law, that have been adopted and adapted from non-Moslem systems.

But Soviet law is, in the eyes of its exponents and practitioners, the
application in the legal field of the philosophy of Marxism. And as
Marxism existed long before the Russian Revolution of 1917, in this
case the philosophy preceded the legal system.

MARX AND ENGELS

The system known as Marxism, elaborated by Karl Marx and his
collaborator Friedrich Engels, is based on the principle of the primacy
of economics over politics, law and the State. By this they meant that
the State, the law and politics (the struggle for power) were human
institutions which arose at a specific time in different human communities as a result of changes in economic relations, or in the relations
between producers and consumers. There was a time when there was
no state and therefore no law, and no struggle between competing
classes of the population; this is known as 'the period of primitive
communism'. But when a minority of the population obtained for themselves exclusive possession of the main means of production in early
times, namely the land, or flocks and herds, which had previously
been held in common, they needed an apparatus of compulsion in order
to protect their exclusive ownership, and this apparatus of compulsion
was the State. Since prehistoric times there have always been exploiting
and exploited classes; in the ancient world, these were the slaveowners
and the slaves; in feudal times they were the lords and the serfs; and in
modern times they are the capitalists or the bourgeoisie and the workers
or proletarians. Thus Marxists speak of slave-owning states, feudal
states and capitalist states; in each case the adjective describes the class
for whose benefit the State exists. There is always a conflict of interests
between the dominant class and the exploited class, and therefore conflict between them; and the State exists in order to keep the exploited
class in subjection. There may indeed be more than one exploited class;
for example, during the later feudal period, the capitalist class was exploited by feudal magnates, although the capitalists were themselves
exploiting their journeymen or labourers, but in such circumstances the
exploited classes are likely to make common cause against the exploiters.

The precedence of economics over politics means that the politically
dominant section in the community are enabled to dominate it precisely
because they are economically stronger. Economic power comes first,
and is protected by political power, exercised through the State and the

law. Nevertheless, conditions never remain stable, and a weaker class may achieve economic power, and, having achieved economic power, will then seek political power; it will seek to overthrow the political dominance of a class that is weaker economically. If, in a particular community we find that the holders of political power are not also the class that holds economic power, there is a situation which Marxists term 'a revolutionary situation', that is, one in which it can be foreseen that an attempt will be made by the class that is politically weaker, but economically stronger, to throw off the dominance of the existing ruling class. The classic example of this is France in the latter half of the eighteenth century, where real economic power lay in the bourgeois or merchant classes in the towns and the peasants in the countryside, while the aristocracy, the politically dominant class, apart from a few isolated individuals, lacked real wealth and economic power. There was therefore a revolutionary situation, which ultimately erupted in the French Revolution; this destroyed the old feudal-aristocratic State, and established a new kind of state with a new kind of law, a State and legal system which enabled the capitalist class to exercise political as well as economic power.

Much or most of this would be accepted by non-Marxists; the latter would mostly agree that the struggle between patricians and plebeians in Ancient Rome, or between Liberals and Conservatives in nineteenth-century Britain, was largely a matter of competing economic interests, though few non-Marxists would now accept the view that there was no 'law' in primitive societies or early communities. The difference between Marxists and non-Marxists lies not so much in the recognition of the fact of class struggle as in what is deduced from this fact.

According to Marx and Engels, the production of food and other goods, and the economic relations between the various parties represented in economic relations, and the relationships between the various classes and between individuals within a class, are the basic realities of the situation in any particular country, and this network of economic relationships is known, in Marxist terminology, as the infra-structure. However, on the basis of this infra-structure of social reality, various 'ideologies' or superstructures are built in order to justify the existing reality. Religion is the most important of these ideologies, for it teaches that 'the powers that be are ordained of God'[1] and this leads easily to a doctrine such as that of 'the Divine Right of Kings', according to which the King must be obeyed because God has appointed him to his position, a view which was officially accepted in Imperial

[1] Romans xiii. 1–4.

F

Russia and which appears in article 1 of the Imperial *Svod Zakonov*.[1] Another ideology is the doctrine of the social contract, the view that the State evolved as a result of a social contract between the governed and the governors. Ideologies usually serve the purpose of buttressing an existing social and legal system, though they are also sometimes elaborated to provide philosophical support for some economically powerful class that is about to make a bid for power in a revolutionary situation. As the term ideology in Marxist terminology covers religion, it is wider than the term political theory, though Marxists would claim that religions are in effect political theories in disguise. Legal philosophy in particular is an ideology in Marxist terms, for like other ideologies, it consists of propaganda, open or veiled, for the support of measures which would promote the interests of some class, usually that of the dominant or ruling class.

From this, it might appear that Marxism is itself to be regarded as an ideology intended to provide philosophical support for the promotion of the interests and aspirations of the working class, the exploited class in modern industrial societies. This, however, Marx and Engels denied vigorously; they were not setting out to provide an ideology, but a science, that is, an objective description of observable facts and laws of social and historical development.

One of the weak points of the whole system, whether considered as ideology or science, is, however, its treatment of law, for Marx and Engels seemed to have confused law with legal philosophy, and this led them to think of law itself as an ideology and therefore part of the super-structure of society. The rules in force at a particular time and place are law; if it be asserted, on the basis of some particular moral or legal theory, that they in fact correspond to justice, this is an attempt to justify them in the eyes of those subject to them and may legitimately be termed 'ideology'. Yet the distinction never seems to have been clear in the mind of Marx, and it may well be that the ambiguities of the German word *Recht*, which can mean either 'law' or 'justice', led to this confusion, which Marx shares with some other continental European writers. It is a confusion which could hardly occur in the case of a person whose mother-tongue was English. Thus at times Marx and Engels write of law as an ideology, and at other times they write of it as a mere reflection of economic facts. Yet economic facts are presented as being part of the infra-structure or basic reality.

Like the infra-structure, law developed in accordance with changes in the means of production, and Marx said of the English Factory Acts,

[1] See p. 12 *ante*.

for example, that they were just as much a necessary product of modern industry as cotton-yarns, machinery and the electric telegraph. If law is a more or less accurate reflection of the economic realities, it can hardly be mere ideology, and the failure to distinguish clearly between law and legal philosophy is of much more crucial importance in Marxism than it would be in some other philosophies, for it raises the question whether law is to be regarded as 'infra-structure' (reality) or 'super-structure' (ideology).

Another source of confusion in the Marxist writings, which has been amply exploited by Soviet leaders, is in the use of the terms 'democracy' and 'dictatorship'. In England and in other Western European countries the term 'democracy' stands for a system of government in which the citizens have a considerable choice in the matters of who is to govern and what policies are to be followed by the government, and the term usually also connotes a considerable degree of civil liberty with regard to matters such as the formation of political parties and the expression of political opinions which may be opposed to those of the government in power: and the term 'dictatorship' is used instead of the older terms of 'monarchy' and 'autocracy' because monarchy has come to be associated with hereditary royalty.[1] The Third French Republic set up in 1870 during the Franco-Prussian war was in ordinary political language a 'democracy'; there was a Parliament, one house of which consisted of elected deputies, and parties and newspapers representing all shades of political opinion flourished. Yet it was described by Marx as being 'the dictatorship of capital'. Similarly, after the power of capitalism was broken, Marx foresaw the workers establishing a 'dictatorship of the proletariat' which, at the same time, would be 'real democracy'. Engels, indeed, seems to have thought that the political form the dictatorship of the proletariat would take, would be akin to the parliamentary forms of the Third Republic; just as these political forms were in his time used to maintain 'the dictatorship of capital' so after the abolition of capital they would serve 'the dictatorship of the proletariat'. Clearly the term 'dictatorship' here is being used to indicate, not the political form of government, but the fact that the class whose interests would dictate the policies to be followed would be the capitalists before the revolution and the workers afterwards.

Thus Marx foresaw a situation in which the most numerous class in a modern capitalist community, the working class (the proletariat), would ultimately throw off the domination of the capitalists, and establish its own society. This society would be a classless community, for

[1] The term 'monarchy' in its original sense means 'the rule of one'.

there would be no exploiting and no exploited classes. It would not be possible to establish this at once, so for the interim period the State would still be necessary, and this would be a proletarian State exercising the dictatorship of the proletariat. During this interim period of the dictatorship of the proletariat the former working class would be the dominant class in society, but there would still be remnants of the former exploiting classes in existence, and these remnants could be expected to try to do what they could to overthrow the dictatorship of the proletariat and to restore the former situation under which they had power, privileges and influence. The main task of the dictatorship of the proletariat would be to crush for ever the remnants of these former oppressing classes, and once this had been done, true communism could be established, and the State and the law, no longer being necessary, would 'wither away'.

During the period of the dictatorship of the proletariat Marx envisaged the continued existence of law, and he thought that this law, the law of the period of the dictatorship of the proletariat, however much an improvement it would be on bourgeois law, the law of capitalist states, would still have certain capitalist features. Marx's phrase is not a happy one: he said that the law during this period would be '*mit einer bürgerlichen Schranke behaftet*' and it is difficult to convey exactly the vagueness of the German in which he was writing, but perhaps 'afflicted with bourgeois limitations' gives the sense of the words, though exactly what he meant is far from clear. Perhaps what he meant was that the law of the period of the dictatorship of the proletariat would still bear a certain formal resemblance to bourgeois law in that bourgeois legal concepts would be employed, and most Soviet jurists in fact understand the expression in that sense; it is also possible, however, that all he meant was that the law would still have coercive functions in view of the fact that during the dictatorship of the proletariat there would still remain hostile class elements to be suppressed. The phrase may also be understood as meaning that until full communism had been reached, when there would be such an abundance of everything that inequality in the distribution of goods and services would cease, there would still be inequalities; the proletarian dictatorship would adopt as its slogan 'From each according to his abilities, to each according to the work performed' whereas full communism would have the slogan 'From each according to his abilities, to each according to his needs'. During the period of proletarian dictatorship, as there would still be inequalities in the quality of work performed by different individuals, their share of goods and services would be different, and the law would still have to regulate the division of commodities on a basis of inequality, and in this respect it would resemble bourgeois law, which perpetuates inequalities in wealth and the right to goods and services.

In a fully communist society there would be no State and no law; the direction of people would be replaced by the administration of things. It must be admitted, however, that Marx and Engels never very clearly described the future communist society of their dreams, and much of what they say appears to be contradictory. They were much more concerned with the means to be adopted for overthrowing the capitalist State than with elaborate predictions of what would happen once this had been achieved. It does seem clear, however, that they envisaged the disappearance of the State and the law, at any rate as at present understood, and that they envisaged some centralized system of 'administration' by which the whole community would participate in the production and distribution of commodities. Exactly how this 'administration' would differ from 'law' as conventionally understood is nowhere explained, but it seems that they thought that once the classless society had been established, there would no longer be need of coercion to enforce the rules and standards required, and that 'public opinion' and pressure from neighbours would replace the coercive apparatus of law courts and prisons. In so far as anything that might be termed 'law' would still exist, it would be law that was completely just, so there would no longer be any possibility of distinguishing between law and justice; and in so far as it realized justice completely, it would be utterly different from all previously known forms of law. Marx and Engels also envisaged, with the disappearance of law, the disappearance of money, for in the communist society there would be plenty for all, and so money would become obsolete as being unnecessary.

The ending of the dictatorship of the proletariat and the achievement of full communism would not be accomplished at a single stroke; it would be a gradual process extending over a generation or more. But gradually the proletarian State, exercising the dictatorship of the proletariat, would be able to relax once the class enemy had been eliminated. Gradually more and more functions would be transferred from the State to 'social organizations', by which seems to be meant voluntary organizations of citizens. Gradually the profession of civil servant would become obsolete as more and more work was taken over voluntarily by the citizens themselves, acting in organized groups.

To most non-Marxists, Marxism seems full of contradictions: the State is in its very essence an instrument for ensuring the exploitation of one class by another, yet a proletarian State will abolish exploitation; the proletarian State will be a dictatorship of the proletariat and at the same time a democracy; the proletarian dictatorship will be necessary in order to crush the exploiting classes, but the exploiting classes will have been deprived of their means of exploitation, namely the ownership of the land and the factories; that Marxism is at the same time a scientific theory of society and a guide to the construction of a new kind of society based on freedom and justice; that all theories of society are 'ideologies' and therefore false but socialist theory is scientifically true; and many others. But strictly this is no defect once the Marxist view is accepted that logical contradictions are inherent in reality, for the Marxist interprets opposite forces in nature or in society as logical contradictions. A theory of nature or society, if it is to reflect reality, must therefore contain logical contradictions. This type of thinking was taken over by Marx and Engels from Hegel's philosophy of history and his theories of logic. This logic of contradictions was termed the logic of dialectics by Hegel, and for this reason Marxist philosophy is known as dialectical materialism. To the Marxist, any criticism of his theories on the ground that they are 'contradictory' misses the whole point; to the Marxist this is no criticism, but the guarantee that his theories are a true reflection of objective reality.

LENIN

Lenin attempted to purge the Marxist movement of errors in the interpretation of Marx's writings, and to restore the 'real' teachings of Marx. While, as we have seen, Marx himself concentrated mainly on an analysis of conditions existing in his own day, and became vaguer and vaguer as he attempted to look into the future, it was essential for his followers to consider how the social revolution was to be achieved in practice. By the time of the First World War the Marxist movement generally was split into two sections, the 'evolutionists' and the 'revolutionists'; the first maintained that society could and, if appropriate action were taken, would gradually evolve from capitalism and without the necessity of violent revolution, while the second group held that the capitalists would never allow themselves to be dispossessed peaceably, and that violent revolution would therefore be necessary; from which it followed that it should be worked for and planned. Lenin came out emphatically in favour of the second approach.

In his book *State and Revolution*, published in 1917, Lenin emphasized that the initial period of the dictatorship of the proletariat would require the suppression by violence of the capitalists and other exploiting classes. For this purpose a strong State would be required, though it would be a State which would gradually 'wither away' as the capitalists were eliminated and there was no longer any need for coercive powers.

Lenin emphasized the necessity of crushing the capitalist elements remaining in the country by the establishment of the dictatorship of the proletariat. He regarded the dictatorship of the proletariat as a necessary measure, but a temporary one; indeed we fail to understand his thought entirely unless we realize that right until his death in 1924, Lenin, like most of his colleagues, believed that world revolution was imminent. It is true that communist revolutions had failed in Germany and Hungary, but there was considerable communist agitation throughout Europe in the early nineteen-twenties and the defeat of the revolution in Germany and Hungary was looked on as a mere temporary setback. In Marxist terminology, there was thought to be a 'revolutionary situation' in Germany in particular in the nineteen-twenties, because the power of the working class, organized in trade unions and political parties, did not receive full recognition from the law. The dictatorship of the proletariat would certainly have to be maintained in Russia until other countries had their communist revolutions, indeed, the fact that the first communist revolution had taken place in what, in capitalist terms, was a rather backward country, Russia, was thought of as something of an historical accident, and it was thought that revolution would soon also occur in the more advanced capitalist countries. The dictatorship of the proletariat, the proletarian State, would of course ultimately wither away, but there could be no question of its withering away while Russia was still surrounded by hostile capitalist countries.

During the transition period, which Lenin thought would be comparatively short, the law would still be partly bourgeois, capitalist law, and partly socialist law, but the law could not move faster than events, and the New Economic Policy meant that to some extent capitalism was given a new lease of life in Russia.

After this first short phase of the dictatorship of the proletariat, there would follow the period of full communism, though Lenin never seems to have thought that full communism could ever be achieved in one country alone, least of all in Russia. Under full communism justice would finally be achieved in human affairs; as there would be abundance for all, there would be no need for law to regulate the distribution of goods and property; everything would be available in sufficient quantities for all, in accordance with the principle 'From each according to his abilities, to each according to his needs'. Lenin never seems to have considered the question how needs would be estimated; even if each individual became the judge of his own needs, there might have to be limits on exorbitant claims, and then there would still have to be some external authority empowered to determine what the needs of each individual were; and if rulings were not to be arbitrary it would seem that law of some kind must survive even in the phase of full communism.

On the more practical plane, Lenin certainly realized that if the New Economic Policy of a temporary restoration of some of the features of capitalism were to work, the need for an ordinary system of civil law was imperative, and he sanctioned the promulgation of the Civil Code of 1922, which, as we have seen, contains nothing that is particularly revolutionary apart from its famous first article, which says that civil rights are protected by law except in cases when they are used in a manner contrary to their social and economic purposes. Even with article 1, most of the Civil Code could have been used as a workable system of law in a capitalist country, and indeed, it was based largely on the German and Swiss Civil Codes and on a Draft Civil Code that had been put before the Imperial State Duma in 1913 and not proceeded with owing to the outbreak of war the following year.

However, Lenin's voluminous writings, sometimes somewhat contradictory, have provided a storehouse of quotations from which later Soviet writers have been able to draw, and indeed, Soviet legal writers tend to decorate their writings with citations from Marx, Engels and Lenin (and, until recently, Stalin) much as seventeenth-century writers interspersed their writings with biblical texts.

STALIN AND VYSHINSKI

During the late nineteen-twenties, after the death of Lenin, it became clear that the proletarian revolution was unlikely to occur in the immediate future in the advanced capitalist countries (though there was much talk of 'a revolutionary situation' existing in Germany); indeed, it was in less advanced countries, such as Spain and China, that revolutionary hopes ran higher. The question whether it would be possible to progress to communism, or even achieve the more limited objects of socialism, in one country alone, therefore, became crucial. This led to considerable conflict between different factions in the Soviet Communist Party leadership, and from these internal disputes one leader emerged victorious – Stalin.

Stalin made it clear that in his view socialism in one country was possible; and therefore the question of the nature of the socialist State and its law became acute. Yet the tendency of some Soviet jurists, and in particular Pashukanis, during the late nineteen-twenties and early

THE FOUNDATIONS OF THE SOVIET LEGAL SYSTEM [73

nineteen-thirties was the reverse of helpful, for they maintained that 'law' was in its essence a bourgeois phenomenon, and that therefore no real 'socialist law' was possible; law and socialism were incompatible. To some extent this view harmonized with the policy then being pursued by the Soviet Government, for this was the period when the NEP was being abolished and the peasants driven into the collective farms; and although as we have seen, these processes were in general conducted within a legal framework, they involved flagrant disregard of vested legal rights. To play down the importance of law and legal rights was, in a sense, to further the measures taken by the Government, measures which were heralded as steps towards the building of socialism. But the idea that law was basically a bourgeois phenomenon concerned with harmonizing private relationships – particularly those of buyer and seller – suggested that now that there were no longer private business-men, capitalists, whom the Soviet State needed to control firmly, there was no longer much need for the law, which could now be expected to 'wither away'.

The views of Pashukanis were in complete conformity with the theo-retical postulates of Marx, that is to say, Pashukanis' theory of law and of the State was a possible one within the general Marxist theory. (Some might say that it was the only possible one; this is probably going too far, for the vagueness and contradictions of Marx and Engels when dealing with the law are so great that many different theories might be formulated and still be able to claim with justification that they were orthodox Marxism.)

Stalin, however, wanted no lapse into anarchy, and he saw that he needed a strong State and a vigorous system of law. He also needed an apologist who would undertake to justify his system of repression in terms of Marxist doctrine, and he found one in the person of Andrey Vyshinski. Vyshinski had taken a prominent part in the preparation of the treason trials of the nineteen-thirties, and had himself been the prosecutor in the most important of them; he was ready to serve Stalin with fanatical loyalty. He undertook to provide a new theory of State and law to meet the needs of the Stalin régime. Clearly, it could not be presented as a 'new' theory; it had to take the form of a restatement of Marxist truths. In Vyshinski's writings the Marxist phrases are found repeated, together with any amount of vituperation of 'bourgeois jurists' and 'bourgeois theories'. Nevertheless the real attack is not so much against 'bourgeois' theories, as against persons such as Pashukanis, who had attempted to develop a legal theory in complete conformity with the teachings of Marx.

Vyshinski, though claiming to be an orthodox Marxist and denouncing those who opposed him as traitors, wreckers and spies, in fact reverts to certain accepted postulates of 'bourgeois jurisprudence'. Law is no longer regarded as a 'system of social relations' but as a system of norms, though these norms must be based on 'life'. Law is not merely a matter of politics; the view that it was had led to the idea that the application of legislation is based on political considerations, and therefore to lack of respect for 'revolutionary legality'. The phrase 'revolutionary legality' now becomes a key one; clearly any State wants its legislation to be respected, but Marxists, having for so long regarded law as a mere instrument of oppression, or of politics, have seldom had much respect for the law as such, and the phrase 'revolutionary legality' was presumably designed to attract them, by drawing a distinction between Soviet law, law based on a revolution, and ordinary bourgeois law, to which no respect was due. To put this in another way, Vyshinski was out to combat the inherently anarchistic implications of the original Marxist doctrine. For Vyshinski, the law and the State will wither away, not with the achievement of communism, but 'only in the highest phase of communism, with the annihilation of capitalist encirclement'.[1] In any case, speculation about the withering away of the State and the law was not in the interests of the Soviet State; the interests of the Soviet State demanded the building up of powerful armed forces and the existence of a powerful system of coercion within the country. It therefore followed, in this logic, that those who were speculating about the withering away of the law were actively undermining the armed forces of the Soviet Union, and were therefore traitors. Pashukanis was condemned as such, though he was rehabilitated 'as a person' (though he was now defunct) during the post-Stalin

[1] The phrase 'capitalist encirclement' is one frequently met with in Soviet writings. The Russian word 'encirclement' translated is however ambiguous, for it may mean either 'encirclement' or 'environment'. If it is understood as 'encirclement', capitalist encirclement will last until all other major States have ceased to be capitalist, when the USSR will no longer be 'surrounded by capitalist states'. But if it is understood as 'environment' it may be maintained that there can still be a 'capitalist environment' so long as there remain 'remnants of capitalism in the minds of men', which, in Soviet terms, may refer to attitudes such as acquisitiveness, a competitive attitude towards others, and even drunkenness. Understood in this sense, a capitalist environment could still continue long after capitalism had ceased to exist. The point may seem unimportant, but as Soviet legal theory still, in the main, adheres to the view that law will no longer be necessary once 'capitalist encirclement' has ceased, it may be that the ambiguity of the phrase conceals genuine differences of opinion about when this may be expected to occur.

period; this, however, amounted only to an acceptance of his good faith and not to an acceptance of the correctness of his views. For the time being, the whole embarrassing question of the 'withering away of the State and the law' was solved by Stalin's declaration that 'the dying out of the State will come not through weakening State authority, but through intensifying that authority to the utmost' (it will be remembered that for Marxists logical contradictions are inherent in 'life'). Vyshinski's role was to persuade the Soviet people that the paramount aim of Marxists was not to get rid of the State, but to build a powerful socialist State; and this was really a distortion of the original Marxist view according to which the State was essentially an instrument for the domination of one class over another.

SINCE STALIN

Since the death of Stalin (1953) Vyshinski's views have been rejected, and he has been denounced for the part he played 'during the period of the cult of personality'. Yet no very decisive new developments have taken place in legal theory.

It is now considered that the period of the dictatorship of the proletariat has come to an end, and the current stage is known as 'the period of the construction of communism'. The dictatorship of the proletariat has been replaced by the State of the Whole People; the ridicule to which Engels subjected the phrase 'People's State' doubtless prevented that expression from being used. Moreover, it is being suggested that certain recent developments, such as the introduction of a 'volunteer militia' to take over some of the duties of the police, the re-establishment of Comrades' Courts, and other transfers of function to 'social organizations' may presage the beginnings of the 'withering away of the State and the law' and it is no longer regarded as treason to speculate about these matters.

Before considering the relationship between Soviet legal theory and Soviet law one point must be made. Soviet writers have, since the existence of exploiting and exploited classes no longer exists in the Soviet Union, found difficulty in maintaining a consistent attitude towards the subject of classes. If the working class is no longer exploited, but is the ruling class, as Soviet theory asserts, it is difficult to see in what sense it is a class at all. In official Soviet theory there are no longer exploiting and exploited classes in Soviet society, but there are two 'friendly, non-antagonistic' classes, the proletariat and the peasantry, together with a 'stratum' (not a separate class), the intelligentsia. A person who accepted the basic tenets of Marxism but who felt no obligation to support official Soviet doctrine might well argue that in the Soviet Union there is indeed an exploiting and exploited class, namely, the proletariat and the peasantry. The forced deliveries of food products which the peasants have been obliged to make to the State, either for nothing or for nominal payment, could well be thought of as 'exploitation', in the strict Marxist sense of the appropriation of the value created by another's labour, by the worker from the peasant, for it enables cheap food to be provided for workers at factory canteens and other places. This, of course, the Soviets cannot admit, but it is significant that although the two 'friendly non-antagonistic classes' (and the 'stratum') form the Soviet population, the population is always 'guided by the working class'. As Vyshinski put it, 'With us the will of the working class merges with the will of the entire people.' No independent expression of the will of the peasantry can officially be admitted or permitted, and indeed the 'will of the working class' is usually assumed to be the same as the will of the Communist Party.

From the theoretical point of view, much of the difficulty arises from the fact that Marx and Engels were concerned mainly with the position of the urban proletariat, and devoted comparatively little thought to the organization of agriculture either during the period of the dictatorship of the proletariat or in the future communist society. From the practical point of view, the difficulty is that the peasantry have never been wholly reconciled to Soviet authority, especially since collectivization; if the peasantry really is the 'exploited class' in Soviet society as some suggest, this is understandable.

Soviet law claims to be based on Marxist theory. Yet the relevance of Soviet legal theory to the actual rules of Soviet law is not always obvious. Some, indeed, suggest that there is no real connection at all; that Soviet academics' exchange polemics about theory, bandying quotations from Marx, Engels and Lenin while Soviet legislators and courts proceed according to the requirements of the immediate situation, or as they would say 'from life'. Soviet writers maintain that there is a close connection, and endeavour to provide a theoretical Marxist foundation for every new enactment; to a considerable extent this is an *ex post facto* rationalization, and so it might be said that here again law comes first and legal theory later.

Yet there is an inner connection between Soviet legal theory and Soviet law. It is not so much that the law is an application in practice of the theory, as is claimed, but rather the fact that Soviet theoreticians, legislators, judges and officials all share a basic faith in Marxism, however differently they may understand it in individual cases. Marxism has often been compared to religion, and the analogies are many and profound; the belief in an original state of 'primitive communism' corresponds to the idea of the Garden of Eden; a 'fall' represented by the introduction of private property and the division of society into classes, a struggle conducted by the Church Militant (the Communist Party) to establish the Kingdom of God on earth, complete with anathemas hurled at 'non-believers', the substitution of quotations from accepted writings for original thought, and the idea that a statement can be 'proved' by a reference to these accepted writings all suggest that the psychology of the communist is basically similar to that of the religious believer. The question alleged to have been put by Khrushchev's son-in-law, 'Does the Pope believe in Christianity?' has often been thought to suggest that the leaders of the Soviet State are mere cynics with no genuine belief in Marxism. Though not impossible, this seems highly improbable; their whole education has been based on Marxism, and their own success has been attributed to understanding of its principles. Moreover, their education has precluded the possibility of any serious understanding of any other possible frame of reference for thinking about the world and its problems. They may well at times feel dissatisfaction with some particular formulation of Marxism, or with some view alleged to follow from Marxist premises; but the suggestion that they are mere cynics out for their own personal power and aggrandizement seems contrary to all the evidence and the psychological probabilities.

The Marxist nature of Soviet law lies, as has been suggested earlier, not in its techniques or terminologies which are common to other systems, but in its purpose. It is the whole bias of the system, as distinct from the nature of individual rules, that displays its Marxist character.

THE JURIDICAL SOURCES OF SOVIET LAW

ENACTED LAW

In most legal systems there is a recognized hierarchy of sources of law. Usually there is a Constitution, which is regarded as basic, and it is from the Constitution that the legislature derives its powers to enact binding laws. The Constitution itself usually provides special procedures by which it can be amended. In other words, should the legislature by an ordinary enactment purport to enact something contrary to the Constitution; for example, should it pass an enactment depriving citizens of a right guaranteed by the Constitution, the enactment will be declared void. Sometimes this can be done in the ordinary courts, as in the USA; sometimes a challenge to the constitutionality of an enactment must go to a special constitutional court, as in the Federal Republic of Germany. Either the Constitution or ordinary laws may give powers to the government or to particular Ministers to issue decrees or regulations within certain limits, but if these limits are exceeded the decrees or regulations may be challenged on the ground that they are *ultra vires*, that is, beyond the power of the authority that promulgated them. The manner of challenge of course varies considerably from country to country, but in most countries of the common law group this can be done in the ordinary courts.

In Great Britain we have no written constitution, so the question of the unconstitutionality of an Act of Parliament cannot arise, but rules or orders made by Ministers of the Crown acting under statutory authority are sometimes declared by the courts to be void on the ground that the Minister has exceeded the powers conferred on him by Parliament. In the United States, however, if it is alleged that a statute passed by Congress, or by a State Legislature, contains provisions that are *ultra vires* the legislature, a dispute about the validity of the enactment called in question may be taken to the Supreme Court of the United States, and if the Supreme Court holds that the enactment is *ultra vires*, this is equivalent to saying that it is a nullity, that it has not and never had any legal effect. For this reason the Supreme Court of the United States is known as the Guardian of the Constitution, for it strikes down as invalid or *ultra vires* all legislation or other official acts which are contrary to the Constitution of the United States. The Constitution of the United States is thus a basic or fundamental law to which all citizens and public authorities, including Congress, the United States legislature, must conform.

The place of the Constitution of the USSR within the Soviet legal system is not so easy to describe. It is certainly described officially as 'Fundamental Law' and its final article, article 146 says:

The Constitution of the USSR may be amended only by decision of the Supreme Soviet of the USSR adopted by a majority of not less than two-thirds of the votes in each of its Chambers.

Moreover article 32 says:

The legislative power of the USSR is exercised exclusively by the Supreme Soviet of the USSR.

These provisions would suggest that rules of law contained in the Constitution itself can be changed only by a formal constitutional amendment. Nevertheless, it is quite clear that rules laid down in the Constitution may be changed by ordinary legislation passed by the Supreme Soviet of the USSR without a formal constitutional amendment being first made. For example, article 119 of the Constitution in its original form in the 1936 version provided that the

> right to rest and leisure is ensured by the reduction of the working day to seven hours for the overwhelming majority of workers.

but the working day was increased to eight hours by a law passed by the Supreme Soviet on 26 June 1940. Similarly article 121 in its original form made all education, including higher education, free of charge, but an enactment of the Supreme Soviet of 2 October 1940 allowed fees to be charged after the seventh year of free schooling, with the result that university education and secondary education after the age of fifteen had in some cases to be paid for. The necessary changes in articles 119 and 121 of the Constitution were only made in 1947 after a proposal by Vyshinski that the Constitution should be amended so as to bring it into conformity with existing law. To the western constitutional lawyer, and in particular to the American constitutional lawyer, this seems a remarkable proceeding, for in the United States while it might be necessary to bring Acts of Congress or of State Legislatures into conformity with the Constitution, the converse could hardly occur, for any Acts of Congress contrary to the Constitution could not be regarded as 'laws' as they would be void on the ground that they were *ultra vires*. The Constitution of the USSR can therefore not be regarded as 'fundamental law' in the sense that the Constitution of the USA is fundamental law. In the United States it would have been necessary first to introduce an amendment to the Constitution in accordance with the special procedures provided for that purpose.

It might be argued, however, that as all laws passed by the Supreme Soviet of the USSR are passed unanimously, they comply with the rule requiring a two-thirds majority, and so amend the Constitution by implication, if not in express words. Yet if this were so, it is difficult to see the reason for the *ex post facto* formal amendments proposed by Vyshinski in 1947.

But there is another point to be considered in this connection. It appears that changes in the Constitution may even be made by an authority officially subordinate to the Supreme Soviet of the USSR.

The Supreme Soviet of the USSR in fact usually meets for only two sessions a year, and each session usually lasts for only about ten days. During the intervals between the sessions of the Supreme Soviet most of its functions can be exercised by the Praesidium of the Supreme Soviet, which consists of thirty-three members elected by the Supreme Soviet. The composition of this body is laid down in article 48 of the Constitution, and its powers are set out in article 49. It has no power to enact a law (*zakon*) but it is given power to issue a decree (*ukaz*); and power to interpret laws.

At the time when the Constitution was adopted in 1936 it seems to have been imagined that, whereas the Supreme Soviet would enact all necessary legislation, the Praesidium would confine itself to the issuance of decrees implementing such legislation, or giving authoritative rulings on the interpretation of laws in force. There was nothing in the Constitution suggesting that the Supreme Soviet would only meet for such short periods that it would be unable to cope with the legislative requirements of the country. Quite soon after the Constitution of 1936 had come into force, the Praesidium of the Supreme Soviet took to issuing decrees which were not merely implementations of existing laws but contained quite new principles, leaving the decrees to be ratified subsequently by the next session of the Supreme Soviet. As the decrees were invariably ratified (no such decree has ever been rejected, though occasionally one or two minor amendments have been made) the Praesidium of the Supreme Soviet became virtually a legislative authority, the formal ratification of its decrees being taken for granted. The decrees come into force as soon as they are made, so in some cases it would be virtually impossible for the Supreme Soviet to refuse to ratify them.

This means that any real distinction between a law passed by the Supreme Soviet and a decree issued by its Praesidium soon ceased to exist. And, as a provision of the Constitution could be amended by a law, so it could by a decree of the Praesidium of the Supreme Soviet. Article 135 of the Constitution in its original form provided that any citizen over the age of eighteen might be elected to be a member of the Supreme Soviet. Before the election of 1946, a decree of the Praesidium of the Supreme Soviet raised the age from eighteen to twenty-three, and the elections were held on the basis of this decree, only candidates over the age of twenty-three being allowed to stand for election. Subsequently the new Supreme Soviet, elected on the basis of this decree, amended the Constitution in order to bring it into conformity with the decree. In this case a fundamental right given by the Constitution was taken away from people over eighteen and under twenty-three by a decree of the Praesidium.

However, the Praesidium of the Supreme Soviet could perhaps in fairness be regarded as merely a standing committee of the Supreme Soviet exercising its powers during the long intervals between the sessions of the Supreme Soviet. But rights given by the Constitution may be altered, not only by the Praesidium of the Supreme Soviet, but also by a purely executive body, the Council of Ministers of the USSR. For example, article 8 of the Constitution says, 'The land occupied by collective farms is secured to them for their free use for an unlimited time, that is, for ever.' This would suggest that a collective farm has a constitutional right to continue to occupy the land originally transferred to it by its original members, or land subsequently allotted to it. Yet a decree of the Council of Ministers of 1950 authorizes the Minister of Agriculture by decree to consolidate two or more collective farms, or to transfer land belonging to one collective farm to another, or to transfer land belonging to a collective farm to some other institution, though his decree needs the formal approval of the Council of Ministers. Yet nothing in the Constitution authorizes the Council of Ministers to withdraw or limit rights enshrined in the Constitution.

It is true that these things occurred under Stalin, and that modern Soviet writers denounce the 'illegalities' of 'the period of the cult of personality' in general: but as they seldom say exactly what occurrences they have in mind, it is not easy for an outsider to understand which practices of this period they are denouncing, and which they regard as 'legal'.

This does not mean, however, that the Constitution is unimportant in practice. Though the rules contained in the Constitution of the USSR will hardly inhibit the Praesidium of the Supreme Soviet or the Council of Ministers of the USSR from issuing such decrees as they think fit, lesser governmental and administrative bodies are usually kept well within their constitutional functions.

Article 20 of the Constitution provides that in the event of a discrepancy between the law of a Union Republic and the Law of the Union the All-Union law prevails. In 1946 an enactment of the Supreme Soviet of the Ukrainian Soviet Socialist Republic concerning divorce was found to be in direct conflict with All-Union legislation on the matter and was withdrawn the following year after the discrepancy was pointed out to the Supreme Soviet of the Ukrainian SSR.

The legislation of the USSR thus consists of the Constitution of the USSR, laws voted by the Supreme Soviet, decrees issued by the Praesidium of the Supreme Soviet, and decrees issued by the Council of

G

Ministers of the USSR and by individual Ministries and other authorities. Similarly the legislation of a Union Republic consists of its Constitution, laws voted by its Supreme Soviet, decrees issued by the Praesidium of its Supreme Soviet, and decrees issued by its Council of Ministers and by individual Ministries and other authorities, and decrees issued by local authorities. In Soviet usage the term law (*zakon*) is reserved for enactments of the Supreme Soviet of the USSR and of Supreme Soviets of Union Republics; a decree issued by the Praesidium of Supreme Soviet of the USSR and by the Praesidia of Supreme Soviets of Union Republics is known as a *ukaz*, and a decree of the Council of Ministers of the USSR or of the Council of Ministers of a Union Republic is known either as a *postanovleniye* or a *rasporyazheniye*; a decree of an individual Ministry or other central or local authority is known either as an *instruktsia* or as a *prikaz*. The differences between these different types of decree are purely technical.

Strictly speaking, however, a *ukaz* may be of three kinds: it may elaborate the provisions of a law without infringing them; this seems to have been the original idea when the power to issue *ukazy* was conferred on the Praesidium of the Supreme Soviet of the USSR. Secondly, it may contain an authoritative interpretation of a law; the power to issue such a *ukaz* is given expressly by the Constitution; and thirdly, it may contain new rules of law, in which case it requires confirmation by the Supreme Soviet at its next session.

A decree of the Council of Ministers of the USSR may sometimes be issued under powers contained in a law, in which case it is a form of delegated legislation as the term is understood in other countries. Sometimes, however, they may be issued without any such delegation, in which case they would be valid if they do not conflict with legislation in force, for the power to issue such decrees is given by article 66 of the Constitution. In the event that a decree of the Council of Ministers of the USSR conflicted with a law in force, it could be annulled by the Praesidium of the Supreme Soviet of the USSR: this is expressly provided for by article 49 of the Constitution. The matter could be brought before it by a protest by the Procurator-General of the USSR; and if it does not choose to annul it, presumably the decree must be regarded as valid law. The Praesidium of the Supreme Soviet of the USSR may also annul decrees of the Councils of Ministers of Union Republics, and the right of annulment in such cases also belongs to the Praesidium of the Supreme Soviet of the Union Republic concerned.

Sometimes a decree is issued as a joint decree of the Council of Ministers of the USSR and of the Central Committee of the Communist

Party of the Soviet Union. In this case technically its legal nature is not altered, but the fact that it is not only a decree of the Council of Ministers but a party directive of the highest authority, would in practice preclude any question of its legality or conformity to law being raised.

COURT DECISIONS

In England and other countries in which the English common law has taken root, an important source of law, besides the enactments of legislative authorities, is *case law*, the decisions of courts in cases coming before them. Once a decision has been given by a court on some disputed point, the decision is regarded as a precedent to be followed for the future, and therefore much of the law in common law countries is to be found in the law reports, in the reports of cases decided by the courts. This case law may be of two kinds. First, it may consist of points of law not covered at all by legislation, and a good deal of the English common law of contract and tort (liability for harm or damage caused) is based not on statute but on the decisions of judges in cases coming before them, and is therefore to be found only in the law reports, and not in the statute-book. Secondly, cases occur in which questions relating to the interpretation of enacted law arise; for example whether a certain provision should be interpreted as covering some set of facts which has arisen in practice. These questions have to be decided by courts, and their decisions will be regarded as precedents to be followed for the future.

On the other hand, the countries of the European continent do not usually regard the decisions of the courts as a source of law, at any rate in theory; the actual position in practice varies a good deal from country to country, but in general we can say that nothing like the same respect or authority is given to the decided case or 'precedent' in the continental countries as in the common law countries.

In the USSR there is no question of any 'common law' growing up unconnected with enacted law, but codes, statutes and decrees require interpretation in the USSR as elsewhere, and the effect of court decisions is discussed by Soviet writers under the topic of 'interpretation' rather than under that of 'sources of law' for it is firmly denied in the USSR that decided cases could be a 'source of law'. Soviet writers distinguish between authentic, judicial and doctrinal interpretation, the classification being based on the authority of the interpreter. As we have seen, the Praesidium of the Supreme Soviet of the USSR is empowered by the Constitution of the USSR to give authoritative interpretations of laws, and similar powers are vested in the Praesidia of the Supreme

Soviets of Union Republics. Such interpretations are deemed 'authentic', for they cannot be questioned. Judicial interpretations are those given by a court. In general, the interpretation placed on an enactment by a court is binding for that case, but not a precedent which other courts are bound to follow for the future. However, the Supreme Court of the USSR is expressly authorized by statute to give directives to other courts explaining the way in which a particular statutory provision should be applied, and the Supreme Courts of Union Republics have similar powers. It seems that this power should be regarded as having effected a kind of compromise between the Anglo-American system of 'case law' and the continental attitude of denying any law-making activity to the courts. In Tsarist times the Ruling Senate, the highest court in the Russian Empire, could give decisions which were binding for the future, so the idea was not unfamiliar to Russian lawyers, and some unifying factor was required if different interpretations of the law were not to arise in various localities; yet suspicion of the lawyer and judge was sufficiently great to prevent the Soviets adopting anything like the Anglo-American system. Hence the idea of giving the Supreme Court limited power to issue 'directives' concerning the interpretation of enactments.

These directives are something between a decree and a law report: the Supreme Court commonly issues these directives as a result of an appeal in a particular case; it states that the law has been misunderstood by lower courts, and then it gives rules about the application of some particular section of a statute or decree. At other times, it issues directives, not as a result of hearing one case only, but because appeals brought to it show that some particular enactment is not properly understood by lower courts, and again it gives detailed rules about its application. These directives are of course binding, because the Court has express statutory power to make them. Some parts of Soviet law have in practice been largely based on these directives: until the Civil Code of 1964 came into force, the law governing contributory negligence was in effect judge-made law. Where a plaintiff is suing a defendant in respect of injuries caused by the defendant's negligence, it may be that the plaintiff himself was partly responsible for the accident, so that the injuries were sustained as a result of the combined negligence of plaintiff and defendant, and in such cases the damages recoverable will be reduced. There was nothing in the Civil Code of 1922 about contributory negligence, but the law was built up by a series of directives of the Supreme Court of the USSR dating from 1926.

However, even where directives are not given by the Supreme Court of the Union, or of the Union Republics, their decisions on points of law, although not perhaps in strict legal theory binding for the future, are normally followed. Cases heard by the Supreme Courts of the Soviet Union, and of the RSFSR, are reported in regular series, and cases decided by other courts are reported in the law journals. There would be no point in reporting them if the decisions were not regarded as offering guidance for the future. The reporting of cases helps to keep the administration of the law uniform, for judges can find out what is being done by other courts in different parts of the country, whereas if no cases were reported, it might happen that different ways of dealing with particular kinds of cases would grow up in different areas, and this is something that the authorities are particularly anxious to avoid. Cases thus have considerable importance, and Soviet textbook writers on the law cite cases more frequently than do the writers of some of the continental countries, though not as much as do English legal textbook writers. In practice, the decisions of the courts virtually amount to a source of law, though they are not officially regarded as such. However, in any system of law gaps may be revealed by a case which depends on facts which do not appear to be directly provided for, and in these cases the gaps must in fact be filled by the courts, for a judge is not entitled to refuse to decide a case on the ground that there is no rule of law governing the matter; he must decide one way or the other. Article 12 of the Basic Principles of Civil Procedure, 1961, provides that in civil cases, the court should apply a provision governing analogous relations, and in default of such, must decide the case in conformity with the general principles and spirit of Soviet legislation. (The rule is repeated in article 4 of the Code of Civil Procedure of RSFSR.) As we have seen,[1] the principle of analogy no longer applies in criminal cases.

Doctrinal interpretation is the interpretation of an enactment by qualified but unofficial persons, for example, academic lawyers. Such interpretation has strictly no binding force at all, but where academic legal opinion is unanimous it will in practice be difficult to ignore.

CUSTOM

Another source of law recognized by most legal systems, though it is of comparatively little importance these days, is custom. If a matter is not directly regulated by statute, but there is a custom prevailing on the matter, under conditions which vary from country to country the custom may be taken into account by a court when giving judgment.

[1] See p. 54 *ante*.

Custom, in practice, was extremely important in Tsarist times, for in the Russian Empire, as in the Soviet Union today, there were, besides the Russians, numerous other ethnic groups, in very different stages of culture and civilization, and in fact the law applied in the *volost* courts which dealt with disputes among peasants was usually the customary law of the area. Indeed in matters of property, inheritance and boundaries it was estimated that something like three-quarters of the population of the Russian Empire were not subject to the official civil laws but to the customary laws applied in the peasant *volost* courts.

The Soviet approach to customary law has been cautious. On the one hand, the Soviet authorities have been determined to stamp out certain primitive customs prevailing among former backward non-Russian ethnic groups, such as the blood-feud, bride-price, polygamy and other customs inconsistent with the principle of sex equality. Indeed, many old customs of this kind are now treated as specific criminal offences and are set out in chapter XI of the Criminal Code of the RSFSR, which is headed 'Crimes constituting Survivals of Local Customs': such are paying or accepting a bride-price, forcing a woman into marriage, bigamy, polygamy and child-marriage. Other types of local custom, however, and in particular local customs about the division of property among the members of a peasant family, constituted no threat to the Soviet system, and the Soviets were not anxious to offend the peasants unnecessarily by forcing them to adopt rules which, however suitable for town-dwellers, were unfamiliar to residents in the country, especially in places where clear and well-established customs existed.

The Soviets have accepted the principle of applying customary law in the settlement of disputes between members of a collective-farm household (the modern equivalent of the traditional Russian peasant household, the *dvor*), and these rules are naturally different from the rules contained in the Civil Code and the Code of Family Law which apply to town-dwellers. In fact the property rights of the members of a family may depend on whether they live within or outside the boundaries of a city, for outside customary law may well apply. In most rural areas the family itself, the *dvor*, the collective-farm household, is regarded as the owner of most of the family property, but a member leaving the household, say going to work in a town, is allowed to take a certain proportion of it with him. The death of the head of the family makes no difference, as the property continues to be owned by the *dvor*, and will be administered by the new head of the family, a principle quite different from the individual ownership recognized in the towns.

A case which came before the courts in 1937 illustrates the position; a man had built himself a house in 1902 in a village where peasant customary law prevailed, under which his children would have equal rights in the house with himself. In 1937 his son sued him, claiming to be entitled to a half-share in the house according to peasant customary law. The son, however, lost the action for the reason that in 1933 the area in which the house stood had been incorporated into a neighbouring city which had extended its boundaries, and so peasant customary law no longer applied. The son could have claimed his share within three years, but his right became statute barred after that time, and as he sued four years after the house had ceased to be subject to peasant customary law, he was too late. Under the ordinary Civil Code, a son has no right to a share of property belonging to his father during his father's lifetime, though under peasant customary law he often had, and the son in this case could, if he had applied in time, have established his right to joint ownership of the house.

Customary law has not been eliminated, though the part it plays in the Soviet system is steadily becoming less important. The Land Code states that local customs concerning the use of land shall be enforced where they do not conflict with the provisions of the Code, so no custom going directly against the Land Code could be recognized. However, Soviet writers often speak of gradually doing away with the distinctions between workers and peasants, or town-dwellers and country-dwellers, and peasant customary law is something that they are likely to get rid of as soon as they conveniently can.

THE SOVIET CONSTITUTION

In the preceding section we saw that the Constitution of the USSR is not in any way an enactment which restrains the authorities from introducing any legislation that they think fit: its provisions do not render void any legislation that may be contrary to them, and in these ways it is unlike the Constitution of the USA, or the written constitutions of many other countries. Nevertheless, despite the fact that it can easily be amended, or can be impliedly amended by the passing of legislation that is inconsistent with its provisions, it does have considerable importance in the Soviet legal system, though not perhaps in the way that western constitutional lawyers would expect.

We should therefore first consider the structure of the Constitution. It contains 146 articles, and is divided into 13 chapters.

Chapter 1, which contains articles 1–12, is headed 'The social structure' but in fact it deals largely with the different forms of property which exist in a socialist state; this topic will be considered in section E of the present chapter.[1] Article 1, however, says: 'The Union of Soviet Socialist Republics is a socialist state of workers and peasants,' which provides a constitutional sanction for the thesis that Soviet society consists of two non-antagonistic classes, and which justifies differences in the rules of law applicable to the two classes. Chapter 2, headed 'The State Structure', is primarily concerned with the powers of the Union as distinct from those of the individual Republics that make up the Union of Soviet Socialist Republics, and covers articles 13–29. Chapter 3, entitled 'The Higher Organs of State Power in the USSR', deals with the highest legislative authority, the Supreme Soviet of the USSR, and covers articles 30–56, and chapter 4, articles 57–63, deals with the Supreme Soviets of the Union Republics, and is headed 'The Higher Organs of State Power in the Union Republics'.

Chapter 5 deals with the Council of Ministers of the USSR and the various Ministries, and comprises articles 64–78; it is headed 'The Organs of State Administration of the USSR'. Chapter 6 deals with the Organs of State Administration in the Union Republics, and covers articles 79–88. Chapter 7 deals with the Organs of State Power in the Autonomous Soviet Socialist Republics: these are areas having a certain degree of local autonomy though considerably less than that of a Union Republic. This covers articles 89–93.

Chapter 8, containing articles 94–101, deals with the Local Organs of State Power, or, as we would say, with local government.

Chapter 9, on the Courts and the Procurator's Office, comprises articles 102–17: these matters are dealt with elsewhere in this book.[2]

Chapter 10, covering articles 118–33, deals with the Fundamental Rights and Duties of Citizens; these provisions will be considered in the Civil Liberties section of this chapter.

Chapter 11 (articles 134–42) deals with the Electoral System, Chapter 12 (articles 143–5) with the Coat of Arms, Flag and Capital, and chapter 13 has a single article, no. 146, which says that the Constitution may be amended only by a decision of the Supreme Soviet of the USSR adopted by a majority of not less than two-thirds of the votes of each of its chambers; we have already seen how little this means in practice.

We now turn to chapter 2 of the Constitution, which deals with the State Structure. Article 13 says: 'The Union of Soviet Socialist Republics is a general state, formed on the basis of a voluntary union of equal Soviet Socialist Republics' which it then proceeds to list: the Russian Soviet Federative Socialist Republic, by far the largest Union Republic

1 See p. 105 *post*.   2 See chapter 5.

in territory, population and economic importance, the Ukrainian Soviet Socialist Republic, the Byelorussian SSR, sometimes referred to in English as the White Russian SSR, the three Baltic Republics (Estonia, Latvia and Lithuania), the three Transcaucasian Republics (Georgia, Armenia and Azerbaijan), the Moldavian Republic (formerly a part of Rumania known as Bessarabia) and the five Central Asian Republics (Uzbekistan, Kazakhstan, Turkmenistan, Khirgizstan and Tadjikistan).

Articles 14 and 15 deal with the division of powers between the Union and the Union Republics.

Article 14 lists fourteen matters which fall within the competence of the Union: these are foreign affairs generally, questions of peace and war, the admission of new Republics into the USSR, ensuring the observance of the Constitution of the USSR and that the Constitutions of the Union Republics are in conformity with it, confirmation of alterations in the boundaries of Union Republics, confirmation of new Autonomous Republics and Autonomous Regions within Union Republics, defence, foreign trade, state security, national economic planning, taxation, banking and the control of industrial agricultural and commercial institutions operating on an All-Union level, transport and communications, direction of the monetary and credit systems, organization of state insurance, state loans, determination of the basic principles of land tenure, determination of the basic principles in the spheres of education and public health, organization of national economic statistics, determination of the principles of labour legislation, determination of the principles of legislation relating to the judicial system and procedure and of civil and criminal codes, legislation concerning citizenship of the Union and the rights of foreigners, determination of the principles of legislation concerning marriage and the family, and the issue of All-Union acts of amnesty.

It will be noticed that in regard to some of the matters referred to exclusive control is reserved to the Union, whereas in other matters, for example with regard to labour legislation, civil and criminal codes, and family law, only the determination of principles falls within the competence of the Union.

Matters not falling within the terms of article 14 are stated by article 15 to be within the authority of the Union Republics.

Each Union Republic has its own constitution, and is accorded the theoretical right to secede from the Union. Its territory may not be altered without its consent.

Articles 18a and 18b are interesting: 18a says that each Union Republic has the right to enter into direct relations with foreign states and exchange diplomatic and consular representatives with them. However, this right is very little exercised in practice, though the Ukraine does have some limited diplomatic and consular relations with Poland. And it is impossible for foreign states to communicate with Union Republics except through Moscow: for many years the United Kingdom tried, without any success, to establish diplomatic relations with the Ukrainian SSR. Article 18b says: 'Each Union Republic has its own Republican military formations.' This looks like a direct statement, but in fact it is only a legal right, and Soviet writers on constitutional law merely state that each Union Republic has the *right* to have its own military formations. In fact, none of them do; there is nothing corresponding to the National Guard maintained by the individual states of the United States of America.

The doctrine of the separation of powers, according to which the legislative, executive and judicial powers are separate in nature and ought therefore to be exercised by mutually independent bodies, a doctrine accepted to some extent at least in most western states, is not accepted at all in principle in the USSR: nevertheless in practice there is naturally a certain division of competence between various bodies, and chapter 3 of the Constitution, which deals with 'The Higher Organs of State Power', is in fact concerned with the supreme legislative functions, and the Supreme Soviet of the USSR.

The Supreme Soviet of the USSR is divided into two chambers, the Soviet of the Union and the Soviet of Nationalities. The Soviet of the Union consists of deputies elected on the basis of one deputy for every 300,000 of the population. The Soviet of Nationalities is intended to represent all the various ethnic groups, and its members are not elected on a basis of one deputy to so many thousands of the population, but on the basis of 25 deputies from each Union Republic, irrespective of size, and also deputies from divisions of Union Republics having specific national features; 11 deputies from each Autonomous Republic, 5 deputies from each Autonomous Region, and 1 deputy from each National Area. Both chambers are elected at the same time for a term of four years, and both have equal rights.

Nothing in the electoral law (decree of 9 January 1950) says that there is to be only one candidate in each constituency; on the contrary, the electoral law rather assumes that on the voting paper there will be more than one name, because it says that the voter must strike out the names of those candidates for whom he is not voting and leave in the name of the candidate for whom he is voting; as far as the electoral law is concerned, it would be perfectly possible to have contested elections, and indeed, the electoral laws have always been drafted in such a way as to permit this. Nevertheless, although various organizations are entitled to nominate candidates, and different candidates may in fact be nominated for a particular constituency, in practice all except one candidate withdraws before the day of the election, so that there is only one name left on the ballot paper.

What appears to happen is that there are discussions between the various organizations that have nominated candidates: they agree finally on one candidate, and the others' names are withdrawn. In any case, a candidate's name cannot be put forward without his consent, and he can withdraw his consent at any time, so a hint to a candidate that he should withdraw his consent to stand may well prove effective; those with political ambitions are not likely to ignore such hints if they come from authoritative quarters.

However, the fact that there is only one name on the ballot paper does not mean, as is sometimes assumed, that a Soviet election is nothing but a piece of play-acting. The law requires that to be elected the candidate must obtain the votes of at least 50 per cent of the registered electors in his constituency, and as voting is not compulsory, it is quite possible for a candidate not to be elected; a candidate will fail to be elected if more than half of the electors do not go to the polls. This does not often happen, but it has happened on occasions, and when it does, a new election is held with a new candidate. Although there are no contested elections as we know them in the West no change in the law would be needed to have them: indeed the law provides for them. But there would have to be changes in the law if political parties other than the Communist Party were to be allowed. Contested elections may well come if the Soviet system develops in the direction of further liberalization, but even if this occurs, they are likely to be within the limits imposed by a one-party system. That other political parties will be allowed to compete with the Communist Party seems unlikely in the foreseeable future. This does not mean, however, that all members of the Supreme Soviet of the USSR and of other elected bodies are members of the Communist Party: many of them are not, but they could not be elected without the support of the Party.

According to the Constitution the Supreme Soviet of the USSR is the supreme authority in the country, but as it is normally summoned for only two short sessions, of ten days each, every year, it is quite clear that it cannot, in practice, act as such. The amount of time available certainly does not permit it to act as a grand forum of the nation in a way comparable to that of the Parliament of the United Kingdom or the Congress of the United States. Between sessions of the Supreme Soviet of the USSR supreme power is vested in its Praesidium, which consists of 32 members elected at the beginning of each four-year term. The Praesidium has a President, 15 vice-presidents (one from each of the Union Republics), 15 ordinary members and a Secretary. This Praesidium issues decrees which have the effect of laws, though they are subject to ratification when the Supreme Soviet meets again. In practice it always does ratify them, and indeed, much of its time is in ratifying the acts of the Praesidium issued in the intervals between the sessions. Deputies to the Supreme Soviet have a number of rights, such as the right to question ministers, to obtain information from public departments, and to make speeches, but the shortness of the sessions prevents these rights having very much significance in practice.

However, each of the chambers of the Supreme Soviet has standing commissions: each has a foreign affairs commission, a budgetary commission, and a legislative proposals commission, and these standing commissions continue their work in the intervals between the meetings of the Supreme Soviet. The members of these standing commissions are elected at the beginning of each four-year term of the Supreme Soviet. In addition to these three standing commissions of each chamber, the Soviet of Nationalities has a fourth standing commission, the economic commission. The reason for this is that the function of the economic commission is to consider whether the economic resources of the country are being fairly allocated among the various ethnic groups within the country. The standing commission have no powers to issue orders, but they prepare reports for the next session of the Supreme Soviet, and report to their appropriate chamber.

In addition to the standing commissions, provisional commissions may be set up, not by each chamber separately, but by the Supreme Soviet as a whole, usually for the purpose of conducting an investigation and for reporting at the next session of the Supreme Soviet. These provisional commissions are used for purposes similar to those entrusted to Royal Commissions in the United Kingdom, and their reports are commonly a prelude to legislation. Much of the time of the sessions of the Supreme Soviet is taken up with hearing the reports of the standing commissions and of any provisional commissions that may have been appointed.

Each Union Republic has its own Supreme Soviet, and a Praesidium, which is the supreme legislative authority within that Union Republic, though it cannot of course enact laws contrary to All-Union legislation.

The body that corresponds most closely to the Cabinet in the United

Kingdom is the Council of Ministers of the USSR. The Council of Ministers is appointed by, and responsible to, the Supreme Soviet of the USSR, and in the intervals between its sessions, to the Praesidium. The Head of the Government is the Chairman of the Council of Ministers. The Council of Ministers of the USSR is quite a numerous body, consisting of some fifty or sixty persons, and there is very little information available about how many members normally attend meetings, what number is required for a quorum, and whether there is any kind of 'inner Council' of specially important members which meets regularly and acts on behalf of the whole Council. Experience in other countries has shown that where the Cabinet becomes as large as this there is a tendency to form an 'inner Cabinet' of ministers holding especially important positions, and perhaps the same phenomenon has occurred in the Council of Ministers of the USSR. Officially, the Council is composed of a Chairman, a First Vice-Chairman, and a number of vice-chairmen, whose number is not fixed by law and varies from time to time: the sixteen Ministers of the USSR, the sixteen Chairmen of State Committees which are directly responsible to the Council of Ministers of the USSR, and the Chairmen of the Councils of Ministers of each of the fifteen Union Republics are *ex officio* members of the Council. Ministers and Chairmen of State Committees are appointed by the Supreme Soviet (or its Praesidium) on the recommendation of the Chairman of the Council of Ministers; other members of the State Committees are appointed by the Council of Ministers themselves.

Ministries of the USSR are of two types, known as All-Union Ministries, and Union-Republican Ministries. The difference is that an All-Union ministry is a single, unified department which administers some particular branch of the administration throughout the country; it may have branches in different parts of the country, but these are responsible only to the Minister at the head of affairs; in other words, it operates without regard to the Governments of the Union Republics in whose territories its branches may be situated. There are six All-Union Ministries, the Ministries of Foreign Trade, Mercantile Marine, Railways, Machine Building Industry, Transport Construction Industry, and Electric Power Stations.

On the other hand, the Union-Republican Ministries operate in conjunction with corresponding Ministries in each of the fifteen Union Republics. For example, there is a USSR Ministry of Public Health, but its functions are mainly co-ordinating and supervising the activities of the Ministries of Public Health in each of the fifteen Union Republics.

In this connection we should note the principle of *dual subordination* which operates throughout all Soviet public administration. Almost every Soviet public authority is subordinated to *two* other authorities. Let us take, for example, the Ministry of Public Health of the Ukrainian Soviet Socialist Republic. The Ministry of Public Health, as a specialized department, is subordinate to a general authority, the Council of Ministers of the Ukrainian Soviet Socialist Republic. This subordination of a specialized branch of the administration to a more general body is known as horizontal subordination: accordingly the Ministries of a Union Republic are horizontally subordinate to the Council of Ministers of that Republic. But the Ministry of Public Health of the Ukrainian SSR is also subordinate to a higher specialized authority, namely, the Ministry of Public Health of the USSR: this is termed vertical subordination. The principle of dual subordination ensures that most public authorities are subject to horizontal subordination, that is to a general authority at the same level, and to a specialized authority at a higher level. So the Union-Republican Ministries exercise vertical authority over Ministries of the same name in each of the fifteen Union Republics, among such Ministries are those of Public Health, Internal Affairs, Education, Foreign Affairs, Mineral Resources, Culture, Defence, Communications, Agriculture, and Finance.

The State Committees of the Council of Ministers of the USSR are like All-Union Ministries in some ways, but their work is of such a nature that it may affect many different branches of administration, and like All-Union Ministries, they may have branches or offices throughout the Union. Among them are the State Security Committee known as the KGB (*Komitet Gosudarstvennoy Bezopastnosti*),[1] and the State Bank of the USSR.[2] Other State Committees are more in the nature of advisory bodies than active administrative organs, for example, the State Committee on defence technique, the State Committee on aircraft technique, the State Committee on economic relations with foreign countries, and the State Committee on scientific and technical research. The importance of these State Committees lies in the fact that they are subordinate only to the Council of Ministers of the USSR, and that their chairmen are *ex officio* members of the Council.

The Council of Ministers of the USSR issues decrees on a number of matters, so that although in principle it is an executive body in fact to some extent it operates as a legislative one. As the doctrine of the separation of powers is not accepted by Soviet political theory this does not appear to Soviet writers as anomalous. The legislative power moreover is based on articles 66 and 67 of the Constitution of the USSR,

---

[1] See p. 143 *post*.   [2] See p. 222 *post*.

which read: 'The Council of Ministers of the USSR issues decisions and orders on the basis and in pursuance of the laws in operation, and controls their execution' (article 66).

'Decisions and orders of the Council of Ministers of the USSR are binding throughout the territory of the USSR' (article 67).

While article 66 suggests that there are limitations on the Council's power to issue decisions and orders, article 67 makes it clear that these decisions and orders are binding throughout the country. In principle, the Council of Ministers might seem to be confined to issuing minor legislation within the framework of laws enacted by the Supreme Soviet, of the kind known as 'Statutory Instruments' in England. However, decrees of the Council of Ministers of the USSR are often of quite major importance, and in this connection we should note that none of the bodies already referred to are really high-level policy-making bodies.

Policy-making at high level in the USSR is not usually a matter for the Supreme Soviet or for the Council of Ministers of the USSR, but for the Communist Party of the Soviet Union, and, in particular, for its Central Committee. The state apparatus is rather the executive agency for carrying out high-level policy decisions arrived at by the Party. This is nowhere mentioned in the Constitution but Soviet writers on constitutional law make no secret of the fact and it is widely understood in the USSR. Therefore, decrees on important matters often start with the words 'The Communist Party of the Soviet Union and the Council of Ministers of the USSR decree . . .' This is a sufficient hint to all politically conscious persons that, whatever the technical position might be or whatever arguments might be advanced that such a decree of the Council of Ministers is not 'On the basis of or in pursuance of laws in operation' the measure has the support of the Communist Party; and this will be sufficient to silence legalistic quibbles. The fact that the Communist Party of the Soviet Union is put first and the Council of Ministers of the USSR second is in accordance with the general view of the respective importance of these two bodies, both in official circles and in the public mind.

During the period from 1961 to 1965 there was much discussion in the Soviet legal press concerning the preparation of a draft for a new Constitution, and it was widely believed that the occasion of the fiftieth anniversary of the Russian Revolution in 1967 would serve for the introduction of a new Constitution, or at least for the publication of a new draft. But the silence which fell on this matter in the course of 1965 had not lifted early in 1968. The two matters which were principally discussed in 1961–5 were the establishment of a clear demarcation line between the rights of the Union and the rights of the Union Republics, with the emphasis on the enlargement of the rights of the latter, and the electoral system, which was criticized as being 'insufficiently democratic'. These were thought to be crucial issues, and we may assume that not until they have been resolved will there be further discussions about a new Constitution for the USSR. Moreover, discussion of a new Constitution is likely to raise questions of fundamental rights or civil liberties, which the authorities would probably prefer not to raise publicly at the present time.

CIVIL LIBERTIES

In this section we shall consider chapter 10 of the Soviet Constitution, which consists of articles 118 to 133, and which is entitled 'Fundamental Rights and Duties of Citizens'. The Constitutions of many countries have a part devoted to the fundamental rights of citizens, and this part of the Constitution is commonly known as a Bill of Rights; certain basic rights are accorded to citizens and these cannot be interfered with by any governmental, executive, police or other authority, nor can they be abridged or taken away by legislation in the ordinary way. We must therefore consider the Soviet attitude to a 'Bill of Rights' and see how far chapter 10 of the Constitution of the USSR can be regarded as a Bill of Rights.

The struggle for a Bill of Rights was an important element in the political life of many continental European countries during the nineteenth century, and was supported by most of the liberal and progressive elements, and indeed, one of the demands of those who supported the unsuccessful revolutionary attempt of 1905 in Russia, was for constitutional guarantees of fundamental civil liberties. The socialist movements in Germany, Austria and other European countries were also in favour of a Bill of Rights being incorporated into the Constitution of their own countries.

Fundamental civil rights were also demanded by various ethnic, religious and other minorities in the Tsarist Empire, and these and other groups were able to put considerable pressure on the communist revolutionaries in the early days of the Soviet régime for constitutional guarantees.

On the other hand, the position of the Soviet Government in the early days of the Civil War was such that it could not afford to allow any opportunities to its enemies, and most communists naturally believed that any concessions would only be utilized by hostile elements to the detriment of the Soviet State. So right from the first there was considerable diversity of opinion about the desirability of a Bill of Rights at all, though one was included when the first Constitution of the RSFSR was drafted in 1918. This first Bill of Rights seems to have been adopted mainly for its propaganda value, however, and not because the establishment of basic civil liberties was regarded as right in itself by the communists. This was particularly the case with the clause dealing with freedom of religion: the clause is said to have been introduced to gain support from the religious minorities in Russia who had endured persecution under the Tsarist régime: certainly freedom to practise religious beliefs was not regarded as a basic right by the communists; on the contrary, they regarded it as important to stamp out religious practices wherever they could.

When the RSFSR combined with other Soviet Republics to form the USSR at the end of 1922, the first All-Union Constitution was adopted, the Constitution of the USSR of 1923. This Constitution contained no Bill of Rights: it was argued that one was unnecessary, because the Constitutions of the RSFSR and the other Union Republics contained Bills of Rights. It was clear, however, that no right given by the Constitution of a Union Republic could prevail if it was contrary to All-Union legislation, so rights given by the Constitutions of the Union Republics were clearly not guaranteed against the Union itself.

When the second All-Union Constitution, the Stalin Constitution of 1936, was drafted, it was decided to include in it a Bill of Rights, again mainly for propaganda reasons, but this time principally to gain support and sympathy for the USSR abroad, rather than for reasons of internal policy. The Bill of Rights then adopted thus forms, as stated above, chapter 10 of the Constitution of the USSR.

The first articles in this chapter deal with social and economic rights rather than with 'civil liberties' as understood in the West. Thus article 118 says: 'Citizens of the USSR have the right to work, that is, the right to guaranteed employment and payment for their work in accordance with its quantity and quality.'

The propaganda value of this provision in the conditions of the nineteen-thirties was enormous, for in most countries of the Western world there was widespread and persistent unemployment, and certainly no Western country undertook to provide employment for all citizens who asked for it. The abolition of unemployment in the USSR during the period of the first two Five Year Plans (1928–36) is certainly one of its major achievements in the realm of human welfare that should

H

not be belittled or misinterpreted in the West, for although the problem of unemployment in the West these days is insignificant compared with thirty or forty years ago, unemployment is still a serious problem in many of the under-developed countries of Asia and Africa in which the USSR hopes to extend its influence, and where many citizens regard a stable job as more important than basic civil liberties. Thus the provision still has considerable propaganda value abroad, and is still deeply significant to the older generation in the USSR itself. The younger generation in the USSR as elsewhere tend to accept full employment as natural, for they have never known anything else.

Article 119 says that Citizens of the USSR have the right to rest and leisure, and provides for the eight-hour working day (until 1940 a seven-hour working day was in force). Article 120 states that citizens of the USSR have the right to maintenance in old age and in cases of sickness or disability. In other words, this merely states that the principle of social security is accepted, as it is in most advanced countries these days, and there is nothing particularly socialistic about this, though inevitably the social services provided in the USSR are a very considerable advance on the very meagre social legislation of Tsarist times. Article 121 say that citizens of the USSR have the right to education (originally it said 'to free education' though this was later amended):[1] but education is still free up to the age of sixteen. Again, this represents an advance on the position in Tsarist times, though even in Tsarist times a majority of the children did in fact receive free elementary education.

The next two articles lay down the principles of sex and race equality, two matters on which the Soviet authorities have never compromised in principle, whatever exceptions may have been made in practice. Article 122 says that women in the USSR are accorded equal rights with men. The importance of this provision is much greater in the non-Russian parts of the USSR than it is in the parts inhabited by Russians, for in Central Asia before the revolution, especially in parts where the Moslem religion was predominant, women were kept very much in the background of affairs, and had few rights and less opportunity of exercising them; the emancipation of women has been a very important factor in the life of the Central Asian Soviet Republics, in which women now hold important positions in a way that would be quite unthinkable in many Moslem countries at the present time. But even in Russia proper the provision is important, in view of the serious disabilities from which women suffered at the hands of the law in Tsarist times, e.g. their

[1] See p. 79 ante.

inability to follow a profession without their husband's consent. Today women even work in industry and transport.

Article 123 of the Constitution provides for equality of rights of citizens of the USSR irrespective of their nationality or race in all spheres of public life, and makes racial discrimination an offence. No discrimination may be maintained against any racial group, nor may special privileges or prerogatives be given to any racial group. This provision of the Constitution has been important in various ways, in view of the fact that the USSR is inhabited by peoples of many different races. It has been used to combat so-called 'Great Russian chauvinism', and to punish Russians who make disparaging remarks about Ukrainians or Georgians, or who attempt to belittle the importance of the smaller ethnic groups inhabiting the country. But it has also been used to stop attempts by groups of people in some of the smaller Republics to exclude Russians and Ukrainians from holding important positions in their Republics. For example, when positions were advertised in the Turkmen Soviet Socialist Republic stating that applicants should be of the Turk-men race the advertisements were ordered to be withdrawn on the ground that the limitation amounted to racial discrimination against Russians or Ukrainians who might apply for such jobs. Article 123 goes on to say 'Any direct or indirect restriction of the rights of, or, conver-sely, the establishment of any direct or indirect privileges for, citizens on account of their race or nationality, as well as any advocacy of racial or national exclusiveness or hatred and contempt, are punishable by law'. This is important too in practice, but we must remember that the law prevents discrimination against Russians as much as it prevents discrimination against the smaller national groups.

Articles 124–8 deal with such civil liberties as are generally under-stood in the West. Article 124 of the Constitution says: 'In order to ensure to citizens freedom of conscience, the Church in the USSR is separated from the State, and the school from the Church.

In the Bill of Rights contained in the RSFSR Constitution of 1918 there was a provision to the effect that freedom of religious and anti-religious propaganda was recognized for all citizens. This provision was repealed, however, during the wave of religious persecution which took place in 1927/8, and replaced by one which provided for freedom of religious belief and anti-religious propaganda. In the Constitution of 1936, freedom of religious worship is substituted for freedom of reli-gious belief.

Separation of the Church from the State does not in practice ensure freedom for the Church even in strictly ecclesiastical matters. Separation of Church and State is interpreted in the sense that the Church may not interfere with the State, not that the State may not interfere with the Church. Church affairs are under the control of the Commission for the Affairs of Religious Bodies, which is directly responsible to the Council of Ministers of the USSR; this Commission was formed in 1966 by the fusion of two Councils, one for the affairs of the Russian Orthodox Church and one for the affairs of other religious denominations. The Commission, which has offices throughout the country, closely supervises all aspects of church life. No new parishes can be formed without its authorization; appointments of priests and bishops are subject to its approval. No priest can officiate without a licence from it, and the licence can be withdrawn at any time. Its representatives attend the oral examinations of students at the theological seminaries, and either directly or indirectly, it can exercise its influence in a variety of ways.

The freedom of the Church is severely limited, and its activities are virtually confined to conducting religious services. The Church may not form study-circles or youth groups, or engage in any missionary or charitable activities. In particular it is not allowed to answer the stream of virulent anti-religious propaganda which is constantly put out by the Soviet authorities. Churches are put at the disposition of religious bodies, but cannot be used by them for any purpose other than the holding of services, and sometimes conditions are imposed, for example, that there should be no disparagement of Soviet theatres, cinemas or other cultural institutions in the sermons preached.

The Russian Orthodox Church is allowed to publish a journal (the Journal of the Moscow Patriarchate), a theological yearbook, religious calendars, and occasionally other works, but the paper allocations allowed are so small that they can have only a very limited circulation. The Baptist Church also publishes a Bulletin, but, like the Journal of the Moscow Patriarchate, it contains mostly reports of the activities of dignitaries of the Church, and contains little theological or controversial matter.

The actual legal position of religious organizations is very obscure, and perhaps the Soviet authorities prefer it that way. The difficulties arise from the fact that new enactments are passed without reference to older ones, and it then remains doubtful whether the new enactments are to be read together with the older ones, or whether the older ones are to be regarded as repealed in whole or in part. In particular, it is not clear whether and if so to what extent the Law on Religious Associations of 1929 is still in force, for some, but not all of its provisions have been reproduced in amendments introduced in 1966 to article 142 of the Criminal Code of the RSFSR. The fact that the legal position is not clear makes it difficult for the Church authorities to exert or press their legal rights, were they minded to do so: in many cases, however, it appears that they are not, and that they are prepared to submit to almost any demand of the authorities so long as they can keep the churches, or some of them, open for public worship. On the other hand, reformist elements in the Russian Orthodox and Baptist churches complain of the illegality of some of the activities of the Commission for the Affairs of Religious Bodies, and of the collaborationist attitude of the higher Church authorities.

There are two articles of the Criminal Code of the RSFSR of which use has been made in certain circumstances for the prosecution of religious believers. One is article 142, which, in its original form in 1960, provided that the violation of laws on the separation of Church and State and of school and Church was punishable by corrective labour for a term not exceeding one year, or a fine. This provision was amended in 1966 to allow persons with previous convictions for such offences to be sentenced to deprivation of liberty for up to three years, and various activities are specified which constitute offences under this article. These include compulsory collections and taxation for the benefit of religious organizations or the clergy, the preparation or distribution of documents calling for non-observance of Soviet legislation on religious bodies, and the systematic teaching of religion to minors, which were already offences under previous legislation; the new offences are the 'commission of fraudulent acts for the purpose of inciting the masses to religious superstitions' (presumably this means the faking of miracles, which was an offence under the Imperial Russian law, and which was an offence under earlier Soviet legislation when done with a mercenary motive) and 'organizing and leading religious meetings and processions and other ceremonies disturbing public order'. This appears to be the response of the authorities to the propagandist activities of certain Baptist groups, which included processions to rivers for public baptisms, hymn-singing on public transport, and other activities displeasing to the authorities. The amendments to article 142, however, also make it an offence to discriminate against citizens on the grounds of their attitude to religion in matters such as employment or acceptance in educational institutions, which appears to be a liberal provision, though it merely repeats provisions contained in earlier legislation.

Article 227, however, is more severe. As its scope and meaning is a matter of some doubt, it is reproduced in full.

The organization or leadership of a group, the activity of which, being carried out under the form of preaching religious doctrines, is accompanied by the causing of injury to the health of citizens or with other violations of the personality or rights of citizens, or with persuading citizens to refuse to participate in social activities or to fulfil their civic duties, or the recruitment of minors into such a group, is punished by deprivation of liberty for a period of up to five years, or by exile for the same period, with or without confiscation of property.

Active participation in the activity of a group referred to in the first paragraph of this article, and systematic propaganda aimed at the accomplishment of the acts therein indicated, is punished by deprivation of liberty for a period of up to three years, or by exile for the same period, or by corrective labour for a period of up to one year.

Note. If the act of persons indicated in the second paragraph of this article, and the persons themselves who have committed them, do not present a great social danger, measures of social pressure may be applied to them.

The original purport and legitimate purpose of such a provision is comprehensible when we think of some of the extreme forms which religious fanaticism has taken in Russia, of groups such as the *skoptsy*, who practised self-castration, and the *khlysty* (flagellants), who practised flagellation of themselves and others. (Soviet literature refers to these sects as still existing, though they are not allowed to register as legal religious groups.) Less extreme religious groups whose beliefs and practices may prove harmful to health include sects which refuse the ministrations of doctors, or which prohibit their members from receiving certain forms of medical treatment or aid, such as blood transfusions. It is clear that the Soviet Government would wish to prevent the propagation of such doctrines, and those which preach opposition to military service. But the provision has been used for prosecutions of members of religious groups who meet in private premises for religious services, on the ground that long hours of standing and praying in premises without adequate ventilation may prove injurious to the health of participants. While it appears that the article is aimed primarily at extremist religious groups, it could perhaps be used against Russian Orthodox groups if they were to preach and practise the full rigour of Orthodox rules about fasting.

The next Constitutional provision is article 124, which says that citizens of the USSR are guaranteed by law

1. freedom of speech,
2. freedom of the press,
3. freedom of assembly, including the holding of mass meetings, and
4. freedom of street processions and demonstrations,

but it is to be noted that these freedoms are stated to be guaranteed 'In conformity with the interests of the working people, and in order to strengthen the socialist system', so that it is quite clear that these rights are not protected if used with the intention or purpose of weakening the socialist system: on the contrary, they may be used to criticize means, but not ends, for the fundamental ends have already been decided, namely, the construction of a communist society. Citizens have freedom of speech, but to use this freedom to attack or discredit the socialist system or the Soviet Government amounts to counter-revolutionary activity, and is punishable as such.[1] The real test of how much freedom of speech exists at any given moment thus depends on the way in which 'counter-revolutionary activity' is interpreted and it is clear that at the present time, for example, there is far greater freedom of speech than existed during the Stalinist period.

Freedom of the press is a different matter, for press freedom is definitely limited by the censorship. All published material has to be passed by the Censorship department before the final order for printing is given. The censorship legislation is an enactment of 6 June 1931, which is still in force, and which makes the Censorship department a branch of the Ministry of Education in each Union Republic. By this enactment the censorship Administration is empowered to forbid the printing, publication or distribution of productions which 1. contain propaganda against Soviet authority and the dictatorship of the proletariat, 2. reveal State secrets, 3. stir up racial or religious fanaticism, or 4. have a pornographic character. All books and journals published in the USSR (except those in foreign languages) carry a censorship mark showing that they have been passed by the censor before being sent to press. (The only exception is the Journal of the Moscow Patriarchate, which is censored by Church officials who know quite well the tolerated limits of their activities.) The extent of press freedom therefore depends on the attitudes adopted by the censorship, which in turn depend on purely political considerations.

Matter is now being published that would have been quite unthinkable in Stalin's time, and although Pasternak's book *Dr Zhivago* was banned, it was only after very careful consideration. Perhaps the

---

[1] See p. 154 *post.*

surprising thing is not that it was banned, but how near it got to publication. However, the relative freedom which the press enjoyed during the Khrushchev era now appears to be waning as the censorship becomes stricter again. Freedom of the press as understood in the West can hardly be considered to be established so long as the censorship exists in its present form. Not only is the press controlled, but there are strict rules governing the sale and use of duplicating machines.

The position is similar with regard to freedom of assembly and the holding of meetings. The law relating to public meetings is an enactment of 15 May 1935, which is still in force. Any meeting at which representatives are to be called from different Union Republics requires permission from the Council of Ministers of the USSR, and any meeting at which representatives are to be called from different regions of a Union Republic needs authorization from the Council of Ministers of that Republic. The Soviet Writers' Union, containing members all over the USSR, for many years wanted to hold a meeting of representatives, but it was not allowed to do so until after Stalin's death, and even the calling of a meeting of writers from different parts of the RSFSR was not allowed for some years after the Second World War, though permission for it was granted shortly after the death of Stalin. All meetings, congresses and conferences must obtain official authorization before they can be held.

Article 126 of the Constitution deals with the right to form societies and associations:

In conformity with the interests of the working people, and in order to develop the organizational initiative and political activity of the masses of the people, citizens of the USSR are guaranteed the right to unite in public organizations: trade unions, co-operative societies, youth organizations, sport and defence organizations, cultural, technical and scientific societies; and the most active and politically conscious citizens in the ranks of the working class, working peasants and working intelligentsia voluntarily unite in the Communist Party of the Soviet Union, which is the vanguard of the working people in their struggle to build a communist society, and is the leading core of all organizations of the working people, both public and state.

The association must be in conformity with the interest of the working people, and no association may be formed without a licence if it is intended to enrol members throughout the Union. Associations of a local character, however, may be formed, but any All-Union society, even such a body as an All-Union dog fanciers' association, has to have a licence to be formed, the licence being granted by the government of the Union Republic in which the society or association has its head office, which of course is usually in the RSFSR.

Chapter 10 of the Constitution of the USSR contains two further articles which are of greater practical importance now than they were in the Stalin era. Article 127 says that no person may be placed under arrest except by decision of a court or with the sanction of a procurator. The Russian word *arest* does not mean exactly the same as the word 'arrest' in English, however: any policeman (militiaman) may 'arrest' a citizen disturbing the public order or committing a criminal offence, and take him to the police station. Temporary detention is not equivalent to the term *arest* in Russian, which means rather detaining in custody prior to trial. If a person is detained by the police, the procurator must be notified within twenty-four hours, together with the reason; the procurator will then sanction an arrest, in which case the detention will continue; otherwise the person detained must be released. This provision was frequently violated by the secret police (NKVD, later MVD) of Stalin's time, as was the inviolability of citizens' homes and the secrecy of correspondence guaranteed by article 128 of the Constitution.

Articles 129 to 133, though included in chapter 10 of the Constitution, have little to do with civil liberties, and enumerate the basic duties of Soviet citizens, such as the duty to safeguard public property and the duty to serve in the armed forces.

Writers and others have protested that even the narrow limits of the civil liberties guaranteed by the Constitution are not always observed in practice by the authorities, and the protest would appear to be justified. It is, however, significant that certain dissident groups in the USSR are using the Constitution itself as the foundation of their protests.

THE SOVIET LAW OF PROPERTY

In Marxist political and economic theory, the ownership of property is the key to both economic power and political power. In the Marxist view the persons or groups that own the basic, productive forms of property, or the 'means of production', control the State and dictate its policies. Control of property was therefore seen as a basic task after the Revolution: without ownership of property, the Soviet State could not hope to last in the struggle with its opponents.

In view of the fundamental importance of the ownership of property in Marxist theory it is not surprising that the first chapter of the Constitution of the USSR contains the basic principles of Soviet property law: some of these principles are elaborated in greater detail in the Basic Principles of Civil Legislation of 1961 (in force since 1 May 1962) and the detailed rules are contained in the Civil Code of the Union Republics.

Article 4 of the Constitution says:

> The economic foundation of the USSR is the socialist system of economy and the socialist ownership of the instruments and means of production, firmly established as a result of the liquidation of the capitalist system of economy, the abolition of the private ownership of the instruments and means of production, and the elimination of the exploitation of man by man.

Socialist ownership of the instruments and means of production leads to the concept of 'socialist property'. Article 5 of the Constitution recognizes two forms of socialist property; property belonging to the State, and property belonging to collective farms and other co-operative organizations. The Basic Principles of Civil Legislation, 1961, recognize a third type of socialist property, the property of public or social organizations, such as trade unions and sports organizations. Article 20 of the Basic Principles of Civil Legislation says:

> Socialist property takes the following forms: State property; property of collective farms, of other co-operative bodies, and their combinations; property of public bodies.

State property is dealt with in article 6 of the Constitution, which says:

> The land, its mineral wealth, waters, forests, factories, mines, rail, water and air transport, banks, means of communication, large state-organized agricultural enterprises (state farms [machine and tractor stations], and the like) as well as municipal enterprises and the bulk of the dwellinghouses in the cities and industrial localities, are state property, that is, belong to the whole people.

The forms of property listed in article 6 are the property of the State: they are not the property of the State enterprises (public corporations) that may be entrusted with their administration: a railroad trust, for example, does not in theory *own* the railway, which is simply put at its disposition by the State.

THE FOUNDATIONS OF THE SOVIET LEGAL SYSTEM [107

For most practical purposes, the public corporations that manage industry and commerce have 'operative management and control' of the state property entrusted to them, and for many purposes this is equivalent to a right of ownership, but what the State has given, the State can take away; a factory, for example, may be transferred from one corporation to another by the State.

Any kind of property, however, may be state property; state property is not confined to the things mentioned in article 6 of the Constitution.

The second form of socialist property is the property of collective farms, which belongs to the farm as such, the farm being recognized as a separate juridical entity with the rights of a legal person. And similarly, there are certain other co-operative enterprises organized on a basis similar to that of collective farms, such as fishermen's co-operatives and co-operatives of small handicraftsmen working for local needs. The often-expressed intention of the authorities is gradually to reduce the differences between these two forms of socialist property; that is, to amalgamate collective-farm and other co-operative property with state property, to make the collective farms more like State farms, though they realize that considerable peasant opposition will have to be overcome before complete amalgamation becomes practicable. Property belonging to unions of collective farms is also socialist property. Article 7 (para. 1) of the Constitution says:

> The common enterprises of collective farms and co-operative organizations, with their livestock and implements, the products of the collective farm as well as their common buildings, constitute the common, socialist property of the collective farms.

Article 8 says:

> The land occupied by collective farms is secured to them for their use free of charge and for an unlimited time, that is, in perpetuity.

Although article 8 of the Constitution says that the land is put at the disposal of the farm free of charge, the collective farm had to make delivery of its products to the State at a comparatively low price fixed by the State, so that the difference between the price at which the State buys and the market price might well be thought of as rent: moreover, the amount taken by the State is definite and fixed in advance by the State, and is not a mere proportion of the actual products of the farm: the proportion is based on the arable area of the farm, regardless of whether the whole area is sown, and of whether or not the harvest is a success. Soviet writers, however, deny that this was a form of rent.

The third type of socialist property is that of public or social organizations.

Property which is not socialist property may be owned by individuals. This type of property is now usually termed personal[1] (*lichny*) property rather than private (*chastny*) property because to the Soviet Russian the term 'private property' (*chastnaya sobstvennost*) suggest private property in the means of production, or capitalist property, and it was much used in this sense during the period of the New Economic Policy. It therefore has derogatory or 'anti-Soviet' implications; the same connotations, however, are not associated with the term personal property (*lichnaya sobstvennost*), which is quite respectable and free from the taint of bourgeois associations.

Two articles of the Constitution deal with personal property. Article 9 says:

> Alongside the socialist system of economy, which is the predominant form of economy in the USSR, the law permits the small private undertakings of individual peasants and handicraftsmen based on their own labour and precluding the exploitation of the labour of others.

Craftsmen may own small businesses, though they may not employ assistants, and business partnerships are allowed only between members of the same family. Thus the size and scope of such private businesses is very restricted, quite apart from the fact that numerous trades and activities are prohibited for the private craftsmen. For permitted private businesses there is an elaborate licensing system. From the point of view of the economy private businesses are now of negligible importance; but private dressmakers and tailors, watch repairers and bootblacks still maintain a precarious existence in a socialist economy. Similarly in a few sparsely inhabited areas individual (non-collectivized) peasants still exist: within limits fixed by law they own their own cattle and agricultural implements. The land of course belongs to the State, but they are given occupation rights. The ownership of individual peasants and craftsmen is still usually referred to as 'private' (*chastny*), and is regarded as temporary and not guaranteed for the future.

[1] 'Personal property' is a literal translation of *lichnaya sobstvennost*. However, as the term 'personal property' has a technical sense in English law, some writers, in order to avoid confusion, prefer 'individual property' as a translation.

Article 10 says:

The personal right of citizens in their incomes and savings from work, in their dwellinghouses and subsidiary home enterprises, in articles of domestic economy and use and articles of personal use and convenience, as well as the right of citizens to inherit personal property, is protected by law.

The term 'savings', often found in Soviet literature, corresponds to some extent to what we might term a person's capital, but the term 'capital' is disliked where private citizens are concerned, so the term 'savings' is commonly used instead. Thus a citizen's 'savings' include property that he has inherited.

Private property of this kind is intended to consist of articles of use and consumption, and not articles from which an income may be derived. In this connection, Soviet law has run into very considerable difficulties due to its being based on rigid doctrines of Marxist economic dogma, which distinguishes between 'the means of production' which are supposed, in capitalist hands, to be a source of unearned income, and articles which are intended purely for personal use and consumption. The idea is that the State should have a monopoly of the means of production, and that citizens should be able to own only those kinds of property that cannot be used in order to derive an unearned income. Clearly some types of property are productive and others are not: but this division of property into productive goods and articles of consumption, however useful it may be for economic theory, is a purely artificial one because it does not necessarily depend on the nature of the property itself, and the law has run into difficulties in trying to formulate an artificial distinction based on theoretical economics in strictly juridical terms.

Take, for example, a car. Obviously, the owner of a car may use it for going to work and for excursions to the country at week-ends, and then the car is an article of use; but the owner may instead hire the car to someone else, and then although the car is an article of use for the hirer, as far as the owner is concerned it is now a form of property from which an unearned income is being derived. Or a person may use his car to operate what is, in effect, a private taxi-service, that is, he may give other people lifts in it for payment, in which case although to some extent the payment is for his services, he is only able to obtain this payment by virtue of his ownership of the car. And in view of the shortage of taxis, as of many other things in the USSR, it is comparatively easy for a person with a car to derive at least occasional supplementary benefit from it by giving people lifts for payment.

The difficulty is to frame legislation which will penalize the speculator who is regularly engaged in such activities without affecting ordinary casual transactions between citizens. Rules of law, particularly rules of property law in a country where these are of fundamental importance, require to be formulated precisely.

Article 25 of the Basic Principles of Civil Legislation, 1961, says 'Property privately owned by citizens may not be used as a source of unearned income'. But when individual payments of a casual nature become an 'unearned income' still remains difficult to say.

Indeed, it is to deal with speculators that, in the last few years, Parasite laws have been enacted in most of the Union Republics, under which individuals who are not gainfully employed and who refuse to take up work after being warned may be exiled for up to three years, compulsory work being provided at the place of exile.[1] This deals with people such as blackmarketeers and speculators whose activities are known, but cannot be proved with sufficient cogency to warrant a conviction in a court of law, and with individuals whose activities are on the fringe of the law, that is, although within its letter, are contrary to its spirit. People who have a job can still be exiled as parasites, if it appears that the job is really only a 'cover' which hides much more profitable activities, legal, quasi-legal or illegal, but which are subject to official disapproval, or regarded as being contrary to public policy.

Even greater difficulties have arisen with regard to houses, which may be privately owned, although the ownership extends only to the building and not the land on which it stands. Here again the authorities have been in a dilemma. In view of the desperate housing shortage, private building has been encouraged, but on the other hand there is a strong fear that houses may be built by people who do not want them to live in, but who want to let them, or let rooms in them, so as to obtain unearned income. To discourage speculation the rule is that a citizen may not own more than one house, and a man, his wife, and their infant children (i.e. children under eighteen) may not own more than one house between them. A person who owns a house, or whose spouse owns a house, cannot buy another, and if a person who owns a house inherits another, he must sell one or other of them; he cannot keep both, living in one, and letting the other. There are also restrictions, laid down by legislation of the Union Republics, about the size of houses that may be privately owned as personal property; in the RSFSR they may not exceed sixty square metres of dwelling-space.

Another measure directed against speculators is the decree of 26 July

[1] See p. 155 *post.*

1962 which provides that houses may be confiscated without compensation if the owner cannot prove that he acquired the house out of legally earned income. If the house was inherited or a gift the question is whether the deceased or the donor acquired it out of legally earned income; if he did not, it can still be confiscated. The person who buys a house in good faith out of his own earnings is protected, but a speculator who has bought a house cannot avoid confiscation simply by selling it to a relative who knows how the purchase money for the house was acquired. Proceedings under this enactment are started by the local authority, which presents its evidence, that the house was acquired out of unearned income, to the people's court, and if the court accepts the evidence, it makes a decree of confiscation, from which there is no appeal. The house is then transferred to the local authority. However, unless the court makes a further decree, the result is that the former owner and his family will still have the right to live there, subject of course to paying rent. If the court finds that the owner has living accommodation elsewhere, it can also make an eviction order.

In many cases where this enactment has been applied, some criminal offence has already been committed; for example, in one case a man had been convicted of theft, but it could not be established what he had done with the proceeds. It later came to light that he had bought a house with them which he had given to his mother. The house was confiscated from the mother. In other cases, no criminal offence has been committed, or at least proved, but this is not important, as once a *prima facie* case is made out the burden of proof is on the owner that he bought the house, or in the case of houses acquired by gift or inheritance, that the previous owner bought it, out of legally earned income; this is done by showing one's income and receipts from all sources. For the ordinary honest citizen, this usually presents no difficulty, but for the man who lives on the fringe of the law this will not always be possible. Nevertheless the enactment can operate harshly, especially with regard to inherited property where it is not possible to show how the deceased came by the purchase price.

The next point to note is that personal property may be in individual ownership, or in co-ownership. Co-ownership is of two kinds, in undivided shares, and without shares. Co-ownership in undivided shares calls for little comment, as it differs little from co-ownership as known in other systems: if two or more people contribute towards the purchase of property, they become co-owners of it in shares proportionate to their contributions towards the purchase price, and if the property is later sold the price received must be divided proportionately to their shares.

Co-ownership without shares exists only in two cases: as between husband and wife,[1] and as between the members of a collective farm household or individual peasant household (*dvor*). The *dvor* is an institution of extreme antiquity, and it is a matter of some interest that it has survived under Soviet conditions. The most important item of property belonging to the *dvor* is usually the private plot of land which each collective farm household has at its disposal. The size of the private plots varies in different parts of the country, and the amount of livestock which may be kept on it varies, but where the main form of farming is cereal production, the rule is that each household may have 1 cow, 2 calves, 2 pigs and their litters, 10 sheep or goats, an unlimited quantity of chickens and rabbits, and 20 beehives. This property, and also the household furniture of a collective farm household, is the common property of all the members of the household, and is governed by special rules. It is referred to in article 7 (para. 2) of the Constitution which says:

> Every household in a collective farm in addition to its basic income from the common, collective-farm enterprise, has for its personal use a small plot of household land and, as its personal property, a subsidiary husbandry on the plot, a dwellinghouse, livestock, poultry and minor agricultural implements—in accordance with the rules of the agricultural artel.

The earnings of the collective farmer are his individual property, but once he devotes them to the needs of his household, they become household property. This household property is not liable to be taken in execution for debts of one of its members; only individual property can be attacked in that way. The household property is only liable for agreements undertaken in the name of the household as a whole. When the head of the household dies, the household property does not pass on succession, but remains the property of the surviving members of the household; it will only pass on succession if the last surviving member of the household dies, when the household comes to an end. On the other hand, a division of household property may be made, for example when sons or daughters of the household get married and set up a household of their own; in this event they are entitled to take a portion of the household property with them. The rules for dividing the household property when this happens are to some extent customary, and in fact are mostly derived from pre-Revolutionary times, when it was the peasant household in many parts of the country that was regarded as the

[1] See p. 176 *post*.

legal unit, rather than the individual. And as investigations in other countries have shown, peasants tend to be extremely conservative in such matters, and to make such distributions according to fixed rules which are well known to them, but which have often never been recorded in writing. Disputes about such divisions then are decided by local customary law; this is the one important instance in which the binding effect of customary law is recognized in the Soviet legal system.

COPYRIGHTS AND PATENTS

Closely akin to ownership of physical things are rights to so-called 'intangible property' such as copyrights and patents. We will first consider the position of the author in connection with copyright law: this is an interesting field, because it shows how the Soviets have adjusted the sphere of private and public interests. The author still works as he pleases; he is not a salaried member of the staff of a publishing house.

The first principle is that, once having given his work, whether novel, play, film or scientific treatise, to the world, the author is not entitled capriciously to refuse further reproductions or performances of it, and therefore the State may take it over: the State being, for this purpose, the Council of Ministers of a Union Republic. Once a work has been taken over by the State, further printings or performances may be permitted without the author's consent. In other words, there is a system of compulsory acquisition of the copyright by the State authorities. However, this right of pre-emption on behalf of the State is limited by two important restrictions:

1. The State may not take over any unfinished work or manuscripts which the author has not thought fit to present to the public. It is only in connection with published work that the right of pre-emption arises.
2. During the lifetime of the author, and for a certain period of years after his death, the work may not be altered without his consent. It must not be added to, or issued in abbreviated versions without his consent, even though the State has acquired the property in the work. But extracts from it may be published in anthologies without his consent, though it must be made clear in the anthology that it is only an extract, and not the whole work. Similarly, shortened versions of the work may be issued for use in schools, dramatic clubs and circles, without the consent of the author, provided that these abbreviated versions are not made available to the general public.

When the State does acquire the copyright compulsorily, the author still has to be paid his royalties on the work. However, it appears that

I

this compulsory purchase of the author's copyright by the State is not a particularly common occurrence, and in practice the author usually retains his copyright. The normal principle is that the copyright lasts for the lifetime of the author and fifteen years thereafter, after which it lapses, and the work can then be published by any publishing house without payment of royalties to anyone. After the death of the author, reduced royalties not exceeding half what would have been paid to the author had he still been alive, are paid to his heirs until fifteen years have elapsed from the author's death.

Translations are not a breach of copyright, and the copyright in the translation is in the translator, so payments of royalties have to be made to him. The underlying principle here is that linguistic minorities should have educational and cultural works made available to them at low cost. Hence author's royalties are not always payable as well.

Copyright exists automatically, and does not have to be claimed, except that in the case of a photograph, the name, address of the photographer and the year must be put in the corner of the photograph if copyright in it is to be claimed.

The amount of royalties to be paid will depend on the contract between the author and the publishing house.

The difficulties experienced in other systems of law in deciding when a work is 'original' also seem to exist in the Soviet system, and the extent to which another author may borrow without infringing copyright also gives rise to the same sort of complications as exist elsewhere. In one case in 1937, two authors had, before the Revolution, composed a German–Russian Dictionary of Technical Terms, in three volumes, and this dictionary had been reprinted several times after the Revolution by a State Publishing House by agreement with the authors. Then another State Publishing House produced a short one-volume German–Russian technical dictionary, and the two authors brought suit against this publishing house for breach of copyright, as they claimed that most of the definitions in the new short dictionary had been lifted from their three-volume one. The case went up to the Supreme Court of the RSFSR, a good deal of evidence was called as to the extent to which the compiler of the short dictionary had 'borrowed' from the larger one, the defendants claiming that any compiler of a dictionary would have to use previous dictionaries, and that original work was done by their compiler in the matter of selection. The plaintiffs claimed that four-fifths of the definitions in the short volume were copied from their work, including a number of definitions which they now admitted were mistaken. However, on an actual count being taken, it was found that only one in four of the definitions in the short dictionary was identical with those in the longer one, though others were very similar. Ultimately it was held that the short dictionary showed sufficient evidence of originality, taking into account the work of selection done by its compiler, and the plaintiffs' action for breach of copyright failed.

Again, difficulties arise in the USSR as they do elsewhere in connection with books or pamphlets produced by people in the course of their employment, in which case it is often doubtful whether the copyright belongs to them or to their employer.

Finally we must consider the position of the inventor. The Soviets, in attempting to industrialize their country in a short space of time, have given every encouragement to the inventive individual who can devise new machines or new processes whereby production can be rationalized. Patents, strictly speaking, still exist in Soviet law, but in practice they have been largely superseded by the 'Inventor's Certificate'.

The Soviet inventor, in practice, now obtains an Inventor's Certificate; to obtain this, he has to satisfy the authorities that his invention is new throughout the world, not merely new in the USSR.

Once the Inventor's Certificate is obtained, the inventor loses all right to the invention, which is assigned to the State to use the idea or not as it chooses. In return, the inventor gets a proportion of any savings in the national economy effected by the use of his invention, subject to a maximum of 20,000 roubles. Moreover, the possession of the certificate amounts to something like a degree or technical qualification and the holder, if he is employed, must be paid as a specially qualified worker.

FURTHER READING

P. Archer, *Communism and the Law*, London, 1963.

A. Denisov and M. Kirichenko, *Soviet State Law*, Moscow, 1960.

S. Dobrin, 'Soviet Jurisprudence and Socialism' (1936), 52 *Law Quarterly Review*, p. 591.

H. Kelsen, *The Communist Theory of Law*, London, 1955.

A. K. R. Kiralfy, 'The Soviet Supreme Court as a Source of Law' (1951), 2 *Soviet Studies*, p. 356.

A. K. R. Kiralfy, 'Attempts to Formulate a Legal Theory of Public Ownership' (1957), 8 *Soviet Studies*, p. 236.

I. Lapenna, *State and Law: Soviet and Yugoslav Theory*, London, 1964.

G. G. Morgan, *Soviet Administrative Legality*, Stanford, Cal., 1962.

B. Rudden, 'Soviet Housing Law' (1963), 12 *International & Comparative Law Quarterly*, p. 591.

R. Schlesinger, *Soviet Legal Theory*, 2nd ed. London, 1951.

CHAPTER FIVE

Criminal Procedure

GENERAL

Soviet criminal procedure differs widely from the Anglo-American system. It resembles in many respects, however, the procedure of Western European countries, in which, in the case of the more serious crimes at any rate, there is a preliminary investigation conducted by an impartial official, the *juge d'instruction* in France or the *Untersuchungs-richter* in Germany. In France and Germany these 'investigators' are under the control of the courts, for it is considered important that they should be quite independent of the procurator, or public prosecutor. In the USSR, however, the investigators are subject to the procurators, not to the courts. Another feature common to Western European and Soviet criminal procedure is that the victim of the offence may, and often does, bring a civil claim for damages as compensation for any injury or loss of property sustained as a result of the offence, so there is a 'civil side' to the proceedings which may complicate the trial.

In Soviet law there may be several parties to a criminal trial; in addition to the prosecutor and the accused, there may be a victim, a civil plaintiff, and a civil defendant. Commonly the victim will also be the civil plaintiff, but in some cases the person who has suffered as a result of the offence is not the person against whom the offence was committed; for example, if the victim was insured and has received the insurance money, the real loser is the insurance enterprise, which may appear as civil plaintiff. Again, normally the accused, if found guilty of the offence, will be the person liable to compensate the victim or the civil plaintiff, but there will be some cases where under civil law an employer is vicariously liable for injuries caused by an employee during the course of his employment; for example, if a lorry driver injures a pedestrian by dangerous driving, he can be prosecuted for the criminal offence and the enterprise employing him will be the 'civil defendant' liable in damages to the injured pedestrian.

Soviet criminal procedure has four main stages: those of enquiry, preliminary investigation, administrative session and the trial.

THE ENQUIRY

When an offence is reported or suspected, the first stage is usually an 'enquiry' conducted by an agency of enquiry. The main enquiry agency is the police, but in certain circumstances other bodies or persons may act as an 'enquiry agency'; thus the secret police (the officials of the Committee on State Security) act as an enquiry agency in the case of serious offences against the State, the fire departments in the case of fires and violations of fire prevention regulations, the frontier guards in the case of frontier violations, and the governors of prisons and labour camps, captains of sea-going vessels, and the heads of Arctic polar stations act as such in the case of offences committed in places subject to their jurisdiction. It is the duty of the police or other enquiry agency to take immediate steps, such as inspecting the scene of the crime, organizing searches, preserving evidence, and detaining a suspect, if there is one. The enquiry agency must decide whether or not to initiate a criminal case within three days[1] of an offence being reported. In comparatively trivial cases, the enquiry having produced a person who is duly charged with the offence, the enquiry agency, with the consent of the procurator, transfers the case directly to court, but in most cases the enquiry is followed by a preliminary investigation.

ARREST

No-one may be arrested except on the order of a procurator (this is considered so important that the rule is included in the Constitution of the USSR)[2] though in certain circumstances[3] the police or other enquiry agencies may detain a suspect (e.g. where he is caught redhanded, or tries to escape, or is identified by an eye-witness, or does not produce his identity papers) and when they do, the detention must be reported to the procurator within twenty-four hours; and within the next forty-eight hours the procurator must either order the suspect to be released on bail or that he should be 'arrested', i.e. that his detention in custody should continue. Custody pending trial is possible only when the offence may be punished by deprivation of liberty; in some cases even then bail may be granted, though in fact it seldom is. Only in

[1] In certain exceptional cases, ten days.
[2] Article 116.
[3] See p. 140 *post.* op. to 'arrest' see p. 105 *supra.*

very exceptional circumstances may a person be detained without a charge having been made against him, and then for not more than ten days.[1]

PRELIMINARY INVESTIGATION

The preliminary investigation usually starts with the charge being read over to the accused by an investigator attached to the procurator's office (or in some cases to the police), and he is first asked whether he admits the charge or not, and then to make a statement on the matter. He is then questioned on his statement. The investigator is forbidden by law to use threats or force to secure a confession, and he is also required by law to elucidate facts favourable to the accused as well as those that tell against him. The accused is entitled to say nothing, and in practice he is sometimes allowed to have a lawyer present during the preliminary investigation, if he wishes, though he is not entitled to this as of right.[2] The investigator will also summon any witnesses, whose evidence is taken down in writing, and the accused is entitled to question them. If the investigator refused to accede to any request made by the accused, e.g. to call a certain witness, he must give the reasons for his refusal in writing. The preliminary investigation must be concluded within two months, though an extension of one month may be granted by a Regional Procurator, who must give his reasons for allowing the extension in writing. A further extension can only be obtained from the procurator of the Union Republic concerned; but in no case may a person be

[1] A person is technically a 'suspect' (*podozrevayemy*) only when he has been detained or allowed bail by an enquiry agency or an investigator before a charge has been made. Should no charge be brought against him within ten days he ceases to be a 'suspect' and must be released. Once a charge has been made against a person he is known as the 'accused' (*obvinyayemy*). From the time that the indictment has been accepted by the court he is referred to by a word, *podsudimy*, which means 'person before the court' but I have continued to refer to him at this stage as the 'accused' because the other words available in English seem unsuitable; 'prisoner' would suggest that he had been brought up out of custody, which is not necessarily the case, and 'defendant' might lead to confusion with the 'civil defendant' who is commonly the accused's employer.

[2] He is entitled to have a lawyer present as of right when he is a minor, or is suffering from physical or mental defects which might make it impossible for him to defend himself. This question of the presence of defence counsel during the preliminary investigation is one that has been hotly debated in most continental countries, and the USSR is no exception in this respect. The Soviet decision to allow participation of defence counsel as of right in the case of minors, etc., and in other cases with the consent of the investigator seems to be something of a compromise, and perhaps also of an experiment.

detained in custody for more than nine months before the case goes to court. The preliminary investigation might be further extended, but the accused would have to be released from custody. If the investigator decides that there is no case against the accused (from which decision the victim or the person who reported the offence may appeal to the procurator) he is discharged: otherwise he declares the preliminary investigation closed, and invites the victim, civil plaintiff and civil defendant to examine the file of the case, and they may ask for further investigations to be made. Finally the accused is allowed to examine the file, and at this stage counsel must be permitted. The accused must be asked if he wants any further enquiries made: if he does, such enquiries must be made, or a reasoned refusal given. It is possible, where the offence is not serious and the accused admits guilt, for the investigator, with the consent of the procurator, to put the accused under 'collective probation', that is, under supervision by some group or organization for the purpose of re-education. This terminates the case. Other possibilities of terminating the case without reference to the court are by transfer to a Comrades' Court, or, where the accused is under eighteen, to the Commission for Minors' Cases.

If the case is to continue the investigator draws up the indictment, which contains not merely the offence charged but also a list of the witnesses who are to be called, with cross-references to the file compiled by the investigator. He then forwards the indictment to the procurator, who may quash it, or send it back for further investigations, or endorse it and transmit it to the court. Although an investigator is part of the staff of the procurator's office and conducts the investigations subject to the supervision of a particular prosecutor, he has a certain degree of independence in that he may disagree with a particular ruling given him by the procurator and appeal to a higher procurator, and the procurator who supervises his work has no disciplinary power over him.

INDICTMENT

When the indictment is received by the court, it is examined by a judge, who may accept the case for trial, but if he does not, an administrative session of the court is held, consisting of a judge, two people's assessors and the procurator. This administrative session may quash the indictment, or may remit the case for further investigation, or it may accept the indictment for trial. If the case is to go to trial, the accused must receive a copy of the indictment and all exhibits to it at least three days before the hearing.

THE TRIAL

The trial takes place in open court. In serious cases the procurator will prosecute, and in less serious cases, the prosecutor may be a trade union official, a factory or health inspector, or the victim of the offence. The accused may be represented by counsel, or by a near relative, or an official of his trade union, or (with the consent of the court) by any other person. The accused must be represented by counsel (who will be assigned to him by the court if he has not retained one), if the procurator is prosecuting, unless he expressly renounces his right to legal representation; he must also be assigned counsel if he is deaf or dumb, and there must be separate counsel where more than one person is accused, unless it is apparent that there can be no conflict of interest between them.

The public hearing usually commences with the accused being asked whether he has any objection to the composition of the court. A judge or a people's assessor may not participate in the trial if he has any direct or indirect interest in the outcome, or is a relative of any of the parties, or of the prosecutor or defending counsel, or of any of the investigators, or if he is related to some other member of the court. A judge or a people's assessor may also be challenged by any other party to the case. A challenge should be made before the actual trial begins, but may be made at any time later, should the fact of interest or relationship only later become known to the challenger. If the person challenged does not admit the validity of the challenge the matter is decided by the other two members of the court. Even if there is no challenge at the trial, if the court is illegally constituted its decision would be quashed, irrespective of the merits, on appeal or review.

There is no such thing as a formal plea of Guilty in Soviet law, but after the indictment is read the accused is asked whether he admits the offences charged. Even if he does so, he cannot be convicted unless his admission is confirmed by other evidence: Powers, the American airman, tried in August 1960 after the U-2 aircraft he was piloting was shot down in the USSR, freely admitted his guilt from the start, but full evidence was called on matters such as the circumstances of his being taken into custody and the equipment carried, and also of circumstances tending to show his knowledge of the purpose of the flight; he was asked if he knew that the aircraft carried no identification marks, and whether he had reason to believe that the flight had been cleared by the Soviet authorities.

The presiding judge then asks if any of the parties have any objection to the witnesses being called in the order decided on at the preparatory session, and if they have, he may agree to witnesses being called in a different order. The witnesses are not regarded as 'prosecution witnesses' or 'defence witnesses'; they come to court to assist in the elucidation of the facts, not to support either side. The first witness called is usually the victim of the offence; he differs from other witnesses in two ways; first, his testimony is given as of right, and the court has no power to prevent him from giving evidence, and secondly, he is entitled to stay in court before he gives evidence; other witnesses are excluded until it is their turn to give evidence.

Each witness, after being warned of the penalties for refusing to give evidence and for giving false evidence, is first asked about his relationship, if any, with the victim or the accused, and about his name, address and place of employment, and is then asked to relate in his own words what he knows about the facts of the case, avoiding statements, the source of which cannot be verified (e.g. remarks made by unidentified bystanders). The witness cannot be questioned while making his statement. When he has finished, he may be asked questions by the members of the court and by the other parties to the case. Usually the judge and people's assessors will begin the questioning, followed by the prosecutor, and then by the other parties to the case. Where a witness has been called expressly at the wish of one of the parties, however, that party may question him immediately after he has finished his statement. However, as there is strictly no such thing as a 'witness for the prosecution' or a 'witness for the defence', there is no sequence of examination-in-chief, cross-examination and re-examination: and this means that no party is entitled to put leading questions to a witness at any stage of the proceedings. Statements made to the investigator cannot be read out at the trial unless the witness is dead or for some other reason unable to give evidence. A party who has already questioned the witness may put further questions to the witness after the witness has been questioned by the other parties, so the questioning of the witness continues until none of the parties or the court has any further questions to put.

The accused is not regarded as an ordinary witness, because his statements in court have a dual purpose: they are indeed evidence of the facts, but they also serve as his defence. For this reason, the rules governing testimony by the accused differ from those governing testimony by ordinary witnesses.

In the first place, the accused is not bound to testify, and if he does not choose to do so, this may not be regarded as an admission of guilt. Secondly, if he does choose to give evidence, he is not criminally liable for giving false evidence. Thirdly, an ordinary witness must confine himself to the facts; the court is not interested in hearing arguments from a witness about the inferences which should be drawn from these facts, or hearing his suppositions or opinions concerning the reasons why these facts occurred; arguments and hypotheses may be advanced by the parties or their legal representatives, but this is not the function of a witness. The accused, however, is not limited in this way in giving evidence; his arguments, explanations and hypotheses must be considered by the court in reaching its decision.

In appropriate cases the opinions of an expert may be obtained. An expert differs from an ordinary witness in that he is called, not because of his special knowledge of the facts of the case, but because of his qualifications; his views, opinions and inferences derive their value from his qualifications, and he may therefore be replaced by some other person with similar qualifications. When an expert's opinion is obtained, it is read in court and the expert is then questioned by the judge, people's assessors, the prosecutor, the victim, the civil plaintiff, the civil defendant, defending counsel and the accused, in that order. The expert's opinion is not binding on the court, though the court must give its reasons in writing if it disagrees with any opinion expressed by the expert. The presiding judge may disallow any question put to a witness, an expert, or the accused, but, if he does, the party putting the question may object to his ruling, and the objection must be recorded so that the matter may be considered, if necessary, by an appellate court.

After all the evidence has been taken, both parties are asked by the judge if they think any further evidence ought to be called, and if not, the prosecutor makes his closing speech, followed by counsel or other representative of the accused. Either can reply to anything said by the other, except that the defence is always entitled to the last word, i.e. if the prosecutor insists on a reply, that gives the defence a right of further reply. The court is not entitled to fix any time limit for the closing speeches. After the closing speeches, the accused himself (whether legally represented or not) may make a final speech in which he must not be interrupted by anyone, even by the presiding judge.

At any time during the trial the court may, if it thinks it desirable, send the case back to the procurator for further investigation.

The judge and the assessors retire to consider the decision, which must be based exclusively on the evidence given in court (this means that they must disregard statements in the investigator's file which have not been verified). A dissenting member of the court may insist on writing out a dissenting judgment which must be annexed to the judgment of the court in the record, but the fact of dissent will not be made public. The dissenting opinion may be useful to a higher court in the event of an appeal or a review.

It is perhaps needless to add that translations and interpreters must be supplied in all cases where there might be any difficulty arising from the fact that many different languages are spoken within the territories of the USSR.

EVIDENCE

The rules of evidence are somewhat lax by Anglo-American standards. Hearsay evidence is totally excluded when the original speaker cannot be identified: in other cases, it is admissible, though any party to the proceedings may require the original speaker to be summoned to give evidence himself. If he is dead or cannot be found, the hearsay evidence is inadmissible. Even during the worst period of Stalinism the Supreme Court of the USSR ruled in 1944 that hearsay evidence alone is insufficient to support a conviction.

Soviet lawyers do not attribute to confessions the excessive value that is sometimes given them by continental lawyers, for they realize, as do all English lawyers, that confessions are unreliable, as they may be made to shield a friend, or even to provide an alibi for a more serious crime committed elsewhere. Soviet legal literature contains many examples of cases where false confessions have been made, quite apart from those extorted by torture or other impermissible practices in political cases during the Stalin era.

In some cases false confessions have been made by alcoholics under the belief that a period of deprivation of liberty would cure their craving for alcohol; in others, they have been made by persons who genuinely believed themselves guilty, as in a case in 1961 when a father had been quarrelling with his daughter one night by the side of a river; he struck her, and heard no more. The body of a girl being washed up later he identified as that of his daughter and confessed to homicide. In fact the identification was mistaken, for the daughter had run off and boarded a goods train, hoping to be sent to a children's home as a waif. The girl identified had been drowned while bathing. Soviet writers admit, however, that at certain periods insufficient attention was given to cases where the accused admitted a lesser offence than that charged; the admission of a lesser offence was often regarded as a mere device to obtain a more lenient punishment, and that some cases of injustice therefore occurred.

Soviet lawyers also realize that the evidence of an accomplice must be regarded with great suspicion, in view of his strong temptation to try to shift the greater part of the blame on to his confederate, and the rule is that no conviction can be supported solely on the evidence of an accomplice, unless it is corroborated; this goes further than the English rule, which merely requires the judge to warn the jury of the danger of convicting solely on the uncorroborated evidence of an accomplice.

Soviet law recognizes no exemption from the duty to testify by reason of relationship or the duty to preserve secrecy, the sole exception being that an advocate may not be questioned about the circumstances of a case which came to his knowledge while acting in the capacity of defence counsel.

THE PEOPLE'S COURTS

The great majority (over 94 per cent in 1960) of trials at first instance come before a People's Court composed of a professional judge and two lay assessors. The higher courts are mainly appellate courts, but, when they act as courts of first instance, the trial is before a professional judge and two lay assessors as in the People's Courts. Appeals and reviews in the higher courts always come before a court composed of three professional judges. These higher courts are the courts of the territorial divisions of a Union Republic: *oblast*, Autonomous Republic, Autonomous Area; the names vary, according to the nature of the district, but for the sake of simplicity they are referred to here as District Courts, whatever their official names may be: they are intermediate courts between the People's Courts and the Supreme Courts of the Union Republic concerned. In most Republics there are therefore courts at three levels: People's Courts, District Courts, and the Supreme Court of the Union Republic, though in some of the smaller Republics there is no court at the intermediate level between the People's Court and the Supreme Court.

The lay assessors are intended to provide an element of lay participation in the administration of justice, a function which is served by the jury in common law countries. In Imperial Russia many cases were tried by jury, for the jury system had been introduced in 1864, but the Russian jury was often notoriously lenient, and commonly acquitted in the face of conclusive evidence of guilt, a fact which some Soviet writers have attributed to 'the sentimentality notoriously characteristic of the lower middle classes, and of the intelligentsia, from which jurors were commonly drawn'. However that may be, it seems unlikely to be a complete explanation; but in any case the Soviets did not want to continue a system under which many criminals escaped their just deserts, and so they adopted the device of lay assessors sitting with the judge, and having equal rights with him: an idea borrowed from certain German courts. Naturally it is from the People's Courts that the ordinary people get their impressions of Soviet justice, for they are far the most numerous, and they deal with most civil cases at first instance as well as with criminal cases.

The Assessors in the People's Courts are directly elected, for periods of two years, though usually only a single panel of names is put forward. Often assessors with special qualifications will be chosen to sit in individual cases, e.g. an engineer in a case involving industrial injuries, or a schoolteacher in cases involving children; there are no special juvenile courts in the USSR where criminal responsibility does not begin until sixteen (fourteen in the case of certain very serious crimes), though there are Commissions for Minors' Cases which serve somewhat the same purpose. Assessors need have no legal training, and in fact the majority have none, but on election they are given a handbook and have to attend at least two lectures a month in a special course for People's Assessors, the lectures being given by judges, practising lawyers or university law teachers.

People's Court judges are elected directly by secret ballot for a period of five years, though in practice only a single candidate is put forward. As in other Soviet elections the candidate still has to get at least 50 per cent of the votes of the electorate, so if too many people abstain (and voting is not compulsory) or spoil their papers, he will not be elected. Considerable election campaigns are carried on by the candidates. This is largely due to the desire to instil the importance of law and the legal system into public consciousness. During the election campaign of 1949, much attention was given to the campaign in the press, the radio, and in street speeches. One judge is reported, without the slightest suggestion of criticism, to have made the principal plank in his platform the fact that, during his previous term of office, in 63 out of the 70 cases he had tried in which private persons were suing railway enterprises, he had found for the plaintiff, and that these 63 successful plaintiffs had collected an aggregate of nearly Rs.150,000 in damages from railway undertakings. Such an attitude appears strange to us, and we have to consider it against the general background of traditional Russian indifference to law mentioned earlier. The traditional Russian tended to be much of a fatalist; if his goods were lost or damaged in transport he would tend to shrug his shoulders and accept it as merely another cruel blow of fate, and perhaps grumble; he would not be likely to think of writing to the railway administration claiming damages for the loss, still less of issuing a writ. It is felt important, therefore, to impress on the general public that they are entitled to sue the railway undertakings if they are injured in accidents, or their luggage or freight consignments are lost or damaged in transit. Another judge in the election campaign emphasized the part he had played in restoring to their jobs workers who had successfully sued for wrongful dismissal, civil actions for wrongful dismissal being quite common in the USSR.

Also important in this connection are the periodical 'reports back' to their electors in which the People's Judges have to give an account of their stewardship. Moreover they may be recalled by the electorate before their term of office has expired, and so are liable to Party pressure.

People's Courts are referred to in article 109 of the Constitution, which says:

People's Judges of District (*raion*) (city) People's Courts are elected by the citizens of the districts (cities) on the basis of universal direct and equal suffrage by secret ballot for a term of five years.

People's assessors of Districts (city) People's Courts are elected at general meetings of industrial, office and professional workers, and peasants in the place of their work or residence, and of servicemen in military units, for a term of two years.

To be elected either a People's Judge, or an assessor in a People's Court, a person must have attained the age of twenty-five.

Less than 50 per cent of the People's Judges are members of the Communist Party, and about 40 per cent of them are women. What is at first sight somewhat more startling is the fact that some of them have, on their election, no legal training whatever.[1] This may suggest a resemblance to the English lay magistrates, but these have a qualified lawyer in the form of their clerk to guide them on questions of law, whereas the Clerk in a Soviet People's Court is not expected to give legal advice to the People's Judge. If a People's Judge has no legal training when elected, he has to take a correspondence course in law. However, the fact that his knowledge of law may be weak at first is of less importance than might appear, because it is the duty of the

---

[1] In 1947 it was reported that about one-third of the total number had, at the time of their election, no legal education. By 1957 the position had considerably improved; in some parts of the country the proportion was lower than 10 per cent, and it is now lower still.

procurator to protest any decision which he thinks is erroneous in law.

Each People's Court has, in addition to its judges, a court secretary, and a sessions secretary. The latter is really the court secretary's assistant and attends to matters such as filing and arrangement of cause-lists; commonly he is a law student who is doing this work, either during university vacations or as part of the practical training which law students are required to undertake during the last two years of their course. There is also a court bailiff, whose main duties are in connection with the execution of civil judgments.

Another noteworthy feature of the People's Courts is their power to issue supplemental directions in addition to giving judgment on the issues directly raised by the case. Where a case has revealed short-comings, the person or organization responsible may be ordered to take appropriate steps to prevent their recurrence: and the courts are also required to satisfy themselves that their supplementary directions have been complied with.

APPEALS

A good deal of the criminal work of the District Courts consists in hearing criminal appeals from the People's Courts. After a People's Court has given its decision in a criminal case an appeal may be lodged within ten days, and there are no formal requirements so long as the appellant makes it quite clear that he wishes to appeal against the decision. He may appeal against the conviction if he has been convicted, either on the ground that it was wrong in law, or that violations of the rules of criminal procedure were committed at the trial, or on the grounds that the decision was wrong in fact, i.e. that the decision was against the weight of the evidence; or he may appeal merely against the sentence, asking the appeal court to substitute a lighter sentence: and he may even appeal against his acquittal, on the ground that wrong reasons for acquitting him were given. In England, when a person is acquitted by a criminal court, the jury or the magistrates simply give a finding of 'Not Guilty' and do not specify their reasons: in the USSR a court acquitting a person must give its reasons, and a person, although acquitted of the offence charged, may feel that the decision prejudices him in some way. For example: a person is charged with stealing someone else's coat. He maintains that he never took the coat at all. The court finds that he did take the coat, but that he mistook it for his own, and that there was therefore no intent to steal but a genuine mistake, and so acquits him of the charge of theft.

However, this finding of the court, although it is an acquittal, may be prejudicial to him, because he may be sued civilly by the person whose coat he is supposed to have taken, for the return of the coat or its value, and if he is, the civil court will be bound by the finding of the criminal court that he did in fact take the coat, although without criminal intent. So although he is acquitted, he thinks the wrong reason was given by the court for acquitting him, and as he may be prejudiced by the wrong reason given, he is entitled to appeal against the reason given for his acquittal.

In England (apart from some trivial exceptions) in criminal cases, only the accused person has the right to appeal. No appeal can be lodged against an acquittal. But in the USSR, the procurator (the official concerned with conducting major prosecutions) may also appeal; he may appeal on the ground that the accused was wrongly acquitted, or that, although the accused was convicted his sentence was too lenient, and even though the procurator does not appeal, the victim of the offence also has a right to appeal either against an acquittal, or against the leniency of the sentence imposed in a case where the accused has been convicted. Equally, the civil plaintiff and the civil defendant may appeal against those parts of the decision which concern them. Whatever the outcome of the case, an appeal against the decision may be brought. The position of the procurator is that although he conducts the prosecution, he is also the 'guardian of revolutionary legality', which means that it is his duty to appeal if he thinks that there is any illegality in the verdict or sentence;[1] for example, if the court has imposed a sentence more severe than it has power to do for the offence of which the accused has been convicted, the accused may not appeal, for he may not know that the maximum has been exceeded, but the procurator should do so.

To English lawyers it may seem reasonable to allow only a person convicted in a criminal case to appeal: but in justification of the Soviet position, under which not only the procurator, but also the victim of the offence has a right of appeal, it must be remembered that some People's Courts are in remote areas and are staffed by persons with comparatively little legal education, and sometimes with little general education either, and that considerable injustice may be done by allowing incorrect acquittals to stand, by reason of the rule that any decision given in a criminal court is binding on a civil court in subsequent proceedings. If a thief is wrongly acquitted, the victim of the offence thereby loses

---

[1] Verdict and sentence are not strictly separated in Soviet practice; the term *prigovor* which is used for the decision of the court in a criminal case covers both.

his right to claim from him the property stolen or its value; the victim may not care whether the thief is punished or not, but he may well want to recover his property or its value. Quite probably in the interests of justice it is desirable, under Soviet conditions, to get as many cases as possible into the appellate courts, staffed by trained professional judges, should there be any doubt about the correctness of the decision of a People's Court in a criminal case.

The victim of the offence usually sues the offender for damages in the criminal proceedings, though he may sue independently in a civil court: but a criminal court which acquits the accused, cannot at the same time allow the civil claim. On an acquittal the civil claim will be dismissed if the reason for the acquittal is that the facts alleged did not occur, or that the accused was not responsible for them; but in the event of an acquittal on the ground that the facts proved do not constitute a criminal offence, the court gives no ruling on the civil claim, leaving the civil plaintiff free to renew the claim in purely civil proceedings if he thinks fit. Sometimes on a conviction the court allows the civil claim in principle, but directs that separate civil proceedings take place to ascertain the exact amount for which the person convicted or the civil defendant should be held liable.

An appeal court, hearing a criminal appeal, is not limited to considering the specific grounds on which the appeal was brought, but may consider any aspect of the case, and it can by its decision do one of the following:

1. dismiss the appeal, that is, leave the verdict and sentence of the People's Court in force; or

2. it can quash the conviction and sentence, thereby acquitting a person found guilty by the People's Court; or

3. it can substitute a more lenient sentence for that imposed by the People's Court; or

4. it may order either that the whole of the proceedings are to be annulled and that there should be a new investigation into the matter by an investigator attached to the police or to the procurator's office, or alternatively that there should be a new trial on the basis of the evidence collected at the original investigation.

It may take this fourth step for various reasons: it may think that the original preliminary investigation was defective, and that a new investigation might lead either to the original accused, or to someone else being accused of the offence, or perhaps some rather different offence; or it may think that the accused was convicted of an offence less serious than he should have been, for example that he should have been

K

convicted, not of petty assault but of attempted murder, and that a new investigation or a new trial might lead to this result. The appeal court cannot itself impose a penalty more severe than that imposed by the People's Court, or convict the accused of a more serious offence, but it can order a new trial, or a new investigation, which may result in the accused being charged with a more serious offence. Again it may order a new trial because of some irregularity in the proceedings at the first trial; in the USSR there is no enthusiasm for the view that an accused person should escape punishment merely because of technical irregularities at his trial: he is entitled to a fair trial under the rules of Criminal Procedure laid down in the Codes, and if he has been convicted as a result of a trial in which procedural requirements were violated, that does not necessarily entitle him to be acquitted; it merely entitles him to have another trial properly conducted with due observance of procedural requirements.

REVIEW

In both criminal and civil cases there is only one appeal as of right for the parties. There can be no second appeal, though if the first appeal results in a new trial being ordered there is a right to appeal against any decision reached at the new trial. But there is a further procedure that is possible, and this is known as review (*nadzor*), which is a matter primarily for the Supreme Courts of the Union Republics, though the District Courts also have certain rights of review. There are two fundamental differences between appeal and review:

1. An appeal can be brought only within ten days after the verdict or judgment appealed against; if no appeal is taken within that time the court decision is said to 'acquire legal force'. If an appeal is taken, the result depends on the outcome of the appeal; if the appeal is dismissed, the decision 'comes into legal force' immediately on dismissal. An appeal can therefore be taken only against a judgment or verdict that has not yet 'come into legal force': review procedure is available only after a decision has 'acquired legal force'.

2. A party to a case is never entitled as of right to obtain a review of a decision that has acquired legal force. The only persons entitled to bring a case up for review are the procurators and the Presidents and Deputy-Presidents of the District and Supreme Courts. In practice cases are often brought up for review because of requests by aggrieved parties; if a person is aggrieved by a judgment or verdict in any case, civil or criminal, which he thinks was given in violation of the law, he can petition the local procurator to have the case brought up for

review; if the procurator refuses, he cannot insist, but he can petition a higher procurator to reverse the lower procurator's decision. He can also petition the President of the District Court to have the case reviewed, and if that fails, he can still petition the President of the Supreme Court of the Republic for a review.

Most of the work of the Supreme Courts of Republics consists of this review work, that is, of reviewing cases on the motion, either of a procurator, or of the President or Deputy-president of the Supreme Court. As far as criminal cases are concerned, a case in which the accused was acquitted cannot be brought up for review if more than three years have elapsed since the acquittal, whatever irregularities may have occurred at the trial, unless additional evidence, not available to the trial court, has since come to light; and in such a case, the review can only take place if proceedings for review are started within a year of the new facts, or fresh evidence, coming to light. (In civil cases reviews are much less common than in criminal cases, and they occur mainly when there are grounds for thinking that a judgment is wrong in law.) In both civil and criminal cases, if the person asking for the review, that is, the procurator or the President (or his Deputy) of the Supreme Court, thinks the decision given on review is wrong, he can have the case reviewed again by more senior judges of the same court. The powers of the court on review are similar to those of an appeal court: it may reject the protest, it can order that proceedings be started again at any stage in a criminal case, i.e. it can order a new investigation, or a new trial at first instance, or a new hearing of the appeal (if there was one); it can mitigate the sentence, though not increase it. In civil cases it can modify the judgment, or send the case back for a new trial. The hearing on review is not in public, and the parties do not have the right to attend either in person or by counsel, though they may be summoned if the review court wished to hear them. The mere fact that the court agrees to hear a review of the case does not of itself suspend a decision that has acquired legal force, though the court may order that execution of the judgment be suspended until the review has taken place.

Apart from this review work, Supreme Courts of Union Republics also act as courts of appeal from cases heard at first instance by District Courts, and they also, in rare cases act as courts of first instance for the trial of criminal and civil cases, and they can order that any civil or criminal case pending within the Republic be transferred to them for hearing, though this power is very rarely exercised. In hearing cases at first instance, they sit with People's assessors just as Peoples' Courts do.

Where a Supreme Court sits as a court of first instance there can be no appeal,[1] but there can be a review as in other cases.

The Supreme Court of the USSR also has review functions, but only where it is alleged that some rule of All-Union (federal) law has not been properly applied by the Supreme Court of a Union Republic. So far as matters of Republican legislation are concerned, the final courts are the Supreme Courts of the Union Republics. (It will be remembered that there are, for example, Basic Principles of Criminal Law, Criminal Procedure, Civil Law and Civil Procedure applying throughout the USSR, and that each Union Republic has its own Civil and Criminal Codes and Codes of Criminal and Civil Procedure in which the rules are elaborated in greater detail.) If it is argued by a procurator of high rank that a decision of a Supreme Court of a Republic on a review is contrary to a rule contained in All-Union Basic Principles, the case can go up for a further review to the Supreme Court of the USSR: or it can be taken there by the President or Deputy-President of the Supreme Court of the USSR. Thus the Supreme Courts of the Republics are the final arbiters on matters concerning the legislation of the Republic, and the Supreme Court of the USSR on matters concerning All-Union legislation applying throughout the country. (Where the accused is charged under an All-Union enactment, he may, in very exceptional cases, be tried before the Supreme Court of the USSR sitting as a court of first instance; a case where this was done was that of Powers, the American U-2 pilot, in August 1960.) And, as in the case of Republican Supreme Courts, a second review by more senior judges is possible in the Supreme Court of the USSR. Theoretically a case could go through five stages; trial, appeal, two reviews in the Supreme Court of a Republic, and two reviews in the Supreme Court of the USSR, and even this does not exhaust the possibilities, for at any stage after the first it may be sent back for a new trial at first instance, and this may be followed by a new appeal and further reviews. Indeed, this is regarded by some as one of the most disconcerting features of Soviet law; one never knows when a decision may be reopened by an application for its review, or how and when the case will end.

THE PROCURACY

The role of the procurators in the Soviet Legal system is of immense importance in the whole system, and, moreover, there is nothing in the legal systems of countries outside the Soviet Union and the People's

[1] No appeal was possible in the case of Sinyavski and Daniel, for they were convicted by the Supreme Court of the RSFSR sitting as a court of first instance: see p. 61 *ante*.

Democracies which quite corresponds to the *prokuratura*; it is a typically Soviet institution.

Officials termed procurators exist in most continental countries, and they existed in Russia before the revolution, but the functions of the present-day French procurator, or the pre-revolutionary Russian procurator, are much more limited than those of the Soviet procurator. On the continent there is a procurator attached to all the higher courts, and the duty of the procurator is to supervise preliminary investigations in criminal cases, and to conduct the prosecution in court where a person is charged after a preliminary investigation. In civil cases he has a 'watching brief' for the State to ensure that where the State or a government department is involved in any way in a civil action, all necessary steps are taken, and he also has to ensure that civil cases in which a minor or a person of unsound mind is concerned, are properly conducted, and to enquire into cases where it is alleged that a marriage is void, to ensure that all the facts are before the court and that, if it is held that the marriage was void, the state records are amended accordingly. Some of the functions of the European procurators are exercised by the District Attorney in the United States and the Crown Attorney in Canada, but in England there is no corresponding official at all: in criminal cases, prosecutions are conducted in most cases by barristers in private practice, instructed by the police or other authority bringing the prosecution; magistrates conduct preliminary enquiries into serious criminal charges and decide whether there is sufficient evidence to justify putting the accused on trial; the Official Solicitor sees that infants and persons of unsound mind are properly represented in civil litigation, and the court itself decides whether a settlement reached out of court in such cases is a fair one. The Queen's Proctor is concerned to see that the machinery of the courts in divorce and nullity of marriage cases is not abused.

The system before the Revolution in Russia was similar to the one prevailing generally on the continent, though the Imperial Russian procurators were required to attend the meetings of certain administrative bodies where they might be asked for advice on the legality of measures proposed. However, the immediate pre-revolutionary system dated from 1864; before 1864 the procurators had had far more extensive powers of supervising the acts of administrative agencies in the provinces, and were in fact regarded as 'the eyes and the ears of the sovereign'. This system had been created by Peter the Great (1689–1725) and the Soviet procurator resembles the procurator of Peter the Great more than the procurator of Nicholas II.

The Imperial Russian system was abolished in 1917/18. During the year 1921, Lenin came to realize that the arbitrary measures taken by local Soviets in different parts of the country often had the effect of alienating the local population, for there was very little central control over the local Soviets of that period, and, moreover, he realized that there would have to be a partial restoration of capitalism, the so-called New Economic Policy, to solve the economic problems of a country devastated by revolution and civil war. New codes of civil and criminal law were in the course of preparation, and if private enterprise were to be permitted for a time, in order to restore the economy, the private businessmen, the NEPmen, must be comparatively free from arbitrary or unjustified persecution by local Soviets, which were often under the control of extreme revolutionary elements which could be expected to resent the partial restoration of capitalism which Lenin saw was necessary. Lenin, who had been trained as a lawyer and knew a good deal about Russian legal history, realized that an organization completely independent of the local Soviets must be created to supervise their activities, and he decided to recreate the *prokuratura*, giving it both the functions that it had had before the Revolution with regard to prosecution of criminal cases, and the supervisory functions of the old *prokuratura* created by Peter the Great which had existed until the Judicial Reforms of 1864.

The Procuracy is now governed by a law of 24 May 1955, a law introduced as part of the measures taken to 'restore socialist legality' after the death of Stalin in 1953. It had previously been governed by laws of 1922, 1923 (after the formation of the USSR), 1929 and 1933.

The essence of the procuracy is that it is an institution operating on an All-Union (federal) basis, completely free from control by any authority other than the Supreme Soviet of the USSR or its Praesidium. The Procurator-General of the USSR is appointed by the Supreme Soviet of the USSR for a term of seven years.[1] His departmental heads are appointed by the Supreme Soviet of the USSR on his recommendation, and all other senior staff in the Office of the Procurator-General are appointed by himself.

Below the Procurator-General of the USSR are the fifteen Procurators of the fifteen Union Republics. These are appointed, not by the Supreme Soviets of the Union Republics, but by the Procurator-General of the USSR, and the Procurators of the Union Republics are sometimes Russians and not members of the national group forming

[1] Article 114 of the Constitution of the USSR.

the majority population of the Union Republic. So-called 'petty bourgeois nationalism' has been quite strong in many of the non-Russian Republics; in Armenia, for example, over the years quite a number of Presidents and Prime Ministers of the Armenian Soviet Socialist Republic have been removed from office and tried or disgraced for 'nationalist' activities, and a Russian procurator can probably keep a check on such tendencies better than could an Armenian procurator. Not only are the Procurators of the Union Republics appointed by the Procurator-General of the USSR, but so are all their major assistants and heads of departments. At the third level, that of the region or district (*krai*, *oblast*, or Autonomous Republic), the procurators are also appointed by the Procurator-General of the USSR, and so are their deputies. Their senior assistants and departmental heads, however, are appointed by the Procurator of the Union Republic. At the fourth and lowest level, the procurators of the sub-divisions of the *oblast*, the *rayon* in the country, and the procurators of towns and cities, are appointed by the Procurator of the Republic, but the appointments have to be confirmed by the Procurator-General of the USSR before they become effective. The senior assistants and departmental heads are appointed by the procurator of the *krai* or *oblast*.

Thus the whole system is a highly centralized one, dependent entirely on the Procurator-General of the USSR, for he makes the appointments at all senior levels, and is responsible only to the Supreme Soviet of the USSR or its Praesidium. The *prokuratura*, then, is something of a state within a state, for it operates completely outside the authority, not merely of local Soviets, but also of the Supreme Soviets and Ministries of Union Republics: as article 117 of the Constitution of the USSR says, 'The organs of the Procurator's Office perform their functions independently of any local organs whatsoever, being subordinate solely to the Procurator-General of the USSR.'

The functions of the *prokuratura* are, generally speaking, to ensure the observance of the law by all persons and authorities, public and private organizations, and to draw the attention of some higher authority to anything that appears to be a breach of the law. A key to the functions lies in the phrase 'It is the procurator's duty to protest, but never to decide.' If a procurator thinks that some act is illegal, he must draw it to the attention of a court or some other appropriate authority. Thus his duty of prosecuting in all but the most trivial criminal cases fits into the picture; the prosecutor is convinced that the accused has committed a criminal offence, for otherwise he would not have endorsed the indictment, so he brings this to the attention of the court; but it is for the court, not for the procurator, actually to decide whether the accused did or did not commit the offence, or whether the acts of the accused charged by the procurator amount, in law, to a criminal offence or not.

The functions of the *prokuratura* are very varied, but they fall into two main divisions termed Judicial Supervision and General Supervision.[1]

Judicial Supervision covers conducting or supervising the preliminary investigation and prosecution in the case of allegations of more serious crimes, but even in this respect it covers much more than we would understand by this in England. For example, in conducting a preliminary investigation into a criminal offence where the accused is in custody, the procurator or an investigator of his department must see that the accused's children are in the care of relatives or are put into a home or boarded out by the local authority, or are otherwise properly cared for; and he must also look after the interests of the victim of the offence, and ascertain, for example, whether he wants to bring a civil claim in connection with the offence, for return of property or its value, or a claim for damages for personal injuries, for example, for loss of wages if he has been in hospital as a result of a criminal attack, and in order to see that the victim's rights are secured, he will have to enquire into what property or other assets the accused has, and to take steps to prevent them being disposed of unlawfully by the accused or his associates in such a way as to make them unavailable for the satisfaction of any award of damages that may be made to the victim of the offence or other civil plaintiff. Considerable assistance is given in this way by the procurator to the victim of the offence, and here it should be remembered that while this assistance is of course available to private individuals who have been the victims of offences against their person or property, in the majority of cases of offences against property, the

---

[1] General Supervision covers the lodging of protests against orders, instructions, bye-laws and decrees which the procurator making the protest considers to be *ultra vires* the authority which has issued them. The protest may be made to the authority concerned itself, or to the authority to which it is subordinate. If the offending instrument is not withdrawn (i.e. the procurator's protest is rejected) a higher procurator may lodge a protest with a still higher governmental authority; ultimately a protest could be taken to the Supreme Soviet of the USSR, though in practice a protest is never taken higher than to the Council of Ministers of the USSR, and even protests to this body are extremely rare. The final decision on whether a decree is *ultra vires* or not never rests with the procuracy. This work of General Supervision is of the utmost importance in keeping lower authorities within their constitutional powers, but it has nothing to do with the courts.

victim is not a private individual but a public corporation; thefts from factories and warehouses are offences against the public corporations in charge of such factories or warehouses, and they will be entitled to recover the property or its value from the offender.

Where the preliminary investigation is conducted by an investigator attached to the procurator's office, the procurator must satisfy himself that the investigation is being properly conducted. Similarly, the procurator supervises investigations into less serious offences conducted by the police or other enquiry agencies, and also preliminary investigations conducted by investigators of the Committee on State Security in cases of offences against the State and counter-revolutionary offences. In all cases the procurator draws or endorses the indictment when it is transferred to the court, and in court he acts as prosecuting counsel in serious criminal cases. However, it is also considered an important part of the procurator's duty to see that no-one is prosecuted without good cause, so if at any stage of the proceedings he becomes convinced of the innocence of the accused, he should drop the proceedings, or, if the case has already reached the court, inform the court that he does not wish to proceed with it.

Now it is this aspect of the procurator's duties which makes it virtually impossible for the 'presumption of innocence' as understood in Anglo-American law to prevail in Soviet law, or indeed, in continental European systems generally;[1] how, it is argued, can a person be presumed to be innocent when an important official, who has supervised a thorough preliminary investigation into the whole case, considers that he is guilty of the offence charged? The prosecutor must certainly prove the offence in court, but the court does not start off with any 'presumption of innocence' such as prevails in England. It is the thorough preliminary consideration of the evidence by a trained and qualified impartial official that is considered the main safeguard of the innocent person in the Soviet system as in continental systems generally. Of course the safeguard loses its value once political pressure is put on procurators and investigators, as happened in Stalin's Russia, Hitler's

[1] The phrase 'presumption of innocence' is capable of giving rise to various semantic confusions in both English and Russian. For a full discussion see H. J. Berman, *Soviet Criminal Law and Procedure*, pp. 79–87; he concludes: 'Soviet law embodies the presumption of innocence in the general sense of that phrase but not in the technical meaning attached to it in English and American law. In any event the RSFSR Code of Criminal Procedure seems to have gone as far as it is possible to go, in a "continental" system of trial procedure, to protect the accused against a conviction supported only by accusations and without convincing proof of guilt.'

Germany and Mussolini's Italy (unfortunately the list could be considerably extended).

THE ORDINARY POLICE

In Tsarist times, even law-abiding citizens commonly felt no great affection for the police; the Russian police before the Revolution were often renowned for their brutality and insensitivity, and there is a Russian word *politseyshchina*, which is a word of contempt meaning police bureaucracy or police brutality, for which there is no equivalent in English, because the thing itself is virtually unknown. After the Revolution the Soviet authorities were anxious to avoid all terms which had any association with the hated Tsarist police, and the very word *politsia*, police, ceased to be used. Instead the word *militsia* came to be used, and like the old word *politsia*, may be used either to mean 'the police' or to denote a police station. At first it was commonly called *narodnaya militsia*, people's militia, but now it is usually termed simply *militsia*. Every effort has been made to get away from the Tsarist police tradition, even, it is said, to the extent of recruiting exceptionally short men for the police, for the Tsarist tradition was to employ only exceptionally tall men. One reason why the Tsarist police was hated so much was that the police had very wide and somewhat ill-defined powers, and that its members in the lower ranks were often illiterate and had no knowledge at all of the law; moreover they were armed, and tended to use their arms on the slightest provocation, or even without provocation. In the countryside there were special mounted police, the *uryadniki* who had power to arrest and detain anyone on little or no suspicion, and who often terrorized the countryside. (They were called *kuryadniki* by the peasants, a word suggesting *kuryatnitsy*, chicken-stealing foxes, which may show the way in which they were regarded by those subject to their control.) The Tsarist police in fact was often recruited from the most ignorant and brutalized sections of the population.

In order to obtain a somewhat better type of recruit, the Soviet authorities enlist in the police only men who have completed their military service, and the significance of this is the educational influence of service in the Soviet Army, where a great deal of attention is paid to education, and especially to teaching illiterates to read and write; the virtual abolition of illiteracy in the USSR has been achieved to a large extent through the educational sections of the army.

The Soviet *militsia* or police force is organized very much on military lines, with the same ranks and titles as those in the army. On joining the police, a recruit must sign on for an initial period of three years, though after three years' service a policeman of any rank can resign on giving one month's notice. All ranks of the police wear uniform while on duty; no plain clothes police or detectives are used. All ranks are armed, but there are very strict regulations about using their arms; a militiaman is entitled to use his gun only if he is attacked by an armed assailant, or if its use appears to be the only way to save an innocent life, for example if he sees an attempt at murder, and shooting the attacker appears to be the only way of preventing the victim from being killed.

As in some other countries, there is still an attempt to keep the police somewhat apart from other citizens. Single men in the *militsia* are accommodated in police barracks, and married men in flats in special blocks, so the police do not live in ordinary houses and flats like English policemen. And, as in most countries, members of the police are not allowed to belong to trade unions.

In each town and other administrative district (usually the *oblast*) there is a Police Board, *Upravleniye Militsii*, and this is subordinated both to the local Soviet, the Soviet of the town or *oblast* (horizontal subordination) and to the Police Board of the Ministry of Public Order of the Union Republic concerned (vertical subordination). The traffic police are organized separately from the main force, being under a sub-committee directly responsible to the Police Board of each city or other administrative district, and it is the traffic police that is responsible in the USSR for conducting driving tests and issuing driving licences; the driving tests are said to be very much more severe than those in England or in most other countries, and consequently there is a much higher standard of driving and road conduct generally.

Apart from the traffic police, the duties of the *militsia* can be classified into three groups: 1. criminal investigation, 2. administrative duties, 3. general duties.

1. Criminal Investigation. This has been referred to above.[1] A criminal offence may be reported to the police, or to a procurator's office, but it makes little difference to which authority it is first reported, for in either case the report is followed by a police enquiry, except where the offence falls within the jurisdiction of some other enquiry organ, such as the fire brigade authorities, or the Committee on State Security in the case of an offence against the State. Once the enquiry has led to some individual being suspected of the offence the procedure varies according to the seriousness of the offence charged; where the offence is a serious one, there must be a preliminary investigation conducted by

[1]See p. 118 *ante*.

an investigator attached to the procurator's office, and the police are no longer concerned with the matter once they have reported the result of their enquiry to the procurator's office; in other cases, the preliminary investigation is conducted by a police investigator. Where the offence is less serious (usually where the maximum penalty is no more than one year's deprivation of liberty) the police continue their enquiry until they have collected sufficient evidence against the suspect, and then, after formal approval by the procurator, forward the charge direct to the People's Court, which will examine it, and if there seems to be sufficient evidence to justify a trial, will accept the case for hearing. In comparatively trivial cases the police can forward the case to a comrades' court, to be dealt with there.

The police may arrest a person on a warrant issued by the procurator's office, or they may arrest without warrant in specified cases, namely,

a. where a criminal is seen and caught by them in the act,

b. where, although the police did not see the offence, they were present shortly afterwards and the culprit is identified by an eye-witness of the offence,

c. where evidence of the commission of an offence is found on a person or at his residence,

d. where a person has attempted to escape and is caught in flight,

e. where a suspect has no fixed place of abode or work,

f. where a suspect refuses to reveal his identity, or for some reason is unable to (e.g. is dumb and has lost his identity papers). In these six cases, arrest without warrant is allowed only if there are circumstances suggesting that arrest appears essential to safeguard the appearance of the suspect in future proceedings. After arrest bail is sometimes allowed. Every case of arrest without warrant must be reported to the procurator's office within twenty-four hours.

The police are entitled to enter any building whatsoever for the purpose of seeking a suspected criminal or a fugitive from justice, but they must obtain a search warrant if they are seeking stolen property, or illicit property such as contraband goods, illicit stills, narcotics, illegal printing presses or firearms. If on a search the police find property which they wish to remove, such as contraband or stolen goods, an inventory of the goods to be removed must be drawn up, and the police must get two private citizens to check the inventories and sign them before the goods are removed. This procedure is intended to forestall complaints of the kind that were sometimes made against the Tsarist police, that in conducting searches they often took away (in fact stole) private property for their own use.

2. Administrative Duties. Like the police in some other continental countries, the Soviet police are entitled to impose fines on the spot for minor administrative infringements which are not treated as criminal offences, e.g. parking offences, pedestrians crossing the street against the lights, walking on the grass in public gardens where this is not allowed. The maximum that can be imposed on the spot as an adminis-trative fine is ten roubles, or twenty in Moscow, and mostly these on-the-spot fines are very much smaller.

A person committing an administrative infringement may be required to go to a police station to explain his conduct, but he cannot be detained there for more than two hours, and if he will not co-operate, or refuses to admit his guilt, the police can then make an enquiry and bring ordinary criminal proceedings in the usual way.

There is also a special procedure for cases of petty hooliganism and petty black-marketeering, which do not seem serious enough to warrant a full-scale criminal charge, but yet seem a little too serious to be left to Comrades' Courts: in these cases the police may take the offender to a People's Court, where he will appear before a single People's Judge without assessors, and he can be sentenced to up to fifteen days' administrative detention by the judge without a formal trial, or up to two months' corrective labour, or a fine. There is no right of appeal. Such a sentence does not form part of a criminal record, *sudimost*, so no notice of it will appear on his identity papers, though of course the offender may have to explain his absence from work to his employers. A very short period of detention like this is thought to be useful in bringing young hooligans sharply to their senses, though the system has been criticized by some Soviet lawyers on the ground that the régime is too soft, as regulations say that people in administrative detention must be supplied with three hot meals a day, and this may well be a luxury that young hooligans, especially if they come from an unskilled labouring environment, seldom enjoy at home. While in administrative police detention, the police are supposed to teach them something useful; what to do with them while in detention seems to be something of a problem for the police.

The police also have the duty of dealing with drunks found in public; they take them to a 'sobering-up' station, and for the sobering-up service a fee is charged. If the bill is not paid within a week it is sent to the employer, so the person concerned may have some further explaining to do; in fact he is usually anxious to avoid this, so these bills are normally paid promptly. Spot fines on persons found drunk in public places may also be imposed by the police.

3. General Duties. There are various miscellaneous duties laid on the police, apart from those already considered, such as maintaining order in public places, summoning first-aid for people injured in traffic accidents or other street accidents, taking lost children to centres from which they can be reclaimed by their parents, and taking insane people into custody until they are transferred to a mental hospital if they are a danger to themselves and others.

One of the most important of these duties is the operation of the passport system. This includes the registration and supervision of foreigners; all foreigners entering the country have to leave their passports in the hands of the police for the first few days for registration, and have to notify the police of their movements. (In the case of tourists, this is seen to by Intourist, the Soviet travel organization concerned with foreign tourists in the USSR.) But there is also the internal passport system for Soviet citizens, which operates in all the most populous areas. The internal passport system is controlled by the police; outside some rural areas where the system does not apply every Soviet citizen over the age of sixteen must have an internal passport. The passport first issued is valid for five years: between the ages of twenty and twenty-one the holder must exchange it for a ten-year passport, and he must get a new ten-year passport when he is thirty. At the age of forty a permanent passport not requiring renewal is given, and such a permanent passport is also given to people under forty who have been awarded certain honours or have reached some high office to which the right to a permanent passport is attached. Temporary passports are issued to people coming temporarily from an area where the passport system is not in force into an area where it is, and also in cases where a passport has been lost, while enquiries are being made until a new one is issued. The internal passport, in addition to matters such as age, whether married or single, and other personal details, contains the name of the institution at which the holder is employed, and contains the dates at which he started work, and left work, at each place of employment. It may also state the holder's *sudimost*, his criminal record, though after a certain number of years without committing an offence a new passport can be obtained which does not contain an account of the holder's criminal record.

The importance of the passport is that to reside permanently in a particular place one must get authorization from the police if one does not already have it from some other authority; in the latter case it must be confirmed by the police. A retired person is not free to live anywhere he likes in the Soviet Union, though of late years much more latitude has been given to people to move about the country than was the case during Stalin's time, when the operation of the passport system was often quite effective in tying people to certain areas.

The powers of the police are clearly defined in most cases, though in public emergencies such as fires, floods and epidemics, the police can take all measures which they think necessary to deal with the emergency, and in these cases they are entitled to suspend all traffic to or from the areas affected.

THE SECRET POLICE

The other police system, the so-called secret police, is the Committee on State Security (KGB). During Stalin's time the secret police under its various names was subject to no restraint at all,[1] and this caused much illegality and apprehension, for no-one could be sure that he would not be denounced by some informer, and after Stalin's death it seemed to be in everyone's interest to bring the State Security Police under proper control.

The present position is that the Committee on State Security is a body attached to the Council of Ministers of the USSR; it is responsible to that body for its activities, and to no other authority, though its individual members are liable for breaches of the law. The Chairman of the Committee on State Security is an *ex officio* member of the Council of Ministers of the USSR. There are local branches of the KGB attached to the Councils of Ministers of Union Republics and other public authorities at lower levels throughout the country.

The main duties of the KGB are counter-espionage and the detection of counter-revolutionary activity. If a person is suspected of a crime against the State the preliminary investigation is conducted by the KGB, but cases must be reported to the procurator's office, and it is the duty of the procurator to see that all legal requirements are complied with by the KGB investigator dealing with the case. The procuracy does not conduct the preliminary investigation, but it has to supervise it, and this renders much less likely the gross breaches of legality which occurred in Stalin's time, when the procuracy had no control in practice (whatever the position might have been on paper) over the State Security Police. If the preliminary investigation results in an indictment the case must be brought before a court, and tried in the usual way under the ordinary rules of criminal procedure; the 'special boards' of the MVD which could exile people for up to five years were abolished shortly after Stalin's death.

[1] See p. 49 *ante*.

In Stalin's time the State Security Police was a law unto itself, and amounted virtually to a private army; it had uniformed detachments, tanks and artillery, and was thrown into any area where there was or seemed to be disaffection; areas, for example, where little local opposition had been organized to the German invaders, and whose inhabitants were suspected of welcoming the German invasion as a liberation from Soviet rule. (These areas were almost entirely areas inhabited by non-Russian populations, for example, certain parts of the Northern Caucasus.)

Detailed information is not available, but it seems that the KGB no longer controls uniformed armed forces. It does, of course, have plain clothes representatives engaged on matters such as counter-espionage work, loyalty checking of personnel engaged on work involving access to military or state secrets, or employed on work abroad, and the provision of bodyguards or private protection forces for highly placed members of the Government and party. It seems that Soviet espionage agents abroad are under the control of the KGB, though in the nature of things we cannot know very much about this side of its work, and some of the information that has been published on the matter may not be reliable.

CONCLUSIONS

Some observations must be made about the way in which the rules of Soviet criminal procedure work out in practice. On paper, and if applied in the right spirit, the rules of criminal procedure should provide a satisfactory system, once the basic assumptions of European continental criminal procedure are accepted. But the best of rules can be perverted, and in the last analysis the quality of Soviet legal procedure, as indeed the quality of legal procedure in other countries, depends very largely on the quality of the people working it. Abuses occur in the Soviet Union, as they do elsewhere, and in the much more liberal atmosphere which has prevailed since the death of Stalin in 1953, abuses are reported much more freely in the Soviet legal and general press. The fact that abuses get more publicity now than they did previously is itself significant; but it provides ammunition for anti-Soviet writers anxious to show that these abuses are inherent in the nature of the system, and it may well be that the abuses publicly reported in fact represent merely the tip of an iceberg. Pro-Soviet writers dismiss these reports as being evidence simply of the desire of the authorities to uncover and eradicate minor defects in a basically sound system. The detached scholar feels that in the absence of any information about the extent of abuses, judgment must be suspended. Even in one's own country it is not always easy to judge of the extent to which events reported in the press should be regarded as typical or exceptional, and the difficulty is greatly increased when one is considering events reported in the controlled press of a foreign country.

To take one or two examples which concern the key figure in Soviet criminal procedure, the procuracy investigator; he can, without breaking any rule of criminal procedure, act in very unfair ways; for example, he may induce a confession by leading the accused to think that if he confesses the investigation will be terminated and he will be released under 'collective probation';[1] in serious cases, where the accused has been detained *incommunicado*, he may dissuade the accused from asking for a defence counsel to study the indictment and the file when the preliminary investigation is terminating, or he may refuse to accept a defence counsel retained by relatives of the accused as one retained by the accused, or he may dissuade the accused from ratifying the agreement made by his relatives by casting doubts on the reliability of the counsel retained by them, or he may allow the accused to call in defence counsel at such a late stage that the right of defence counsel to ask for further evidence to be taken becomes virtually worthless because counsel has insufficient time to consider the file. Some accused persons have suspected an investigator of having made a secret arrangement with a defence counsel, and then persuaded the accused's relatives to retain that counsel for the defence, and for this reason have rejected the services of such counsel. All this appears from the Soviet press itself. Yet the fact that it is reported shows both that such cases have occurred, and that the authorities are anxious that they should not occur.

Some western critics have regarded it as a fundamental defect in the Soviet system that the investigators are subject to the procuracy and not to the courts, as is usual in Western European countries. While this criticism is not entirely without reason, it rests on the assumption (which could well be true in Western Europe and untrue in the Soviet Union) that judges are necessarily more fair-minded than investigators. Though the vast majority of both investigators and judges are now law graduates, there is not the slightest doubt that a career in the procuracy tends to be the first choice of the most able law graduates, and that the procuracy recruits from the upper reaches of the law school pass lists. Transferring the investigators to the supervision of the courts rather than of the procuracy would, under Soviet conditions, probably result in their coming under the control of persons of lesser ability than at

[1] See p. 119 *ante*.

L

present. Ability is not synonymous with fair-mindedness, but generally speaking the better the lawyer, the more able he is to see a problem from different points of view. Moreover, Soviet People's Courts are often criticized, both by Western and Soviet critics, of being too 'prosecution-minded' and so long as there remains something in this criticism the transfer of the investigators from procuracy to court control could hardly help; the fact of the matter is that the prestige which, in the West, and particularly in England, surrounds the judiciary, tends in the USSR to be attached to the procuracy. The appellate judges in the Soviet Union are naturally aware of the state of things in lower courts, and they do not mince their words: in an article in *Izvestia* on 2 December 1964 the President of the Supreme Court of the USSR had some harsh things to say about People's Courts which 'blindly and un-critically follow and in effect rubber-stamp indictments'. He found it necessary to remind People's Courts that an acquittal is not necessarily a reflection on the work of an investigator. Certainly the fair-minded Soviet lawyer is aware of the fact that there are abuses in his system which need remedying; but could not the same thing be said about the fair-minded lawyer in any other country?

FURTHER READING

H. J. Berman, *Soviet Criminal Law and Procedure*, Cambridge, Mass., 1966.
A. Trusov, *An Introduction to the Theory of Evidence*, Moscow, 1962.
E. L. Johnson, 'Compensation for Victims of Criminal Offences in English and Soviet Law' (1964), 17 *Current Legal Problems*, p. 144.
I. Lapenna, 'The New Russian Criminal Code and Code of Criminal Pro-cedure' (1961), 10 *International & Comparative Law Quarterly*, p. 421.
P. B. Taylor, 'The Role of the Investigator in Soviet Criminal Procedure' (1966), 7 *Journal of the International Commission of Jurists*, p. 20.

CHAPTER SIX

The Criminal Law

GENERAL THEORY OF CRIME

Seeing that crime, in the original Marxist doctrine, was a reflection of the class struggle, Soviet writers have found it difficult to explain its continued existence in a society in which socialism has been achieved, and which is on the road to communism. For long it was possible to explain that crime was due to a survival of attitudes derived from capitalism, but with every passing year this explanation seemed less plausible, and at the present time in most parts of the USSR only persons approaching the age of sixty have even childhood memories of capitalism. Yet crime persists, and the typical Soviet criminal seems to be a man in his middle twenties. Of recent years, although the doctrine that crime is a 'survival from capitalism' has not been discarded, a much more realistic attitude has been adopted, and a science of Soviet criminology is being developed. Work is being done in particular at the All-Union Institute for the Study of Crime and for the Elaboration of Measures of Crime Prevention, the founding of which in May 1963 showed that the question of crime prevention was being taken seriously at the highest levels, for this is a high-powered Institute directly subordinated to the Procurator-General of the USSR, and it works in close collaboration with the Supreme Court of the USSR; from a more academic standpoint, a department for the study and prevention of crime has been functional since November 1960 in the Institute of State and Law of the Academy of Sciences of the USSR. Whatever the causes of crime in the USSR may be (and the non-Marxist will see no reason for supposing that they are much different from the causes of crime in 'bourgeois' states) one thing seems clear; there is a very close connection in the USSR between crime and alcohol. Some years ago it was reported that of persons convicted of rape, 67 per cent were intoxicated at the time of the offence; for murder, the figure was 85 per cent and for hooliganism, 96 per cent. And it seems that a desire for the means to indulge a craving for alcohol is the motive for many petty thefts and frauds. Further than this, speculation is hardly profitable.

However, the Marxist view that crime is a survival from capitalism is reflected in Soviet jurisprudence in the view of crime as a 'socially dangerous act'. The importance of this was much greater in former times than it is now, for the equation 'crime equals socially dangerous act' could be reversed, and under the doctrine of analogy any socially dangerous act could be regarded as a crime and punished as such.[1] At present the only legal significance of the principle that a crime is a socially dangerous act lies in the provision that even though there may be the elements of a crime present, that is, even though an act formally comes within the definition of an offence set out in a particular article of the Criminal Code, it is not to be considered a crime if owing to its insignificance there is no social danger present or if the act or the offender can no longer be regarded as socially dangerous at the time of the trial. These provisions seem to lack the importance attributed to them by Soviet jurists, for most systems of criminal law provide some general escape clause to cover cases where even the minimum punishment provided by law would be inappropriate in view of the triviality of the act. They do, however, provide an exception to the minimum sentence often prescribed by Soviet law.

AGGRAVATING AND MITIGATING CIRCUMSTANCES

When considering what sentence to impose, a criminal court must consider whether there are any aggravating or mitigating circumstances. If there are aggravating circumstances, it must apply the maximum fixed by the Code for the offence, or at any rate a penalty near the maximum; in some cases, however, the Code allows penalties greater than the ordinary maximum in cases where there are aggravating circumstances. Where there are mitigating circumstances it should apply the minimum fixed by the Code, or something near the minimum; it may even apply a milder penalty altogether.

The following are regarded by the Criminal Code of the RSFSR as aggravating circumstances:

1. that the convicted person has a criminal record; (the court may, however, in its discretion ignore this circumstance);
2. that the crime was committed by an organized gang;
3. that the crime was committed for mercenary or other base motives;
4. that the crime had serious consequences;
5. that the crime was committed against a minor, or an elderly person, or a person in a helpless situation, or against a person who was dependent on the guilty party financially or otherwise;

[1] See p. 39 *ante*.

6. that the convicted person has incited or instigated minors to commit an offence;

7. that the crime was committed in a manner which was specially cruel or humiliating to the victim;

8. that in committing the crime advantage was taken of some public calamity;

9. that the crime was committed in a way endangering public safety;

10. that the crime was committed by a drunken person using dangerous objects; (e.g. a gun or a car)

11. that the convicted person deliberately attempted to shift liability for the offence on to an innocent person;

12. that a further crime has been committed by a person put under 'collective probation'[1] while still under probation or within a year after it has ended.

The following are regarded as mitigating circumstances:

1. that the offender averted harmful consequences of the crime, or voluntarily made compensation for any loss caused, or made good any harm done;

2. that the crime was committed following a combination of difficult personal or family circumstances;

3. that the crime was committed under the influence of threats or duress, or on account of financial, professional or other dependence;

4. that the crime was a. a first offence, b. committed as a result of a fortuitous combination of circumstances and c. not representing any great social danger;

5. that the offence was committed under the influence of strong emotional disturbance caused by the unjustified acts of the victim;

6. that the crime was committed as a defensive measure against a socially dangerous attack, though it exceeded the limits of permissible self-defence; (5 and 6 are not applicable in cases of murder and assault, for their general effect is covered by particular rules in connection with these offences, having the same general effect of mitigating liability).

7. that the offender is a minor;

8. that the offender is a pregnant woman;

9. that the offender has shown sincere remorse or spontaneously gave himself up, or gave active assistance in bringing the crime to light.

The court, however, may but is not bound to recognize any other circumstance as a mitigating circumstance; thus the courts on occasion have recognized illness or old age, previous good conduct at work or a good war record, domestic troubles, lack of intelligence or education,

[1] See p. 119 *ante*.

or unselfish motives, as constituting mitigating circumstances in particular cases.

Both aggravating and mitigating circumstances may exist in the same case; it appears that they are then regarded as cancelling each other out.

PUNISHMENTS

The various punishments which may be imposed by a criminal court will now be considered.

The death penalty, carried out by shooting, may be imposed for fourteen separate offences in all. It may be imposed on persons convicted of treason; espionage; political assassination of a Soviet public figure; political assassination of a foreign public figure; the creation of organizations for committing especially dangerous offences against the State or against another 'working people's state'; the organization of armed gangs. In other cases the death penalty may be imposed where there are aggravating circumstances, either those referred to above or some other aggravating circumstance set out in the article of the criminal code dealing with the offence in question; these are premeditated murder; disrupting the work of corrective labour colonies; making or passing counterfeit money or securities; violation of rules relating to exchange control; stealing state or social property on a very large scale; rape; acceptance of a bribe by an official; and killing or attempting to kill a policeman or people's guard in the performance of his duties. Only in the last case, however, killing or attempting to kill a policeman or people's guard in the performance of his duties, where there are aggravating circumstances, is the death penalty mandatory; in this case, the aggravating circumstances are those referred to earlier. In all other cases the court may, in its discretion, impose some lesser penalty. In wartime there are other offences which may be punished by death, e.g. desertion, evasion of the call-up, insubordination.

There has clearly long been a strong division of opinion about the death penalty in the Soviet Union, for it has several times been abolished only to be restored shortly afterwards.[1] Even the Criminal Code of 1960 makes a passing obeisance to abolitionist sentiment by referring to it as 'an exceptional measure of punishment, pending its complete abolition'.

Deprivation of liberty for a determined period is the punishment normally imposed for serious offences. In most cases the minimum period which may be imposed is three months, and the maximum ten

[1] In fact there have been similar vacillations with regard to the death penalty in Russia ever since the middle of the eighteenth century.

years. Apart from cases of quasi-crime,[1] a period of less than three months can be imposed only when a sentence of corrective labour has been changed to one of deprivation of liberty because the offender has failed to carry out the instructions given; but a period of up to fifteen years may be imposed 'for especially serious crimes and on especially dangerous recidivists'. The Criminal Code contains a definition of 'particularly dangerous recidivist'; it is highly complicated, depending in part on the number of previous convictions and in part on the seriousness of the previous offences. In cases where the offender is not an 'especially dangerous recidivist' the normal ten years' maximum may be exceeded where the relevant provision of the Criminal Code expressly allows this: examples are numerous offences against the State, murder under aggravating circumstances, rape under aggravating circumstances, and some forms of offences against property, in which cases sentences up to fifteen years may be imposed; in the case of intentionally inflicting grievous bodily harm from which the death of the victim has resulted, a maximum of twelve years is provided.

A sentence of deprivation of liberty is served either in a prison or in a corrective labour colony. The court may sentence persons convicted of 'serious crimes' and 'especially dangerous recidivists' to serve the whole or part of the sentence in a prison. There are four types of corrective labour colony régime: ordinary, strict, very strict, and special. As a general rule, offenders convicted of less serious crimes are sent to ordinary corrective labour colonies, and those convicted of more serious ones to those with a strict régime. The colonies with very strict régimes appear to be reserved for persons who have previously served sentences of deprivation of liberty, and the colonies with a special régime are for persons classified as 'especially dangerous recidivists'. The court passing sentence states in which type of labour colony the sentence is to be served, and the only subsequent administrative variation possible (i.e. without reference to the court which imposed the sentence) is that offenders may, if their conduct justifies such a measure, be transferred from colonies with a special régime to colonies with a very strict régime.

In addition to the corrective labour colonies strictly so-called, there are also 'corrective labour colony-settlements'. These are intended for persons who have served part of their sentence in a corrective labour colony and who 'have made good progress on the road towards correction' and in these colony-settlements conditions are more relaxed in the sense that they are more like conditions outside. The idea is to accustom prisoners gradually to a return to normal life.

[1] See p. 157 *post.*

Deprivation of freedom in one form or another is one of the punishments very commonly imposed by courts. In no case is deprivation of liberty an alternative to a fine.

A penalty very frequently imposed in the case of less serious offences is that of corrective labour, and this penalty is one of the more original features of the Soviet penal system. The offender either continues his ordinary work, or is directed to some other work at a place within reasonable travelling distance from his residence, and in either case there is a deduction from his wages up to a maximum of 20 per cent. In both cases, too, the time covered by the sentence (which ranges from one month to one year) cannot count for purposes of seniority, pension-entitlement and so forth. Under the milder form, continuing at one's previous job, the offender may, if he wishes, change his job, but he will still be subject to the disqualifications inherent in this form of punishment; under the more severe form, working at a designated institution, he cannot change jobs during the period of the sentence, and the work designated is usually of a heavy manual type.

Two other punishments which are rather special features of the Soviet system are exile and banishment. In cases provided for by the Criminal Code either may be imposed from a minimum of two up to a maximum of five years. Neither punishment is strictly a deprivation of liberty in the general sense of detention in a prison or a labour colony, but the person sentenced to exile is required to take up his residence in a specified area, which is often located in Siberia. In the case of banishment no area is specified, but the offender is prohibited from residing in a certain place or places; very commonly there is a prohibition against residence in the five or six largest towns in the country. Sentences of exile or banishment may be imposed as a sole punishment, but more often they constitute a subsidiary punishment which comes into operation after a sentence of deprivation of liberty has been served.

Fines are seldom imposed as a punishment[1] except in cases where a sentence of corrective labour would be inappropriate because of the offender's inability to work or for some other similar reason. In any case where a fine is imposed, either as a main or a subsidiary penalty, the court must consider the financial position of the offender before fixing the amount, and may allow up to six months for payment if he is unable to pay it at once.

In comparatively minor cases the penalty may be a public reprimand.

---

[1] That is, as a punishment for offences dealt with in the Criminal Code. Small fines are often imposed for 'administrative infringements' which, not being regarded as criminal offences, are not dealt with in the Criminal Code.

The court may give such directions as it thinks fit for giving publicity to the reprimand by means of the press or in other ways.

Confiscation of property and deprivation of rank are subsidiary penalties; this means that they may only be imposed in addition to some other penalty. Confiscation may be of the whole or of an aliquot part of the offender's property; confiscation of the whole is sometimes imposed as additional to the death penalty. Confiscation of a part is often imposed as an additional penalty in cases where there have been extensive frauds at the expense of the State. In addition the instruments used to commit a crime, money and valuables acquired by means of a crime, and objects the ownership or use of which is not permitted (e.g. narcotics, illegal stills or printing presses) may be confiscated.

Dismissal from a job may be ordered by the court in appropriate cases as a main or subsidiary penalty, and so may reparation of the damage caused by the offence. Reparation may take the form of an order to repair the damage, or to pay money damages where the amount does not exceed 100 roubles; where it is more it should be the subject of a separate civil claim. Another form of reparation of damage is an order that the offender apologize publicly to the victim in a manner prescribed by the court.

SPECIAL OFFENCES

Soviet criminal law has to deal with the same sort of conduct that calls for repression by criminal courts in other countries, the offences against life, limb and property which occur everywhere. The law governing offences against the State, however, has certain peculiarities which will now be considered.

Chapter 1 of the Special Part[1] of the Criminal Code deals with 'Offences against the State' and is divided into two sections, the first dealing with 'Especially dangerous offences against the State' and the second with 'Other offences against the State'. Some of those in the first category, such as Treason and Political Assassination, carry the death penalty (which, however, is not mandatory), while others do not. Treason is defined as including 'flight abroad or refusal to return from abroad to the USSR', a somewhat unusual provision. An offence which does not carry the death penalty, but which is treated as an 'Especially dangerous offence against the State' is anti-Soviet agitation and propaganda, defined in article 70 of the Criminal Code. In view of the fact

[1] i.e. the part dealing with individual offences, as distinct from the General Part which deals with punishments, complicity, aggravating and mitigating circumstances, and other matters of general application.

that article 70 has been relied on in recent trials which have aroused considerable attention, it is set out here in full:

> *Anti-Soviet agitation and propaganda.* Agitation or propaganda carried on for the purpose of subverting or weakening Soviet authority or for the purpose of committing individual especially dangerous offences against the State, or circulating for those purposes slanderous fabrications which defame the Soviet State and social system, or circulating, preparing or keeping, for the same purpose, literature of such content is to be punished by deprivation of liberty for a term of from six months to seven years, with or without an additional period of exile for a term of from two to five years, or by exile for a term of from two to five years. The same acts committed by a person previously convicted of especially dangerous offences against the State, or committed in wartime, are to be punished by deprivation of freedom for a term of from three to ten years, with or without additional exile for a term of from two to five years.

Gerald Brooke, the Holborn lecturer, was sentenced under this article in July 1965 to a period of five years' deprivation of freedom, the first year to be spent in prison and the four succeeding years to be spent in a correctional labour colony with a strict régime. His offence appears to have been smuggling into the Soviet Union and attempting to distribute literature produced in the West by an anti-Soviet organization of Russian émigrés. He made no attempt to deny the charges, and according to Soviet reports, was caught in the act. The full regulations in force at the camp have apparently not been made available even to the British Embassy and Consulate staff who have been concerned with the case, but it appears that at the labour camp to which he was removed after the year in prison he is required to do eight hours' work a day at a lathe, that he may receive one food parcel every six months during the first half of the sentence and one every four months during the second half, and that he may receive an unlimited number of letters, though he may write only two a week. He is not allowed English newspapers. He is allowed to visit Moscow once a year to see relatives.

Another recent case under article 70 was that of the writers Sinyavski and Daniel, which, as it raised more general points about the present-day administration of justice in the case of offences against the State, was discussed earlier.[1]

[1] See p. 59 *ante*.

Speculation, which is defined as the buying and reselling of goods for the purpose of making a profit, is clearly an offence which could threaten the socialist economic system. The essence of the offence lies in buying goods in greater quantities than are required for personal use with the intention of selling them at a profit; merely selling second-hand articles for which one has no further use is no offence even if a profit should incidentally be made, and indeed the local authorities manage special 'commission shops' at which citizens can expose for sale unwanted articles, the shop taking a commission on each sale effected in this way. The provisions are aimed rather at people who try to make a living by dealing with goods in short supply (and shortages have long been endemic in the Soviet economy). Nevertheless many innocent people have aroused suspicions by buying quantities of goods in shops and markets and have found that they have had to justify their activities before criminal courts when all that was involved was a person from a village buying things for neighbours when on a casual visit to a large town.

The punishment for speculation can be severe; the Criminal Code provides a maximum of two years' deprivation of liberty in the ordinary case, or seven years when conducted on a large scale, but speculation in foreign currencies or securities, if conducted as a form of business or on a large scale, or by a person with a previous conviction for a currency offence (violation of the rules governing exchange control) may be visited with the death penalty. Several cases have been reported of the death penalty having been carried out for large-scale speculation in foreign currencies.

Another unusual chapter of the RSFSR Criminal Code deals with 'Crimes constituting Survivals of Local Customs' which is applicable in non-Russian areas, and deals with matters such as refusal to renounce a blood-feud, payment or acceptance of a bride-price on marriage, forcing a woman into marriage, agreeing to marry a woman under age, and bigamy and polygamy. The offences of bigamy and polygamy are committed only where a person cohabits in a common household with two or more women, and are punished by a maximum of one year's deprivation of liberty. Outside the areas where this chapter applies bigamy, as such, is not a specific offence, though it would be caught by an article of the Code which makes the concealment of circumstances which are an impediment to marriage or the furnishing of false information to the agencies which register acts of civil status an offence punishable by a maximum of one year's corrective labour.

CRIMINAL LAW AND MORALITY

It will be convenient at this stage to say something of the Soviet view of the relationship between criminal law and morality. The trend of legal thought both on the continent of Europe and in Anglo-American thought, during the nineteenth and twentieth centuries, may generally be described as 'positivism' (in England this trend is associated with the names of Jeremy Bentham and John Austin), which leads to a sharp distinction between law and morality. The criminal courts are concerned with punishing offences against the law, and are not courts of morals, though a moral element often comes in when it is a question of deciding the appropriate punishment. The Soviets would in general accept this view, but they do not emphasize it; it seems clear that a deliberate attempt is being made to blur the line drawn by nineteenth-century jurisprudence between law and morality. This can be seen in several connections; for example, the Constitution of the USSR says, 'It is the duty of every citizen of the USSR to abide by the Constitution of the USSR, to observe the laws, to maintain labour discipline, honestly to perform public duties, and to respect the rules of socialist inter-course.'[1] Again, the Criminal Code lays down that it is to be regarded as an aggravating circumstance that an offence was committed 'from mercenary or other base motives'.[2] This clearly leads into the realm of morality, for the law does not define a 'base' motive. Soviet moral views are not always easy to ascertain, and moreover are apt to lack stability; for example, sexual jealousy was at one time considered 'immoral' and the murder of an unfaithful wife or her lover was therefore a murder committed under aggravating circumstances, because of the 'lowness' of the motive, but it appears that a different view now prevails. However, that may be, it is clear that this provision opens wide the door to a moral evaluation of the conduct of the accused. It should perhaps be stressed here that the view that a criminal court is basically a court of

[1] This constitutes the whole of article 130 of the Constitution of the USSR. Its legal significance appears to be small, though it has been suggested by a Soviet academic writer that it could serve as an excuse for breach of contract in certain cases, e.g. a contract by a musician to perform at a concert where since the date of the contract circumstances have arisen, such as illness or accident, which would not make performance strictly impossible, but where performance could only be rendered at the expense of pain and suffering. The argument is that it would be contrary to 'the rules of socialist intercourse' to try to hold a man to a contract under such circumstances. If a Soviet court would take this view this would support the argument about the blurring of law and morality.
[2] See p. 148 *ante.*

morals is not one imposed on the Russian people by the Soviet Government; on the contrary, this attitude is one that is traditionally and typically Russian, and one which the Soviet Government makes use of for its own purposes.

QUASI-CRIME

One of the main features of the present time is the revival of Comrades' Courts to deal with comparatively minor matters. Comrades' Courts were set up in a number of factories and apartment blocks in 1919 to deal with minor matters, and they functioned quite effectively during the nineteen-twenties, but during the nineteen-thirties they gradually fell into disuse, and after 1939 little was heard of them until they were revived in 1959. At present there are enactments governing Comrades' Courts in most of the Union Republics: in the RSFSR the matter is now governed by a Decree of 3 July 1961, and the jurisdiction given the Comrades' Courts by the decree has been increased by a decree of the Praesidium of the Supreme Soviet of the RSFSR of 23 October 1963 which amends it in some respects. The fact that the jurisdiction of Comrades' Courts has thus been widened suggests that the policy at present is to encourage these rather informal tribunals, and to relieve the People's Courts of a number of minor matters which it is thought can best be disposed of by a Comrades' Court.

Comrades' Courts can be set up at factories, apartment blocks, collective farms, schools, and wherever there are at least fifty people living or employed, and, in certain specified cases, even where there are less. The matters they deal with are set out in article 5 of the Decree of 3 July 1961, and include being late for work, poor quality work, failure to observe safety regulations or fire precautions, carelessness involving damage to machinery, stock, etc., drunkenness, use of foul language, spreading malicious and unfounded rumours about colleagues, disputes between neighbours about amenities in apartment blocks, and civil disputes up to fifty roubles where both parties consent to the matter being heard by a Comrades' Court; and the decree of 23 October 1963 adds other matters, such as illicit use of transport belonging to factories, farms, etc., for private purposes, and (in the case of people with no criminal record) petty thefts from workmates or neighbours (in the case of a man with a record, the case would have to go to the People's Court), illicit manufacture of intoxicating drinks, where done only for private use and not for sale (if in large quantities for sale, it would be a matter for the People's Court) and also for various rather vaguely defined moral offences, such as 'unworthy conduct towards women, failure to care properly for one's children or parents' and, added by the decree of 23 October 1963, 'failure to give proper assistance to a sick or injured colleague'. In fact, it seems that the Comrades' Courts are, to some extent at any rate, definitely intended to function as courts of morals as well as courts of law, and that this is part of a deliberate attempt to blur the distinction between law and morality so carefully drawn by nineteenth-century jurisprudence and philosophy. It appears that this attitude is based on the Marxist theory that ultimately in a communist society law will 'wither away' with the State, and public opinion, expressed through groups of neighbours and workmates, will take the place of legal coercion, and that the Comrades' Courts are therefore a foretaste of the kind of social control which will exist in the communist society of the future.

The Comrades' Courts may impose certain sanctions; they may make the offender apologize in public, or give him a 'comradely warning', or a public reprimand, or a public reprimand with publication in the press, or impose a fine of up to ten roubles, or order compensation to any victim of the offence up to fifty roubles: they may also recommend, but not require, that the management at his place of work demote him, or put him on unskilled manual work for up to fifteen days, and they may recommend his dismissal if they find that he is having a harmful effect on young apprentices, or that he cannot be trusted to handle money or safety appliances properly.

Despite their comparatively informal character, Comrades' Courts are required to have a secretary and to keep proper records, and they are given power by law to summon witnesses, so they must be regarded, to some extent at least, as official bodies. Moreover, if any orders given in a decision by them are not complied with, e.g. to pay a fine or pay compensation for damage done, the matter can be reported to a People's Court which can then get its bailiff to levy execution in the same way as execution is levied on property belonging to people who have not complied with the civil judgments of a People's Court. There is therefore a real sanction in the procedure. If any case coming before a Comrades' Court appears more serious than was at first thought, or needs a more thorough investigation, the Comrades' Court is always entitled to transfer the case to a People's Court.

Another innovation of the last few years is the public meeting which can be called to pronounce judgment on 'parasites' under the Parasite Laws of the various Republics, which were enacted to deal with people who, while keeping within the letter of the Civil and Criminal Codes, were nevertheless in fact living off unearned income. While 'parasites' can be sentenced to exile for from two to five years by a public meeting, a number of safeguards have been introduced, largely as a result of pressure from the legal profession, that charges must be confirmed by the *militsia*, that the sentence must be confirmed by the local authority, and that the procurator's office can, if it thinks fit, protest confirmation of a sentence to a higher regional authority; the latest reports suggest that in fact the system has not been a success, and that the parasite legislation is now being enforced by the courts rather than by public meetings.

Much of what we would call petty offences in England are termed 'administrative infringements' in the USSR and do not come before the criminal courts. Administrative sanctions are normally imposed by administrative authorities, and although there is no right of appeal to the courts there is normally a right of appeal to a higher administrative authority. Administrative sanctions consist of warnings, fines (not exceeding fifty roubles, or 100 roubles where the offender is a civil servant, and in most cases very much less, e.g. up to five roubles for being drunk in the street) and corrective labour; but in some cases administrative offences may be dealt with by a single People's Judge and in these cases, deprivation of liberty of up to fifteen days may be imposed. In some cases a repetition of an administrative offence may amount to a criminal offence, e.g. hunting without a licence is a criminal offence under article 166 of the Criminal Code in the case of a person who has already been subjected to administrative sanctions for such an offence. Driving while drunk will normally result in suspension of a driving licence for from one to three years, the sanction being imposed by an administrative authority.

JUVENILE DELINQUENTS

The general age of criminal liability is now sixteen. Some special rules apply in the case of persons over sixteen and under eighteen; thus no-one who was under eighteen at the date of the offence may be sentenced to death, and, where the offence does not represent a great social danger, and the court thinks that the offender can be reformed without a punishment, it may apply 'compulsory educational measures' instead of imposing a punishment, or alternatively, it may refer the case to the Commission for Minors' Cases which can then apply 'compulsory educational measures' if it thinks fit. The 'compulsory educational measures' which may be imposed by the court or the Commission for Minors' Cases include: requiring the offender to make a public apology to the victim, reprimand or warning, transferring the minor to the 'strict supervision' of his parents or some other person, or to the care of some organization or individual, or committing him to a special educational institution or educational colony. Where any loss not exceeding twenty roubles was caused by the offence, the minor may be required to make compensation up to that amount if he has an independent wage.

In the case of some very serious offences, however, the age of criminal liability is reduced to fourteen, but even in these cases the above-mentioned 'compulsory educational measures' may be applied either by the court, or by the Commission for Minors' Cases if referred to them by the court, though compensation may not be ordered in the case of a person under fifteen.

The Commissions for Minors' Cases deal with all offences committed by persons below the age of criminal responsibility, and can take certain measures against the parents or guardians of such children, though they cannot deprive them of their parental rights; this can be done only through a court.

FURTHER READING

R. Beerman, 'Soviet and Russian Anti-Parasite Laws' (1964), 15 *Soviet Studies*, p. 420.

R. Beerman, 'The Anti-Parasite Law of the RSFSR modified' (1966), 17 *Soviet Studies*, p. 387.

F. J. Feldbrugge, *Soviet Criminal Law*, Leyden, 1964.

D. P. Hammer, 'Law Enforcement, Social Control and the Withering of the State: Recent Soviet Experience' (1963), 14 *Soviet Studies*, p. 379.

I. Lapenna, *Soviet Penal Policy*, London, 1968.

R. Schlesinger, 'The Criminal Code of the RSFSR' (1961), 12 *Soviet Studies*, p. 456.

T. Taras, 'Social Courts in the USSR' (1963), 14 *Soviet Studies*, p. 398.

CHAPTER SEVEN

Contract and Tort

THE CIVIL COURTS AND CIVIL APPEALS

Civil litigation comes before the same courts in the USSR as criminal cases. The court system has already been described in chapter 5, and there is little to add here.

The rules about appeals in civil cases are basically the same as in criminal cases. An appeal against the decision of a People's Court may be taken providing that notice of appeal is lodged within ten days of the decision appealed against. However, not only may the parties to the action appeal; the procurator may also appeal the case to the District Court on a point of law, even though the unsuccessful party does not want to appeal. The procurator cannot appeal against the decision merely because there was conflicting evidence and the court chose to believe one witness rather than another, but he can appeal if he considers that on the facts accepted by the People's Court the judgment was wrong in law, or he can appeal on the ground that there was a violation of the rules of civil procedure at the trial. The procurator is entitled to be present at any civil trial at which a disputed question of law arises, and he will often give his observations on the law or the procedure during the course of the trial. He might appeal a decision, for example, because the court refused to call a witness whom one party wanted to be heard, or because a witness refused to answer a question and the court did not press him to answer, or for any other procedural irregularity. This appeal is by way of 'cassationary protest'.

With regard to procedural irregularities there is a difference between criminal and civil cases: in a criminal case, any infringement of the rules of procedure, except the most trivial, means that the appeal court must set the proceedings aside and order a new trial, or a new investigation; it cannot allow a criminal verdict, whether of conviction or of acquittal, to stand if it appears that there were irregularities at the trial. In a civil case the mere fact that there were irregularities does not of

M

itself oblige the appeal court to declare the trial and judgment a nullity; the court will do this only if it thinks that the irregularity might have affected the actual outcome of the proceedings. Where it is convinced that the whole truth of the matter was revealed, despite the irregularity, it can allow the decision to stand, that is, it can dismiss the appeal while admitting the procedural irregularity and bringing it to the attention of the People's Court concerned.

In civil appeals the appellate court may either:

1. dismiss the appeal, allowing the judgment of the People's Court to stand;

2. allow the appeal, in full or in part, on the ground that there was an error by the court below, and remit the case for a new trial in the People's Court from which it came. In such a case the appellate court may, if it thinks fit, direct that the case should be re-heard by a differently constituted court, that is, that the People's judge and the assessors who first heard the case should not hear the case at the new trial. A new trial is ordered when the appellate court considers that further evidence should be heard before the case can be properly decided;

3. allow the appeal, quashing the decision of the People's Court and terminating the proceedings;

4. modify the judgment given by the People's Court: this can be done when there is no need for any further evidence to be heard, the District Court being satisfied that the People's Court correctly established the facts of the case but came to an erroneous conclusion concerning the law applicable.

The basic rule is that an appellate court cannot act as a trial court, that is, hear further witnesses and come to conclusions itself on disputed questions of fact; its task is rather to see that the decision arrived at by the People's Court was arrived at correctly and to remit the case for re-hearing if further facts should be investigated before a correct decision can be given. However, there are a few exceptions to this basic principle, and they vary from Republic to Republic: in the RSFSR in cases involving labour relations, for example actions for wrongful dismissal or actions for unpaid wages, the appellate court may itself obtain further evidence and decide the case without sending it back for retrial to a People's Court.

And, as in criminal cases, civil cases may also be taken to the highest courts, the Supreme Courts of the Union Republics and the Supreme Court of the USSR, by way of review (*nadzor*) on the initiative either of the procurator or of a Supreme Court itself. As in criminal cases, the District Courts also have some review jurisdiction. In civil cases, however, there is no time limit within which an application for review may be brought.

CONTRACT

The civil courts hear contract cases in which either the plaintiff or the defendant or both is a citizen. Where both parties to a contract are public corporations, however, the ordinary civil courts have no jurisdiction and disputes arising out of the contract are heard by state or departmental arbitration tribunals. Clearly under Soviet conditions most important economic contracts will be concluded between public corporations, and the ways in which disputes arising out of them are settled will be discussed in chapter 11: in this section we shall consider those contracts which are subject to the jurisdiction of the civil courts.

Contracts between a citizen and a public corporation are of many kinds. A citizen may wish to supplement the benefits payable under social security legislation by private insurance and enter into a contract for life or accident insurance with the State Insurance Corporation, *Gosstrakh*, or he may agree with a publishing house to write a book, or he may hire a car from a car-hire service corporation. From the point of view of the ordinary citizen, however, the most common contracts which he concludes with public corporations are those of employment and those under which he purchases goods in retail stores managed by public trading corporations. Employment creates a labour law relationship, and this is considered in chapter 9; sale creates a civil law relationship, and the law relating to it will now be briefly considered.

Article 246 of the RSFSR Civil Code of 1964 provides that a person who has bought defective goods is entitled to one of the following remedies:
1. that the seller should replace the defective goods by proper ones;
2. a reduction in the price;
3. free removal of the defect by the seller;
4. reimbursement by the seller if the buyer has removed the defect at his own expense;
5. rescission of the contract together with damages for any loss caused by the defect.

The buyer can choose which of these remedies he wishes; where the defect has caused damage, e.g. if a defective washing machine has damaged shirts being washed by it, the fifth remedy will normally be appropriate, as damages will be recoverable for the shirts destroyed. However, this fifth remedy is excluded should the seller be able to prove (and the burden of proof is on him and cannot easily be discharged) that he was in no way at fault in not knowing of the defect, though this would seldom be the case in practice. The claim must be made as soon as the defect is discovered, and in any case within six months, unless a longer period has been provided in an express guarantee.

Some consumer durables can be purchased on credit from the retail stores; the system is not strictly 'hire-purchase' as understood in Anglo-American law, as ownership in the thing purchased vests at once in the purchaser, but rather 'credit sale'. The purchaser has to pay a deposit of from 20 to 25 per cent of the cash price, and a credit charge of 1 or 2 per cent of the cash price as consideration for the credit facility, and the balance of the cash price is paid by means of deductions from the purchaser's wages, which are paid directly by the purchaser's employer to the store. The contract signed by the purchaser includes a form of authority to the purchaser's employer authorizing the deductions, and this is forwarded by the store to the employer. Most articles sold on credit are guaranteed; this entitles the purchaser to free repairs within the guarantee period; if the article breaks down a third time within the guarantee period after having been repaired twice, it must be re-replaced; and if this is impossible, the deposit, credit charge and all payments made must be returned to the purchaser. Even in the case of non-guaranteed goods, the buyer is entitled to have the article exchanged if he returns them within seven days if latent defects have appeared, and if the shop cannot replace the article at once, the contract is rescinded and the deposit and credit charge must be refunded. In the case of clothes bought on credit, even in the absence of defects in manufacture the goods will be exchanged for others of a different size, colour or style if returned clean and unworn within five days.

Contracts to which both parties are citizens are comparatively rare and unimportant in practice. A person with a spare room in his house may let it, but the amount of rent chargeable is regulated by law. A person may lend money to another, but interest is no longer allowed in dealings between citizens. A person may sell a house or furniture to another but private sales of used cars are severely restricted.

In connection with sales of houses, one type of contract arose in practice and caused a certain amount of difficulty: this was where a person transferred his house to another in consideration of an under-taking that the purchaser would provide board, lodging and attendance for the vendor for the rest of the vendor's life. This was obviously a convenient arrangement in the case of an elderly person with no family,[1]

---

[1] Usufructs or life-interests in property are otherwise unknown to Soviet law. It is therefore not possible for the owner of a house to sell it reserving a life interest for himself.

but the Civil Code of 1922 contained no special provisions about such contracts, though there was no reason for regarding them as illegal. The matter was therefore regulated by articles 253 and 254 of the Civil Code of 1964, which provide that such contracts may be made where the vendor is unable by reason of age or health to work. Where such a contract has been made, the buyer remains bound to maintain the seller even though the house is accidentally destroyed, and he is not permitted to dispose of the house during the lifetime of the seller. If the buyer dies during the lifetime of the seller the house reverts to the seller and no compensation is payable to the buyer's estate in respect of the period during which the seller was being maintained by the buyer. The contract can be rescinded at the demand of the seller if the buyer fails to comply with his obligations, or at the demand of the buyer if through unavoidable circumstances he is no longer able to provide the seller with the services contracted for, and in both such cases the house reverts to the seller without any compensation being payable to the buyer. If the contract was entered into as a result of the seller's ill-health, and the seller's health improves to such an extent that he is now able to work, the buyer may demand to be exempted from the obligation to provide board and attendance, with the result that the house remains the buyer's, the seller having merely a right to reside in the part agreed upon rent-free for the rest of his life. This seems rather unfair on the seller, as he has parted with the ownership of his house and is not getting the consideration he contracted for: the rule clearly reflects a typical Soviet anxiety lest private property be used to permit an able-bodied person to live without working. Soviet commentators on the Code explain that the reason why no compensation is payable to the purchaser in cases where the contract is rescinded, is that during the period up to the time when rescission took effect, the purchaser had the benefit of the use of the house, except for the portion reserved to the vendor.

TORT

The provisions of the Civil Code of 1922 concerning tort (civil injury) had two basic principles: first, liability in damages for harm or loss to another person was based on causation, not fault. The early Soviet jurists took pride in the fact that, unlike most systems of 'bourgeois' law, a plaintiff in tort merely had to show that the defendant had caused the harm suffered in order to recover damages. Quite possibly the prevailing views of economic determinism affected the adoption of this principle, which was also in line with the attempt to exclude 'guilt' from the criminal law. The defendant, however, could escape liability if he could show that he could not have prevented the harm, or that he was entitled to cause it, or that it had arisen as a result of the intention or gross negligence of the plaintiff himself. The second basic principle was that of liability for extra-hazardous activity. Persons and enterprises whose activities involved 'increased hazard' for bystanders were liable for harm caused by the source of increased hazard unless they were able to prove that the harm arose as a result of insuperable force (*vis major*, a Roman law concept roughly equivalent to Act of God and inevitable accident in the common law). This increased hazard rule was a genuine juristic achievement, for whereas most legal systems (including the Imperial Russian law) impose stricter liability on the owners or users of certain particular dangerous things (railway engines, aircraft, wild animals) the early Soviet jurists generalized the principle behind these various special cases and imposed liability on the owners of all sources of increased hazard. The reasons for imposing this stricter liability on the owners of sources of extra hazard were that the person who derives the benefit from the use of such sources of extra hazard should bear the resulting losses, and that, in general, some accidents are foreseeable as likely from the mere fact of the use of such dangerous objects.

During the period of the New Economic Policy it was felt that these rules would benefit ordinary workers, who would be able to recover damages when they had been injured without having to prove fault or negligence on the part of the defendant, as they generally would have to in most bourgeois systems of law.

However, the first rule, that the person who caused harm or damage was liable to make reparation, meant that jurists and judges were liable to get entangled in philosophical theories of causation. The elaboration of theories of causation soon became a popular occupation with Soviet jurists; they endeavoured to construct a specifically Marxist theory of causation, though without achieving any specially noteworthy results. However, to this day every theoretical Soviet jurist is expected to make some contribution to this most difficult of all legal and philosophical problems.

One causation theory espoused by the earliest Soviet writers, known as the theory of the equivalence of conditions, held that, if the act of the defendant, however reasonable, was an essential condition (condition *sine qua non*) of the plaintiff's loss, the defendant could be said to have 'caused' that loss. This view was supported by the earliest Soviet jurists on the ground that the widest possible interpretation of the principle of causation was in the interests of the working masses. The courts rejected this approach. For example, in the case of *Tikhomirov* (1930) the defendant, a doctor, had told the plaintiff that he was suffering from syphilis, and had sent him to a clinic. At the clinic the plaintiff was told that he was not suffering from that disease. After obtaining a further medical opinion, the plaintiff went to Moscow for a Wassermann test, which proved negative; he then sued the defendant to recover the costs of his trip to Moscow. Under the theory of the equivalence of conditions it would have been held that the doctor had 'caused' the plaintiff to incur the expenses of his Moscow trip, because without his diagnosis of syphilis the plaintiff would never have incurred these expenses. The Supreme Court of the RSFSR ruled that he could not recover, as 'the doctor did not send him to Moscow'.

Rejection of the 'theory of conditions' thus led to a limitation of the number of cases in which a plaintiff could recover. Recovery was also restricted as the courts made greater use of the provision that the defendant could avoid liability if he could show that he could not have prevented the harm; in this way the courts gradually came to reintroduce the requirement of fault into the law by the back door.

Although the law provided that the gross negligence of the plaintiff excluded recovery, it did not explicitly refer to cases where the plaintiff had himself been guilty of some negligence not amounting to gross negligence; as early as 1926 the Supreme Court of the RSFSR ruled that in such cases damages could be reduced, thus accepting a principle of contributory negligence known as 'mixed liability'. Similarly in a case in 1929, where the plaintiff sued for damage to her house caused by a fire that started in the defendant's factory, the Supreme Court ruled that although the defendant had been negligent, and there was a causal connection between their negligence and the fire which damaged the plaintiff's house, the extent of the damage had been aggravated by a strong wind (*vis major*) for which the defendant was not responsible, and as the plaintiff's loss was caused only in part by the defendant's negligence, full recovery from the defendant could not be allowed.

By the late nineteen-thirties, lack of fault by the defendant was fully accepted as a defence: thus, the position reached was that once the plaintiff proved that the damage or loss had been caused by the defendant (however 'cause' might be interpreted) this raised a presumption that the defendant had been at fault: it was then for the defendant to rebut that presumption if he could. This principle is now expressed in article 444 of the Civil Code of 1964:

Harm caused to the person or property of a citizen, and also harm caused to an organization, is to be compensated in full by the person who caused the harm. He is absolved from liability if he proves that the harm was not caused by his fault. Harm caused by lawful acts is to be compensated only in cases provided for by law.

The increased hazard rule came to be somewhat restricted in practice during the nineteen-twenties and nineteen-thirties: as measures of socialization progressed, more and more sources of increased hazard came to be owned by the State or by public corporations, which were usually the defendants in such cases, and it was realized that the increased hazard rule, if widely interpreted, might place an undue strain on their resources. For example, in 1928 the Supreme Court of the RSFSR ruled that the Moscow–Kazan Railroad was not liable under the extra-hazardous activities rule for fires started by sparks from railway engines, though the early commentators on the Civil Code of 1922 had assumed that this was just the kind of case covered by the extra-hazardous activities rule: the Supreme Court ruled that the extra-hazardous activities rule envisaged the activities of a railroad in actual transport and did not include the mere heating of boilers, which was not an extra-hazardous activity: fires caused by sparks from an engine were therefore to be treated as purely accidental events. The increased hazard rule appears in article 454 of the Civil Code of 1964:

> Organizations or citizens whose activity involves increased hazard for other persons (transport organizations, industrial enterprises, building works, possessors of cars and the like) are bound to make compensation for harm caused by the source of increased hazard unless they prove that it arose as a consequence of insuperable force or the intention of the victim.

TORT AND INSURANCE

As in many other modern systems of law, questions of tort liability are intimately linked with questions of insurance, and discussions of tort liability divorced from insurance aspects tend to lack practical reality. The connection is particularly close in relation to the amount of damages recovered by a successful plaintiff in an action for tort, for in many cases the plaintiff will already have received benefits under social security legislation.

Damages in personal injury cases are normally calculated on the difference between the plaintiff's former flat rate earnings (i.e. excluding overtime and bonuses) and his present earnings plus social security benefits, and are payable by way of periodical payments and not in a lump sum. Thus if a skilled worker was earning 200 roubles a month before the accident, and can now earn only fifty, and is receiving 100 roubles a month as social security benefit, damages will be in the form of an order for periodical payments of fifty roubles a month. Reviews are possible if the plaintiff's earning capacity alters. Thus it will be seen that nothing is allowed for pain and suffering or shortened expectation of life, and nothing for loss of promotion prospects. The amount payable will, of course, be reduced if there was contributory negligence by the plaintiff.

An important point is that the increased hazard rule does not apply where the injured person is an employee of the owner or organization making use of the source of increased hazard; this is explained on the ground that dangerous machinery and appliances are not a source of increased hazard to those actually using them, as persons are not employed to use them without having undergone appropriate instruction in their use. Soviet jurists have frequently pointed out the anomalies and injustices to which this rule gives rise: thus, where the driver of a taxi and his passenger were both injured in an accident, totally losing their earning capacity, the enterprise owning the cab and employing the driver was liable to the passenger under the increased hazard rule, and the passenger's social security pension plus damages amounted to 926 (old) roubles a month, while the driver could not recover damages from his employer, and had to be content with his social security pension of 526 (old) roubles a month. The Soviet authors who report the case dryly observe, 'It is hard to convince the injured driver, or anyone else, of the justice and humanity of such a decision.'

It would appear that the early Soviet leaders considered that social insurance legislation would ultimately do away with the need for tort actions, and that the provisions for tort liability in the Code of 1922 constituted merely an interim measure to deal with the situation until the State was able to assume financial responsibility, by means of insurance, for all injuries and losses. Certainly in the early days, tort actions were discouraged, except when they were brought against private entrepreneurs (NEPmen). The picture changed in the nineteen-thirties, and the growing emphasis on fault as a condition of liability showed that the tort action was regarded as having deterrent value. Even liability for extra-hazardous activities is felt to have a deterrent effect, for although such liability may not technically depend on fault, it encourages those who are in control of dangerous things to seek out additional ways of taking safety precautions, and indeed, the deterrent effect of tort liability, even in the case of liability for extra-hazardous activities, is considered a good reason for allowing *vis major* to constitute a defence in this case, for the deterrent effect would be lost if the defendant were liable for something quite beyond his control.

Finally, we should note the position of the private motorist. A car is regarded as a source of increased hazard, and the owner as such is liable for injuries caused by it under the extra-hazardous activity rule, that is, irrespective of fault in the ordinary sense of the term. But he cannot insure against such liability, for to allow such insurance, it is felt, would detract from the deterrent effect of tort liability. The fact that it is the owner who is liable, as such, and not the driver at the time of the accident, doubtless makes the Soviet car owner somewhat unwilling to lend his car to his teenage sons, which may well have some useful results in accident prevention. Where the owner is liable under the extra-hazardous activity rule and someone else was driving at the time of the accident, the owner will have a right of recourse against the driver only where he can show actual fault on the part of the driver.

FURTHER READING

E. L. Johnson, 'No Liability without Fault – The Soviet View' (1967), 20 *Current Legal Problems*, p. 165.

A. K. R. Kiralfy, 'Employers' and Employees' Civil Liability in Soviet Law for Industrial Accidents' (1965), 14 *International & Comparative Law Quarterly*, p. 969.

B. Rudden, *Soviet Insurance Law*, Leyden, 1966.

B. Rudden, 'Soviet Tort Law' (1967), 42 *New York University Law Review*, p. 583.

CHAPTER EIGHT

The Soviet Family

INTRODUCTORY

In pre-revolutionary Russia, marriage (and therefore divorce) was a matter which fell within the sphere of competence of the ecclesiastical authorities of the church to which the parties belonged. Religious marriages were recognized by the State, and if any question arose concerning the validity of a marriage it was determined by the ecclesiastical courts of the church concerned, whose decision the State would accept. Although the vast majority of the population of the Russian Empire were Orthodox Christians, there were also Roman Catholics, Lutherans, Baptists, Jews, Mohammedans and Buddhists, as well as some smaller religious bodies, but in all cases in matters of marriage the parties were bound by the law of their religious denomination; the possibility of divorce therefore depended upon the attitude adopted by each particular church. For Roman Catholics there was of course no divorce, for their ecclesiastical courts applied the canon law of the Roman Catholic Church. The ecclesiastical courts of the Russian Orthodox Church did grant divorces in certain cases, for example in the case of adultery by a wife, and where the husband had committed certain serious criminal offences, but the procedure was long and expensive and certainly beyond the means of the vast mass of the population.

After the Revolution the Orthodox Church was separated from the State, and religious marriages celebrated after the establishment of the Soviet régime no longer had legal validity, though religious marriages celebrated before the Revolution remained valid. The new leadership was anxious to make as complete a break as possible with the old religious ideas associated with marriage, and before the end of 1917, a decree providing for easy divorce and for the official registration of births, marriages and deaths was passed. Some confusion followed, for the machinery necessary to implement the decree did not at first exist, and more detailed regulation followed in the Code of Family Law of 17 October 1918. Under this enactment marriage was treated as a question of fact rather than as one of law; if two people cohabited with the intention of living as husband and wife, they were, as far as the law was concerned, married. (There was, incidentally, a precedent for this in the ancient Roman Law.) However, the law did provide for the possibility of registering marriages, and statistics released in 1925 showed that the great majority of people who got married did in fact register their marriages: the proportion of unregistered to registered marriages was one to eighteen.

The principle that marriage was a question of fact, and registration merely optional, seems to have been based on both ideological and practical considerations. From the ideological point of view it was felt to be important to break away from the old religious associations of marriage as much as possible, particularly in view of the fact that by tradition and by the Imperial Russian law the husband was in a position of considerable authority over the wife; the communists were anxious to establish the principle of sex equality as soon as possible, and this is in fact reflected in most of the provisions of the Family Code of 1918. The recognition of cohabitation as marriage was of practical value, too, for in the troubled period of the war, the Revolution, and the Civil War, many men had disappeared and many irregular unions were formed; by recognizing these unions as marriages, the woman became entitled to maintenance should she be in need and unable to work, and both she and any children born would have inheritance rights if the man died.

The system, however, was only suited to emergency conditions, and it was probably only because of the ideological considerations that it lasted so long. It was preserved when a new Code of Laws governing Marriage, the Family and Guardianship was promulgated in 1926 to replace the Code of 1918; the new Code however allowed a *de facto* marriage to be registered retrospectively to the date when cohabitation commenced, but as conditions became more stable the lax attitude towards marriage caused a good deal of confusion, for it was not always easy to say when a *de facto* marriage existed, and it was abandoned entirely when an enactment of 8 July 1944 came into force.

The law of 8 July 1944 was an All-Union enactment, and therefore prevailed over the rules contained in the Family and Marriage Codes of the Union Republics, so some of the provisions of these Codes ceased to have effect. The main change introduced by the law of 8 July 1944 was that for the future only registered marriages were to be recognized by the law as giving rise to the status of husband and wife and to matrimonial rights and duties. Factual unions which had commenced before the law came into force could be registered with retrospective effect, but apart from any question of rights acquired prior to July 1944, cohabitation outside registered marriage no longer has any legal effect.

The law of 8 July 1944 has now been replaced by new Basic Principles of Marriage and Family Law, which were promulgated on 27 June 1968, and came into force on 1 October 1968. These Basic Principles apply throughout the USSR, and this means that as a consequence the Codes of Marriage and Family Law of the Union Republics will have to be remodelled in order to bring them into line with the Basic Principles. The Basic Principles do not affect the rule that only registered marriages create legal rights and obligations between the parties, though in other respects they have introduced new rules, which will be noted in due course.

MARRIAGE AND NULLITY

Registration of marriage is now essential. Apart from the confusion caused by the earlier system, one suspects that the law of 8 July 1944 was also designed to reduce the influence of the Orthodox Church. It is true that in itself a church marriage had had no legal effect since the early days of the régime, but if parties were married in church and then commenced cohabitation, they were regarded as married in law, not by reason of the church ceremony, but by reason of the cohabitation. To the unsophisticated it therefore appeared that the State was recognizing religious marriages as valid, and in cases where parties cohabited after a religious marriage service they had no particular incentive to register their marriage at the Registry of Civil Status.

A registered marriage is celebrated at the offices of the Registry of Civil Status. In some large towns these are in the form of Wedding Palaces, at which an attempt is made, by means of attractive surroundings, to counter the romantic appeal of the very beautiful Orthodox marriage service, and the Basic Principles of Marriage and Family Law, 1968, says that marriages are to be celebrated with solemnity. The Basic Principles also lay down one new requirement: that at least one month's notice must have been given before a marriage can be celebrated (exceptions may be allowed by legislation of the Union Republics). The reason for this is that in the past some couples have contracted marriage after a very short acquaintance, and this was believed to be a factor contributing to a number of divorces. In one reported divorce case the parties decided to get married the day they first met, went to the Registry of Civil Status the next day to arrange their marriage, and were married a few days later. That, of course, was highly exceptional: nevertheless, sociological investigations showed that in 2 per cent of divorce cases the parties had only known each other for a few days before they made arrangements to get married. The new rule will allow for a 'cooling off' period.

Both parties must be at least eighteen years of age, and as eighteen is the age at which a minor comes of age for all legal purposes, there is no question of parental consent being required. However, the local authority may give special permission for a marriage to be solemnized where the girl is at least seventeen and there are special circumstances; even in this case it does not appear that parental consent is required. The parties to the marriage must not be within certain 'prohibited degrees' of relationship; but the prohibited degrees of Soviet law are minimal. Marriages cannot be celebrated between ascendants and descendants, or between brothers and sisters of the whole or of the half-blood. There are no other restrictions, and in particular, there are no rules preventing marriage with a relative of a former spouse. Marriage cannot of course be solemnized where one party is already married, and it cannot be solemnized without the full consent of both the parties to it.

Occasionally marriages are solemnized in violation of these rules. In such cases, the principle is that the marriage must be treated as valid until it is annulled by a judicial decree of nullity. Proceedings to declare a marriage null and void may be brought by one of the parties, or by any person, such as a relative, with a legitimate interest in showing the marriage to be void, or by a procurator; and such proceedings may be brought even after the death of one or both of the parties. Where the ground on which annulment is sought is that one or both of the parties was under the age of eighteen, however, no decree can be made if the party under eighteen has reached that age at the time when the court is asked to make such a decree, or if the woman has conceived or given birth to a child. In the latter case, it makes no difference which party was under age; the purpose of the rule is to protect the interests of the child, who benefits by reason of the fact that his parents' marriage cannot now be treated as invalid.

Where it is alleged that, despite the fact that a marriage was solemnized and registered, one party did not in fact give his consent, a distinction has to be drawn between total lack of consent, and defective consent.

Cases have occurred, when as a result of a mistake by the official and carelessness on the part of the other people concerned, a marriage has been registered as having taken place, where in fact the official mistook a witness or a friend for one of the parties to be married, so that the register shows, for example, that the intended bridegroom was married to a bridesmaid. Clearly here there was a complete absence of consent of the parties to intermarry, and in such a case the marriage is regarded, not as a marriage which must be treated as valid until it is annulled, but as a 'non-existent marriage'. The remedy, when the facts come out, is not judicial proceedings for a decree of nullity but administrative proceedings to have the entry on the marriage registers cancelled.

Defective consent, on the other hand, is where one party verbally agrees to marry the other, but the consent was procured by means of force, threats or fraud. Another kind of case coming within the category of defective consent is that of the 'sham' or 'fictitious' marriage. If both parties agree to get married, not because they wish to live together as husband and wife, but for some ulterior motive, such as obtaining a passport or a residence permit (*propiska*), the view taken is that they did not really consent to marry each other, but only consented to going through a marriage ceremony with each other. Such marriages can be annulled, provided that neither party ever intended the marriage to be a real one. If only one party intended a sham marriage, or even if both parties originally intended a sham marriage but have in fact cohabited as husband and wife, the marriage cannot be annulled.

A marriage can also be annulled if it is shown to have been bigamous, that is, that one of the parties to it was at the time already married to a third party. However, there has been some difference of opinion about the position where the first marriage has, since the celebration of the second, been annulled. In principle, although a registered marriage must be treated as valid until it is annulled, if it is annulled the annulment is retrospective. This is the basic difference between annulment and divorce; a decree of nullity pronounces the marriage void from the start, whereas a decree of divorce merely dissolves it for the future. This raises the question of the status of a second marriage contracted before the first has been annulled. Clearly such a second marriage could not be contracted if the officials of the Civil Status Registry were aware of the first, for the first must be treated as valid until it is annulled. But people do manage to commit bigamy in the USSR just as they do in other countries. But when the first marriage is annulled, this is equivalent to saying that it never existed:[1] does this now make the second marriage valid? In the case of *Topunov* v. *Topunova* in 1958 the Moscow City Court said No: despite the annulment of the first marriage the second marriage was void for bigamy.

[1] With the exception that any children born of it are the legitimate children of both parents.

However, in a recent case, *Frolov* v. *Frolova* (1967), the Supreme Court of the USSR has ruled that a decree of nullity will not necessarily be made even though a marriage was bigamous at its inception. Here the parties had married in 1948, and in 1965 the husband petitioned for a decree of nullity on the ground that he had contracted a previous marriage in 1944 and that his first wife was still alive at the time of his marriage to the respondent in 1948, and that the second marriage was bigamous. Frolov's first wife had divorced him in 1954. After passing through a number of lower courts, the case was taken to the Supreme Court of the USSR as it was seen to raise an important point of principle, namely, whether a person who had committed bigamy in full knowledge of the facts could later take advantage of his own wrong by petitioning for the bigamous marriage to be annulled, and the Supreme Court held that he could not. The petitioner had continued married life with the respondent for ten years after his first marriage had been dissolved, and he could not now disown her. Although his marriage with the respondent was originally void for bigamy, the defect was regarded as having been cured by the dissolution of his first marriage in 1954. Though not entirely *in pari materia* this decision of the Supreme Court of the USSR must make it doubtful whether the decision of the Moscow City Court in the case of *Topunov* v. *Topunova* would still be followed.

COMMUNITY OF PROPERTY

We now turn to the question of property as between husband and wife. This is still governed by the Family Code of 1926, which, as we saw,[1] substituted a régime of community of property for the complete separation of goods established by the first Family Code of 1918, under which the wife was said to be freed from domination by her husband. This, however, seems to have been propaganda for foreign consumption, because under the Imperial Russian law the property of husband and wife was already separate, and a husband had no right to deal with or administer property belonging to his wife. The Imperial Russian law did not apply to the peasants, but neither did the Soviet Family Codes, as property relations between husband and wife are still governed by the law relating to collective farm households.[2] But complete separation of property in fact, under Soviet, just as under Imperial conditions, usually gave the husband a privileged position, for he would go out to work and earn wages, and the wife commonly stayed at home and did the housework and looked after the children.

Hence it seemed that the principle of sex equality would be better

[1] See p. 38 *ante*.   [2] See p. 112 *ante*.

served by community of property. Under the system of community established by the Family Code of 1926, property acquired after the marriage belongs to both spouses jointly; the husband's and wife's wages, and furniture and other articles bought out of their wages. The Family Code of 1926 does not regulate the community in very great detail, and therefore a number of supplementary rules have grown up in court practice. The basic principle is that property owned by either before the marriage remains the individual property of that spouse, but property acquired afterwards is community property. However, some exceptions have been established by court decisions: property which is acquired by inheritance after the marriage belongs as individual property to the spouse who inherited it, and does not fall into the community, and the same applies to gifts received by either spouse. This resembles Western European law. Equally, property acquired after the marriage for the exclusive use of one spouse, such as clothing and footwear, belongs exclusively to the spouse for whom it is acquired.

Under the Soviet law of intestacy, the widow takes an equal share with any children of the deceased, so if a man dies leaving a widow and two children, they will each take a third: but before the estate is distributed in this way, the widow is entitled to her share of the community property; thus she will first get her share of the community property, after which her late husband's share of the community, together with the property owned by him individually, will be divided among the widow and the two children; so the widow will normally get more than the children in fact, because she gets her share of the community property.

The community property is owned by the spouses as co-owners, so if property, such as a house bought out of community funds, is to be sold, both must agree to the sale, and the notary certifying the conveyance will have to satisfy himself that this has been done.

The community property can be divided only in the case of death or divorce, or at the instance of a creditor. If a creditor has obtained judgment against the husband and cannot satisfy it out of assets belonging to the husband individually, he can apply to the court to have the community fund divided and then get the judgment satisfied out of the husband's share. The division of the community property on divorce will be considered in connection with divorce.[1]

DIVORCE

There have been many changes in Soviet attitudes towards divorce. Under the Code of 1918, divorces were granted with little formality by

[1] See p. 182 *post*.

N

the People's Courts, but the Code of 1926 made divorce even easier: all that was necessary was for one party to go to the Civil Status Registry and announce that he wished to terminate the marriage: the other spouse then received a postcard from the Registry informing him that the marriage had been dissolved, and of his right to apply to a People's Court for the settlement of any dispute about the children or maintenance. The era of 'postcard divorce' for a nominal fee (three roubles) lasted until June 1936: after this date, both parties had to attend at the Registry and the fees were raised considerably—fifty roubles for a first divorce, 150 for a second and 300 for a third or subsequent divorce. These fees brought about a sharp reduction in the divorce rate, but there was no infringement of the principle that divorce could be had for the asking if one was prepared to pay the fee.

A fundamental change was made by the enactment of 8 July 1944. This established complicated judicial procedure for divorce, under which there had first to be proceedings in a People's Court to see whether it was possible to reconcile the parties; only if the People's Court found this to be impossible could the case go to the District Court (the city or *oblast* court) and it was only the District Court which had jurisdiction actually to pronounce a decree of divorce. This two-staged procedure, which entailed considerable expense,[1] did have the effect of further reducing the divorce rate, which was what the authorities at the time wanted; they were concerned with encouraging the stability of family life, which had of course suffered considerably during the war.

Later this two-stage procedure was abolished by an enactment of 10 December 1965, which to a large extent restored the position to what it had been before 1926, restoring the jurisdiction of the People's Courts (the ordinary courts of first instance) to grant decrees of divorce.

The reasons officially given for the change were that the District Courts, situated in the *oblast* capitals, were further from the place of residence of the spouses, and that there were therefore greater difficulties and unnecessary expenses involved in summoning the parties to the court, arranging for the presence of witnesses, and in particular, of hearing evidence from workmates and neighbours of the spouses, and from the social and official agencies connected with matters such as child care. The *oblast* and city courts were 'further from the people' and by reason of this, were less able to get at the real reasons which led to

---

[1] One hundred old roubles on presentation of the petition, and a fee of from 200 to 2,000 roubles if a divorce were granted, the fee being divided between the parties in such proportions as the court thought fit.

the divorce petition being presented, so that it was easier for 'sham' cases to get through. It is also true that the city and *oblast* courts are 'further from the people' in the literal sense that, for people not living in the *oblast* capitals, to get a divorce meant a troublesome and possibly costly journey to the *oblast* capital; so many spouses separated without bothering to get a divorce. They often contracted new *de facto* unions which sometimes proved quite stable, but if they broke down there was no question of any liability for maintenance. The prevalence of *de facto* unions, with the resulting increase in the number of illegitimate children, may have been a major factor behind this reform: without saying so, the authorities wish to make divorce easier, and to encourage divorce in cases where there has been a breakdown of the marriage. There is no doubt that the new law has resulted in a very great increase in the divorce rate: in 1966, the first year in which the new law was in operation, the number of divorces granted in the Leningrad *oblast* was three times the number granted in 1965.

Under the law of 10 December 1965 a divorce petition may be presented to the court by either spouse, or by the spouses jointly. The court having jurisdiction is normally the People's Court for the district in which the respondent resides. However, the People's Court for the district in which the petitioner resides has jurisdiction in certain cases, namely:

1. where the petitioner has charge of infant children and it would be difficult for him or her to travel to the place of the respondent's residence;
2. where the whereabouts of the respondent are unknown;
3. where the respondent has been sentenced to a term of deprivation of liberty for at least three years;
4. where the respondent agrees to the case being heard in the court of the petitioner's residence. Where a joint petition is presented by both spouses, and they reside in different districts, the fact of the joint petition being presented to the court of the area where one resides is taken to amount to the other's consent to that court hearing the case.

The petitioner in the first place must present his petition in the People's Court for the area of his own residence and a fee of ten roubles is payable. If this is also the area in which the respondent resides, the respondent is summoned to a preliminary session of the court, so that he can say whether there is any possibility of a reconciliation, and also what witnesses he wishes to call.

Where the respondent does not reside in the same area, the court will, in the ordinary case, transfer the petition to the court for area in which the respondent resides, unless the petitioner can show that the court for his own area has jurisdiction. If the case is transferred to the court for the respondent's area, the petitioner will have to travel to that court when the actual case comes on: where the court for the petitioner's area has jurisdiction, the court for the respondent's area may take his evidence on commission, and forward it to the court having jurisdiction.

When the decree of divorce is granted, a fee of from 50 to 200[1] roubles is payable: the court determines the amount in accordance with the financial position of the parties, and the proportions in which they have to pay in accordance with their respective degrees of responsibility for the break-up of the marriage. And in certain cases the procedure will now be even simpler, for the Basic Principles of Marriage and Family Law, 1968, have effected a breach with the principle which has prevailed since 1944, namely, that divorce can be decreed only by a court. There will be no return to the 'era of postcard divorce' but where both spouses want a divorce and they have no children under age, they can present a joint petition for divorce to the Registry of Civil Status, which will register the divorce after the expiry of three months if the spouses do not withdraw their petition. A similar procedure will be available when one spouse presents a petition on the ground that the other has been officially declared missing, or has become insane, or has been sentenced to a term of deprivation of liberty of at least three years. In these cases if any dispute arises the matter will be transferred to a court.

On the other hand the Basic Principles provide that a man is not entitled to petition for divorce when his wife is pregnant or within a year after the wife has given birth to a child, unless the wife consents.

There is no list of formal grounds on which a divorce may be granted. The view accepted by court practice and by writers is that the court should grant a divorce in any case where two things are established:
1. that the marriage has broken down, and
2. that it is impossible to reestablish matrimonial relations between the parties; this is confirmed by the Basic Principles of Marriage and Family Law, 1968.

Statistics recently published show that in fact 96 per cent of divorce petitions are granted. Of the 4 per cent of cases in which the court refuses to make a decree, there are two classes:
1. the majority, where the court comes to the conclusion that the trouble between the spouses has arisen mainly because of interference by their relatives, e.g. the evidence tends to show that the real trouble is not so much disputes between husband and wife but between wife and mother-

---

[1] The fees payable are the same as under the former system, as the new rouble introduced in 1961 is equivalent to ten old roubles.

in-law or husband and mother-in-law, and the court feels that if the parties were left to themselves there is a chance that the marriage could be saved;

2. where it feels that for propagandist, or as the Soviets would term it, educational reasons, it should refuse a divorce. This arises where the quarrels have been due to one spouse adopting an attitude which is felt to be contrary to 'communist morality' and that if this spouse reformed, the marriage could be saved. This may happen when the respondent does not want the divorce, and the petitioning spouse is the 'guilty party' according to the principles of communist morality, especially where he refuses to recognize equality of the sexes. For example, a husband petitions for divorce and says that his marriage broke down because his wife refused to do the housework and cooking. If both parties have full-time jobs, he will be asked if he did any housework, or offered to do any. If he says that he did not, he will be told that if both parties have full-time jobs, both are expected to share in household chores, and that if he is not willing to do any housework he cannot complain that his wife is not willing to do any either.

In fact, however, as in England, most divorce cases are not contested: both spouses want the divorce. Sociological research workers in Leningrad and Kiev have recently conducted enquiries into divorce, and in Leningrad it was found that only 15 per cent of divorce cases were defended, though in Kiev it was 32 per cent. Another interesting fact that resulted from the research work was that, even though the courts may refuse divorces where they think the marriage could be saved if relatives could be prevented from interfering, in fact, interference by relatives has a good deal to do with the quarrels that lead to the break-up of a marriage. In Leningrad, it was found that in 41 per cent of cases there had been quarrels between a divorcee and his 'in-laws', whereas in Kiev it was found that the figure was 61 per cent. These figures relate only to quarrels and 'scenes' between a person who was later divorced and the relatives of his then spouse, and do not say of course whether it was a dispute between the spouses which led to a quarrel with the relatives of one of them, or a quarrel with relatives that ultimately led to a dispute between the spouses and a break-up of the marriage. This happens elsewhere, too, of course; but the fact that shortage of accommodation often compels young married couples to live with the parents of one of them, and the fact that the three-generation family is traditional and still very common in Russia, probably makes this a more important factor in the USSR than it is in other countries. And in addition we must bear in mind, that while marrying for money is not common in the USSR, marrying for a *propiska* or residence permit is by no means unknown, and so is marrying for a flat: an unmarried woman with a flat in Moscow or Leningrad is unlikely to lack suitors.

Sometimes it happens that one party to a marriage simply disappears, and the other party may never hear from him again. To meet this kind of case, Soviet law provides special procedures for pronouncing a person missing (or 'disappeared without trace' as the Russians put it), and for pronouncing that a person is to be presumed dead. The effect of pronouncing that a person is missing is to bring into effect measures for securing his property and allowing payments to be made out of it to those whom he is under a duty to support. Such a decree does not dissolve his marriage, but is regarded as giving the other spouse a sufficient ground for a divorce: after a decree of divorce has been made, either spouse will of course be free to remarry. After a person has been declared missing, further proceedings can be taken in order to have him presumed dead; or proceedings for a presumption of death can be taken independently. A decree of presumption of death operates in any case to dissolve the marriage, even if it should later appear that the person presumed dead is in fact still alive. Thus after a decree of presumption of death either party is free to remarry. If a man presumed dead does reappear and finds that his wife has contracted a second marriage he cannot contest the validity of the second marriage, for his own was dissolved by the decree presuming him dead. In such cases, however, if the wife only contracted the second marriage in the belief that the first husband was dead, and wishes to resume relations with her first husband, it is accepted that this will be sufficient ground for bringing divorce proceedings against the second husband in order to enable her to remarry the first one. In a distressing situation such as this, it is felt that the woman should be able to decide which husband she wishes to live with. As the first marriage was dissolved, however, it cannot be revived, and if she prefers to live with the first husband, she should divorce the second one and go through a new ceremony of marriage with the first.

On a decree of divorce being pronounced, property acquired by the spouses ceases to be community property. In the vast majority of cases the spouses are able to agree on its division, so the property now becomes the individual property of one or other of the former spouses. When the parties are unable to agree on the division of the community property (which occurs in about 4 per cent of divorce cases) the court has to proceed to a division. There is no rule of law in the RSFSR that the property must be divided equally between the former spouses;[1]

[1] Equal division is provided by the Codes of some of the other Union Republics.

the court is entitled to take all relevant factors into account, and the fact that all the property may have been acquired from the earnings of one spouse by no means indicates that the spouse in question should have all or even a major portion of the community property, for a wife who has remained at home as a housekeeper to look after young children is regarded as doing work of social value equal to that of a man engaged in gainful employment. In practice disputes often concern the house, which is likely to be the major item of value in the community property. The court has no power to order a sale of property: it has to divide it in kind between the parties, and sometimes the court will order a house to be divided between the parties, allocating to each a share. Accommodation is still in very short supply in many parts of the Soviet Union, and divorced spouses are commonly reluctant to give up living accommodation even if this means living in close proximity to a former husband or wife. Where division in kind is not practicable, the court may order a balancing money payment, taking into account the means of the party ordered to pay, and may allow time for payment. In deciding which articles should be allocated to which spouse, the court will of course take account of factors such as, which will have custody of any children of the marriage, which spouse needs articles for the purposes of his employment, and similar matters.

In the absence of special circumstances the court will usually try to effect an equal division, so the important question in practice is what the court will regard as special circumstances. In one case a husband argued that he was entitled to a larger share of the house than his wife on the ground that it had been built from material allocated to him without payment as a disabled ex-serviceman. The court did not accept this view, on the ground that allocations of building materials to disabled ex-servicemen were intended to benefit the families of such persons as well, and this decision was upheld on appeal to the Supreme Court of the USSR.

The Basic Principles of Marriage and Family Law, 1968, have not basically affected the position, though they have brought about a reasonable compromise between the rule of equal division in all cases, which was the rule in some Union Republics (e.g. Byelorussia) and the rule that division is in the discretion of the court, as in the RSFSR. They provide that in principle, division is to be equal, but that the court may order an unequal division where this would be in the interests of children under age, or in the interest of one of the spouses, the interest being 'worthy of consideration'. The principle of equal division, though fair in the ordinary case, can work great hardship in the exceptional case. In a case from Byelorussia the husband had been sentenced to a long term of deprivation of liberty; the wife hoped that on his release he would return to her, and during the period of imprisonment was able to save enough out of her earnings to buy a house. On his release the husband petitioned for and obtained a divorce, and was able to claim a half share in the house, though he had made no contribution at all towards its acquisition. Under the new rule, the interest of the wife would presumably be sufficiently 'worthy of consideration' to allow a departure from the principle of equal division.

FAMILY MAINTENANCE

Under Soviet law husbands and wives have a mutual duty to maintain the other. But the law imposes no duty of cohabitation on spouses, and desertion is therefore not treated as a matrimonial offence. The mere fact that her husband has left her gives the Soviet wife no right to claim maintenance from him, for citizens are supposed to be able to support themselves out of their own earnings. If a wife is to obtain a maintenance order against her husband, she must prove three things: that she is unable to work, is in actual need, and that the husband is in a position to be able to make payments to her. A husband may obtain an order against the wife on similar grounds. Inability to work is conclusively presumed in the case of a man over sixty, or a woman over fifty-five, or a person of either sex in charge of a child under the age of seven. A wife can also obtain a maintenance order against her husband to cover a period during which she is pregnant and for a year after a child is born.

If a maintenance order is made during marriage, it remains in force despite a divorce: this is a recent innovation confirmed by the Basic Principles of 1968; it was introduced by an All-Union decree of 21 July 1967, which replaced the former rules which varied from Republic to Republic: in the RSFSR all maintenance obligations between former spouses ceased one year after divorce.

Moreover there are now two cases in which a former spouse may apply for a maintenance order against the other: these are, first, where a disability making work impossible arose within one year after the divorce, and secondly, where the marriage was of long standing and the plaintiff reached pensionable age within five years after the divorce. This meets the former unhappy situation of the woman who devoted many years of married life to looking after her family and was divorced in late middle age with no right to a pension because she had never been gainfully employed.

Where there are children and the husband and wife separate or are divorced, a maintenance order may be made against the father for the maintenance of the children, if they are in the custody of the mother. (Equally it can be made against the mother where the children are in the custody of the father.) The amount of maintenance payable is fixed by law and amounts to a quarter of the father's income for one child, a third for two children, and a half for three or more. If the father is earning high wages, this sometimes means that the mother can live off the maintenance money that she receives from the father on behalf of the children without working herself, and some Soviet writers have criticized the position on that ground and have advocated the fixing of an upper limit. This has not been done, but the Basic Principles of 1968 provide that the court may reduce the amount of maintenance payable where the person liable has other children to support as well, and the position of these other children is worse than that of those in respect of whom maintenance is to be paid.

Where the parents of a child are dead, maintenance obligations fall on other relatives: grandparents, step-parents, and brothers and sisters.

Adult children are liable to maintain incapacitated parents and parents are liable to maintain incapacitated adult children.

A person who is unable to work and is in need may, if he has no spouse, parents or adult children, claim maintenance from grandchildren and from sons-in-law and daughters-in-law.

A person who cannot work may be in receipt of a disability pension or a retirement pension and it was for long a moot point whether a person in receipt of a pension, of an amount considered appropriate under social security legislation, could be said to be 'in need'. However, the pensions are not always adequate, and it has been held by the Supreme Court of the USSR that the mere fact of receipt of a pension does not debar a person from bringing a suit against his relatives for maintenance if they are in a position to support or contribute towards his support.

CHILDREN

In the early years of the Soviet régime, the Soviet authorities tended to look on the family with disfavour as a centre in which the old attitudes would be preserved, and family life and discipline tended to break down. However, waves of juvenile delinquency in the early nineteen-thirties brought about a change, for it was realized that a stable home background, especially where the parents were in sympathy with the régime, was a potent factor in preventing delinquency. Consequently in the nineteen-thirties parents were made civilly liable for damage done by their children and were also made criminally liable if they allowed their children to run wild and failed to exercise proper care and supervision over them; and parents who neglected their children could be completely deprived of parental rights.

The matter of homeless children was for long a major problem for the Soviet authorities, for after the Revolution and Civil War there were large numbers of homeless children, who often roamed the country in gangs, living on what they could find or steal. Homes and orphanages were quite inadequate to deal with the large numbers involved, and various measures were taken to persuade people to take waifs and orphans into their homes. Legal adoption had existed in Imperial Russian Law, but it was abolished in the first Family Code of 1918 because it was thought to be a means of evading rules about succession to property. But it was restored by the second Family Code, 1926, and people were encouraged to adopt homeless children. An adopted child under Soviet law has all the rights of a legitimate child of the adopter, and the adopter has all the rights and duties of a parent towards him, and he ceases to have any legal connection with his blood relations.

However, some people were not prepared to go to the length of adoption, although they were prepared to help a homeless child, and in 1928 a procedure less than full adoption was introduced, termed dependency. The child, who is accepted as a dependant, does not change his name or lose any family rights that he may have, but the person who accepts him assumes full responsibility and care for him until he comes of age, after which there is no longer any legal connection between him and the person who brought him up, and so no question of any rights of succession or mutual support.

There is a third system, introduced in 1936, known as *patronat*. Under this system a person agrees to act as patron for a homeless child, and does so by means of a contract with the Ministry of Health where the child is under four, or with the Ministry of Education where he is over that age. The Ministry pays a small monthly sum to the patron as a partial return for his services, and the patron undertakes to act as the child's legal guardian until the child is sixteen. The child acquires no rights in the family of his patron, and the relationship ends when the child attains the age of sixteen. In fact it is very like the English system under which homeless children are boarded out by local authorities, and seems to have been equally successful. The problem of homeless children arose again during and after the Second World War, and the *patronat* system was widely adopted to deal with it. The problem of homeless children is of course of much less importance at the present time.

The Soviet authorities have always been anxious to remove any stigma attaching to illegitimacy, and to equate the position of the illegitimate child with that of the legitimate child as far as possible. Before 1944 affiliation proceedings were possible, but they were abolished by the law of 8 July 1944. Under this enactment the mother of an illegitimate child could surrender the child completely to the State to be brought up as an orphan, or she could keep the child and receive maintenance grants from the State, but no proceedings against a putative father were possible.

The Basic Principles of Marriage and Family Law, 1968, have adopted a new approach. The parents of an illegitimate child may, if they agree, have their names registered as parents of the child, in which case they will stand in the same relationship to the child as parents who are married to each other stand in respect of legitimate children. If the father of a child born out of wedlock does not consent to being registered as the father, proceedings for the establishment of paternity may be commenced by the mother. Evidence of paternity, however, can be established only by showing either that the mother and the putative father were living together before the birth of the child, or that the putative father contributed towards the maintenance of the child, or that the putative father has admitted paternity. If paternity is established in such proceedings, the name of the father is registered as being the father of the child, and his rights and duties in respect of the child are the same as those of the father of a legitimate child.

The reasons for limiting the kind of evidence that can be given in affiliation proceedings are that the authorities are anxious to avoid the scandals and injustices that arose under the system which prevailed before 1944, and to distinguish between cases where a child is born as a result of purely casual relations and cases where a woman was living with a man in the belief that he wished to found a family with her, only to find that he left her when she became pregnant. In the latter case it is felt that the woman has a moral claim to receive maintenance for the child from the father: in the former case, she preserves her rights against the State under the law of 8 July 1944, and will not be allowed to get a legal declaration of paternity. However, to avoid prejudice to the child by reason of the blank space in the birth certificate where the father's name appears, it is provided that this space should be filled up with the surname of the mother and with such other names as she may choose. This fictitious statement of paternity is purely to avoid embarrassment to the child; it will not of course prejudice any man who happens to bear such a name.

INHERITANCE

Succession on death may be testate, that is, when the deceased leaves a will, or intestate, when he does not do so, in which case his property devolves according to rules of law set out in the Civil Code.

Wills have to be notarially certified. If a person wishes to dispose of his property by will he informs the notary of his intentions, and the notary drafts the will in the appropriate form, and gives a copy to the testator, the original being kept in the notary's office. The notary has to see that the dispositions in the will do not contravene the law in any way. Since 1962, when the Basic Principles of Civil Law came into force, Soviet law has been much less rigid than it was about freedom of testation, in that now a Soviet citizen can leave his property by will to anyone he likes. Before 1961, powers of testation were very limited, and a testator could only leave his property to people who would be entitled on an intestacy. For example, if he had two sons, if he died intestate, they would be entitled to divide the property equally. By will he could leave the whole to one son, and disinherit the other, or he could vary the proportions, say, leave three-quarters to one son and one-quarter to another, but he could not leave it to anyone else; consequently wills were not very important.

Even now, liberty of testation is far from complete, because a testator must leave two-thirds of his intestate share to any child under age (majority is reached at the age of eighteen in the USSR) and any person who would have taken under the law of intestacy, if that person is unable to work. So a bachelor, who has no relations apart from an elderly mother, cannot disinherit her by will, as if he dies she could be entitled under the law of intestacy. A man over sixty and a woman over fifty-six are irrebuttably presumed to be incapable of work, whatever the actual position may be. These rules must be explained by the notary to the testator, and in fact the will must contain a statement that this has been done.

In general, the Soviet law of succession on death is not very different from the systems prevailing in other continental countries. Where there is more than one heir, which of course is very common, Soviet law shows a distinct preference for what we might call 'the heir on the spot' as distinct from an absent heir. The 'heir on the spot' is favoured in two ways:

1. Of two or more heirs, the one who was actually living with the deceased at the time of his death is entitled to all ordinary household

furniture and utensils, and only the rest of the estate has to be divided with other heirs. As many Soviet citizens possess little more than house-hold goods and utensils, this means that often the 'heir on the spot' will get the whole estate to the exclusion of an absent heir.

2. An heir becomes entitled only when he accepts; acceptance is signi-fied either by taking possession of assets forming part of the estate or by notifying the notarial office at the place of the last permanent residence of the deceased. Acceptance has to be signified within six months of the death, which gives an obvious advantage to the 'heir on the spot'. Where a family is scattered it may well be that absent heirs do not hear of the death of the deceased until after six months, and there is certainly no incentive for the 'heir on the spot' to inform other relatives of the death. And even if the matter comes to the notice of a notarial office, all that the notarial office is bound to do, if it appears that there may be other heirs entitled, is to take steps for the preservation of the assets for the period of six months to allow other heirs to come in, that is, to prevent the 'heir on the spot' from disposing of them to the prejudice of absent heirs. Any measures taken to secure the property, however, lapse when six months have expired from the date of the death.

The absent heir is not necessarily absolutely deprived of his rights if he only appears after six months from the death, but, if he wants to claim his share and the heirs on the spot will not divide with him, he will have to bring a claim in court and the court will consider whether he had a good excuse for not making his claim within six months. Excuses such as absence on military service or other official duties, or illness or absence due to hospital treatment, are accepted, but mere ignorance of the death of the deceased or ignorance of his right to make a claim does not seem to be sufficient. The result in a number of cases is that only the 'heir on the spot' takes.

A second special feature of the Soviet system is the special treatment afforded deposits in banks and savings banks. As far as this form of property is concerned, a person may make provision for its devolution after his death, either by will or by a special nomination form free from all restrictions. Even when the power of testation was more restricted than it is now, it did not apply to disposition of deposits held in banks. Why this special exemption is given is not very clear; in the nineteen-twenties it may have been introduced to encourage people to use the savings banks and other banks, for at that time there was not always a great deal of confidence in Soviet institutions, but at the present time the rule is not very easy to explain.

A third special feature of Soviet inheritance law is the fact that persons who were *de facto* dependants of the deceased at the time of his death are regarded as heirs equally with others recognized by law, even though they may not be related to him at all. This means that if the deceased had adopted a child *de facto*, without going through the procedures for legal adoption, the child would be regarded as an heir equally with the deceased's own children.

There are no death duties in the USSR and in many cases it is not necessary for anyone to go to a notary's office at all; the heirs succeed automatically by operation of law, and they may be able to agree among themselves how the estate should be distributed. However, in many cases, in order to obtain property belonging to the deceased, they will need an inheritance certificate to prove their entitlement, and, if the estate included a house or a car, they will need a certificate in order to be registered as owners. To obtain the certificate recourse to a notary will be required. Where there are several heirs, they may continue as co-owners, but, if they can agree among themselves, the notarial office will issue separate certificates for different parts of the estate.

Inheritance was frowned on in the early days of the Soviet régime, and the legal provisions about inheritance have not been fully worked out; it has never been a matter to which great importance has been attached by the Soviet authorities. This means that a number of rules of notarial practice have grown up, and rules have been issued to notarial offices to cover points which arise in practice. In fact many minor disputes over inheritance are settled by the notarial offices, by the notaries explaining to the parties just what their rights are. The matter is often complicated by reason of the Soviet matrimonial property régime, under which property acquired by either spouse after the marriage vests in them jointly, so, where the deceased leaves a widow or a widower, the surviving spouse's share of the community property has first to be taken into account before the amount of the estate can be ascertained. This often causes considerable complications, because the surviving spouse may be entitled to a share in property in the name of the deceased (e.g. a house registered in the name of the deceased alone), but on the other hand, the deceased may have been entitled to a share in any property registered in the name of the surviving spouse alone. There is, of course, always an appeal to the court from any decision by the notary on the way an estate should be divided.

FURTHER READING

E. L. Johnson, 'Matrimonial Property in Soviet Law' (1967), 16 *International & Comparative Law Quarterly*, p. 1106.

D. & V. Mace, *The Soviet Family*, London, 1963.

A. E.-S. Tay, 'The Law of Inheritance in the new Russian Civil Code of 1964' (1968), 17 *International & Comparative Law Quarterly*, p. 472.

CHAPTER NINE

Law and the Soviet Worker

HISTORY

Labour Law is a distinct and important branch of Soviet Law. The protection of the worker against exploitation was an essential point in the original Bolshevist programme, and many Soviet workers regard the kind of protection given by Soviet labour law in much the same light in which basic civil liberties are regarded in Western countries. Soviet workers have told Western visitors 'The Labour Code is our Magna Carta'. Yet the elaboration of detailed rules of labour law has proved a matter of considerable difficulty. The original Soviet Russian Labour Code of 1922 was enacted at a time when private capitalists (NEPmen) were operating, and many of its provisions were later repealed as the public corporations became the main employers of labour. Indeed in the early nineteen-fifties a copy of the Labour Code was something of a bibliographic rarity, and it was clear that the Code of 1922 was no longer applicable to prevailing conditions. It was announced that Basic Principles of Labour Legislation were to be adopted on an All-Union basis, and that the Union Republics would then enact their own Labour Codes in accordance with the General Principles. Draft Basic Principles of Labour Legislation were published in 1959, and much discussion then followed in the law journals and the general press. The discussion then ceased: the Draft was never enacted, and so the Labour Code of 1922, though much amended, still remains in force in the RSFSR, with similar enactments in the other Union Republics. Certain particular matters, however, have been dealt with by individual enactments.

As the role of the trade union is predominant in many spheres of labour law, it will be convenient to examine the matter by considering the functions of the Soviet trade union.

TRADE UNIONS AND LABOUR DISPUTES

Until the Revolution of 1905 trade unions were illegal bodies in Russia, though this does not mean that they did not exist. The Revolution of

1905, though it did not succeed in achieving all its aims, did lead to considerable improvements, and trade unions began to grow quickly in the industrial areas, and were playing quite an important part in the life of the ordinary urban worker by the time of the Revolution in 1917. In the early days of the Civil War, under 'war communism', the trade unions were often responsible for running factories, but after the introduction of the New Economic Policy in 1921 with the limited restoration of private enterprise the trade unions reverted to their former role of protecting the worker against the employer, in particular, in ensuring that the employer complied strictly with the rules laid down in the Labour Code, 1922, and other enactments. Infringements were reported to a body then termed the Workers' and Peasants' Inspectorate, which was charged, among other things, with seeing that the labour laws in force were strictly applied.

The Soviet Trade Union movement faced a crisis, however, in 1927/8 with the ending of the New Economic Policy, and the adoption of the first Five Year Plan. This followed from the decision of the Communist Party and the Soviet Government to industrialize the country as quickly as possible, the intention being to turn what was then still largely a backward peasant economy into a modern industrial one. This important decision meant heavy concentration on capital goods, and therefore that for the time being the workers' standard of living had to be drastically reduced, as more and more labour was drafted into heavy industry and the manufacture of machine tools, military equipment, and the building of factories and plants, and away from clothing, agriculture, food-processing, furniture and other consumer industries. Under these conditions, the proper role of the trade unions in Soviet society became a vitally urgent question. There was a stormy meeting of the All-Union Congress of Trade Unions in 1928, at which the president, Tomski, maintained with vigour that 'it was the duty of the trade unions to ensure that they should not lose their freedom to press for improvements in the material conditions of their members and that workers should not be required to increase production without increased remuneration'. Tomski maintained that rationalization and the increase of production were tasks for the State and management, not for the unions. The adoption of this principle however would have led to a slowing down of industrialization; if the worker had to receive compensation for increased productivity, savings for capital investment would have been reduced: Tomski was forced to resign, and he was transferred to work outside the trade union leadership; ultimately he committed suicide in 1937 to avoid arrest during the purges.

o

Thus after 1928 the trade unions were fully committed to the government policy expressed in the Five Year Plans, and were prepared to accept temporary sacrifices in workers' standards of living. As the planning of the economy continued to become more intensive, more matters came to be decided by *Gosplan*, the central planning authority. The trade unions after 1935 lost their power to make collective contracts with management concerning hours, wage-rates and other matters until they were revived in a rather different form in 1947.

Other functions had to be found, and in 1933 the Central Council of the Trade Unions was merged with the Ministry of Labour, and given the task of administering the social security system and also of ensuring observance of laws governing conditions in factories, safety regulations and the like. To some extent, the trade union movement thus became part of the State apparatus.

A requirement that there had to be a trade union representative on the management board of every enterprise was repealed, and even the obligation of management to consult the trade union representatives on all important decisions was dropped in 1937. A clear line was then drawn between the respective functions of management and the trade unions, as follows: it was the function of management, as such, to press for greater efficiency in production, including the lowering of operating costs; for these, the management was responsible solely to the Ministry under which it worked, and the unions were not to interfere with management in its specific tasks. On the other hand, the task of the unions was to see that the laws were observed: it had to report illegalities and it also had to administer social service schemes.

However, the trade unions were given somewhat wider powers in 1947, and the trade union organization at factory level is now divided into seven committees, each of which carries out a specific task.

1. Wages Committee. The duty of this committee is to check on wage-payments and to see that each worker gets the amount to which he is entitled. This is important, because wage-payments are often calculated in accordance with complicated formulae, depending on time, piecework rates, fulfilment of output norms, quality of goods produced, bonuses, and so on. (In 1958 it was said that 4 per cent of the entire labour force in the USSR was engaged solely in calculating the wages due to the other 96 per cent: despite considerable simplification of the wages system since then, much accountancy work still has to be done.)

2. Labour Protection Committee. This is concerned with seeing that factory legislation is observed, including proper standards of heating, lighting and ventilation, with the running of first-aid stations, and in

general with safety precautions and the health of the workers. It also has to ensure that the workers actually use the protective clothing and goggles issued to them; workers on piece-rates (a high proportion of the Soviet labour force) are often tempted to discard protective clothing which slows down their activity and so reduces their earnings.

3. Pensions Committee, and

4. Benefits Committee. These committees are concerned with the administration of the social security and state insurance legislation in cases of permanent and temporary disability. This topic will be discussed later.[1]

5. Welfare Committee. This is concerned with general workers' welfare, and in particular, with such matters as canteens, lockers and changing rooms, provision of lavatories and showers, and also with supervision of factory flats and houses. Although the majority of workers in the larger towns rent flats or houses from the local authorities, many factories have their own blocks of flats and workers' houses, and some provide loan facilities for workers buying their houses; this is often done in order to attract skilled labour, which, at any rate until very recently, was in short supply. Supervision of all such facilities and arrangements is a function of the Welfare Committee of the trade union. Another matter with which the Welfare Committee is concerned is the use of the Welfare Fund (also known as the Enterprise Fund and formerly termed the Director's Fund). Sums varying from 2 to 10 per cent of the planned profit of the factory, and sums varying from 25 to 75 per cent of profit obtained in excess of the plan (i.e. where the plan has been over-fulfilled), are paid into this Welfare Fund. Half the amount in the Welfare Fund is normally used for general welfare, and the other half for the payment of bonuses to the workers whose efforts have made the over-fulfilment of the plan possible. The way in which the bonuses are allocated is largely determined by the general law and certain percentages have to be paid to various workers according to their rank and position: but the Welfare Committee is concerned with making suggestions to management on how the other half should be spent, e.g. in improving the club, or acquiring sports grounds, or building more houses and flats for workers. When many facilities seem desirable, great weight will be given to the order of priorities suggested by the Committee.

6. Cultural Committee. The Cultural Committee is responsible for supervision of educational and recreational activities, e.g. the maintenance of sports grounds, organization of factory football teams, provision of factory club facilities, arranging lectures and concerts.

[1] See p. 203 *post.*

7. Inventions and Rationalization Committee. Workers who have thought out ideas for rationalization, or for the improvement of machinery, or who make inventions, can submit them to this committee, which is bound to take them up with the management with a view to their introduction, and if they are accepted, to see that the worker concerned receives the benefits to which he is entitled, and to advise him how to obtain an 'inventor's certificate' if the invention is really a new one; an 'inventor's certificate' is a very valuable qualification which brings considerable financial rewards.[1]

There are two further functions of the Soviet trade unions that we must notice. One is in connection with collective contracts, which were restored in 1947. These have little relation to the collective contracts which American labour unions negotiate with employers. In the USSR wage-rates are fixed by law, and by regulations made by the various ministries, which in spite of recent simplifications, are often extremely complex. There is little room for negotiation on wages, pensions, or compensation for sickness or accident. But there is some opportunity for agreement, for example, on how the welfare half of the Welfare Fund should be spent, or how the work that is planned for the factory should be distributed between the different shops; in the main, therefore, these collective contracts merely repeat matters that have already been laid down for the factory in the plan, but they have the advantage of binding the union to see that the planned production tasks are fulfilled. In form the collective contracts are negotiated between the management of a factory or works and the factory or local trade union committee, but in fact the contracts are based on drafts supplied by the Ministry concerned and the Congress of Trade Unions: when signed by management and the local trade union, they have to be confirmed by the Ministry and the Congress of Trade Unions before they are ratified, in order to ensure that they are in full compliance with the plan. Once signed, the collective labour agreement lasts for one year. It seems that the main reason for restoring collective bargaining in 1947 was the propaganda effect; such contracts help to convince the workers that they have a real incentive to work harder, and guarantee that a proportion of the extra profits gained will be applied for their benefit in definite ways. But the collective contracts seem to give the worker comparatively few rights that they would not have under general labour law.

The other important function of the Soviet trade unions is in connection with labour disputes. This matter is governed by a law of

[1] See p. 115 infra.

31 January 1957 which is of considerable importance and which made several improvements on the previous system. The law requires Labour Disputes Commissions to be set up in factories and other places of work for the settlement of labour disputes to replace the Rates and Conflict Commissions which had existed under an earlier system introduced in 1928. A Labour Disputes Commission consists of an equal number of members appointed by management and the trade union, the management members being appointed by the director, the trade union members by the trade union committee.

Most labour disputes must in the first instance be submitted to the Labour Disputes Commission, and the law gives a long list of examples of the kind of disputes in question. These specially enumerated cases are:
a. Disputes concerning production and payment. The factory will have its total output planned for it, but how this is to be divided between different shops may have been laid down in a collective contract, and there may be disputes arising from the application of the allocation agreed upon.

b. Dismissal or transfer to another job. Many disputes arise over dismissals and transfers. The grounds on which a worker can be dismissed are laid down by law (the Labour Code 1922, as amended) and even where a ground exists no worker may be dismissed without the consent of the trade union.

The grounds are:
1. absenteeism, i.e. not turning up for work without adequate excuse. Even one occasion is a lawful ground for dismissal. (Leave without pay, if asked for beforehand, is normally granted as a matter of course for getting married, and on the death of a parent or a child, but not on the death of other relatives);
2. being late. A worker who is more than ten minutes late three times in one month, or four times in two consecutive months, can be dismissed;[1]
3. closing of the factory, or reduction in staff, or suspension of work for more than one month (e.g. for re-tooling);[2]
4. unsuitability of the worker for the work concerned;
5. persistent disobedience to orders, or other infringements of labour discipline;

[1] It is interesting to note that while the law expressly provides for the case of arriving late, it does not deal with the case of leaving early; this was the legal point involved in the case referred to on p. 202 *post.*
[2] Suspension of work for more than one month is said to be obsolete in practice as a ground of dismissal.

6. conviction by a court of a criminal offence which is either connected with his employment, or which has led to a sentence of more than two months' deprivation of liberty;

7. more than two months' absence owing to sickness (except where due to pregnancy and childbirth);

8. reinstatement of a worker wrongfully dismissed, or of a worker released from the armed forces within two months of being called up; this allows a worker taken on to replace him to be dismissed;

9. because the trade union requests his dismissal.

This does not mean of course that a worker must be dismissed in these circumstances: it only means that management has power to do so, provided that the trade union committee agrees, so that dismissal under these circumstances is not illegal.[1] In practice as skilled labour is still scarce, dismissals are not likely to occur except in bad cases. Often, however, the facts of a case are in dispute, and usually it is when a worker is maintaining that management is mistaken about the facts, that a case goes to the Labour Disputes Commission. In practice, it is 'unsuitability for the work' that is the most common cause of a dispute; obviously there is room for a good deal of difference of opinion here.

With regard to transfer to other work, a worker can complain, not only if he is transferred from one shop to another, but also where he is transferred from one job to another within a shop or department. Owing to the complicated nature of the Soviet wage-system, this may seriously affect his wages, as there are good and bad jobs in most plants, that is, jobs where a certain amount can be earned more or less easily than in others.

c. Payment for idle time and for rejects, i.e. for sub-standard work.

d. Payment for work requiring different qualifications. This deals with a grievance that previously existed. It may be that in an emergency, say because a chief engineer is ill, another engineer has to take over his job for a day or two. Formerly, if that occurred, the substitute would be entitled to the pay for the job that he had taken over only if he had a written request from management to do it. This meant that if a man on arrival at work was told by the head of the shop to do a job normally requiring higher qualifications, he had the alternative of complying at once, in which case he would not be entitled to extra pay, or demanding an order in writing from the management to do the job, in which case there might well be delays, and he might even be accused of sabotage by holding up production. The written request is now unnecessary.

[1] Trade union committees are said to refuse consent to dismissal more often than they grant it.

e. Payment for unfinished work on a cancelled order: this provision again is due to the complicated wages system.

f. Payment for time lost from work: this covers cases where a worker is delayed in returning from outside work.

g. Payment for overtime. In law, overtime can only be ordered by management either with the consent of the trade union, or where there is a serious emergency, e.g. if a consignment arrives late and has to be unloaded. Overtime by law has to be paid at time-and-a-half for the first two hours, and double time for the next two; more than four hours' overtime is illegal. In some cases overtime was arranged directly by agreement between the management and the workers concerned, without getting prior permission from the union, and in such cases it was held that the workers had no rights to overtime pay, as it was in effect illegal overtime. Sometimes this was done because management and workers both wanted to fulfil the plan in time, because pay rates depend to a large extent on fulfilment of the plan, and by informal or unofficial overtime this result might be achieved. Unscrupulous managements, to cover up their own blunders, might order certain workers to work overtime without permission from the union, with perhaps some privilege for the workers concerned, but without proper overtime pay. The worker is now entitled to proper overtime pay whether the overtime was regular or irregular.

h. Stoppages from wages. Where a worker has caused loss to the enterprise by damage to plant, machinery or documents, and the loss arose as a result of his carelessness or breach of the law or of internal regulations or specific instructions, he is liable to have an amount not exceeding one-third of his basic monthly wage deducted as compensation to the enterprise. Where the damage was caused to materials, semi-finished or finished products, up to two-thirds of his average monthly earnings may be deducted, though in neither case may the deduction exceed the actual loss to the enterprise (limited liability). The worker is liable for the full extent of the loss caused irrespective of the amount of his wages (unlimited liability) only where the act causing the damage amounted to a criminal offence, or where this liability was voluntarily assumed by him under a special written agreement with the management in cases where he was entrusted with articles of value, and in cases specially provided by law, e.g. storekeepers in certain cases where losses have resulted from their negligence in the performance of their duties, under a decree of 20 July 1930.

i. Disputes in connection with severance pay.

Some cases are excluded from the competence of the Labour

Disputes Commissions. The rules contained in the Labour Disputes Law of 31 January 1957 do not apply to managerial or highly skilled workers, or to civil servants, or to the application of disciplinary measures in cases coming within special statutes. In occupations where elaborate safety precautions are essential, e.g. in mining, management is empowered by statute to impose disciplinary sanctions (other than dismissal or transfer to other work) without any right of appeal. Although such 'disciplinary sanctions' may amount to no more than a reprimand, a note of all such sanctions is entered in the worker's labour passport, which he takes to his later jobs. Notes of these sanctions can be removed if no other sanctions are incurred within a year.

Disputes about the actual fixing of wage-rates and scales cannot go to the Labour Disputes Commissions. Wage scales are determined by the Ministries concerned. Commonly the rates for piecework are altered after experience with new machines; if it is found that the machines are easier to work than was first thought, and that high wages are being obtained as a result, the rates are lowered.

In any particular case, if the Labour Disputes Commission cannot agree, the matter is referred to the trade union, and the worker can also appeal to the trade union if the Labour Disputes Commission decides against him. When the matter is decided by a trade union, the worker, if the decision is against him, can appeal to the court in any case, whereas management can only appeal to the court on a point of law, not on the ground that the trade union made a mistake on the facts.

This is a great improvement from the point of view of the worker, as he is entitled to appeal to the court in any case where the decision is against him. Before the law of 31 January 1957 a worker had to get the permission of the trade union to appeal to the courts except in cases of wrongful dismissal: permission was sometimes granted, but there is some evidence that at times the unions were not doing their proper job of looking after the workers' interests, the union leaders wishing to remain on good terms with the management ('sweethearting with the management' as an American worker would express it). This meant that a worker who was out of favour with the union would not get permission. As he can now appeal in any case, neglect of workers' interests by trade unions may receive more publicity than formerly, and victimization of a worker by his union may be more difficult, but it is still possible, for discharge of a worker at the request of his union is still a lawful ground for dismissal.

The position of the Soviet worker *vis-à-vis* management is good: his position *vis-à-vis* his union could still do with some improvement, especially as elections to union posts are usually on the single-list principle, that of only one candidate for each vacancy.

If the case goes to court, a procurator is required to be present. The part played by the procurator in a labour relations case may be illustrated by an account of a case which I heard in a Moscow People's Court in September 1954.

The plaintiff, a geologist, was suing the organization which had formerly employed him, for wrongful dismissal. The court consisted of a People's Judge (a woman), and two lay assessors. The plaintiff conducted his case in person, and the defendant organization was represented by its jurisconsult, i.e. its salaried legal adviser. The procurator was present as *amicus curiae*. After the witnesses who were to give evidence had been sworn and had left the court-room, and after it had been ascertained that neither party objected to the composition of the court, the plaintiff addressed the court at considerable length and with considerable eloquence. The burden of his grievance was that he had been dismissed with a bad testimonial, which meant that he would have great difficulty in getting another job in his own special line, and that the person who had given the testimonial was not himself a qualified geologist and was therefore not in a position to judge the quality of his work. The plaintiff was cross-examined by the defendant's representative, who then called his witnesses. The first witness for the defendant stated that the plaintiff had shown himself unable to fulfil the tasks assigned to him, which required very high qualifications: but when the judge asked him if he had any direct knowledge of the plaintiff's work, he admitted that he could not himself give any opinion as to its quality, and that his evidence was, in effect, hearsay. This witness was then cross-examined by the plaintiff. The second witness for the defendant told the court that he had given the plaintiff full instructions concerning the work to be done, but the plaintiff had not been able to do it properly. This witness was cross-examined very thoroughly by the plaintiff[1] concerning the conditions prevailing when the plaintiff started his work with the defendant, and the witness admitted that they were unsatisfactory, but he said he had given the plaintiff advice about how he should reorganize the work and deal with the arrears, and that the plaintiff had not followed his advice. One of the assessors then asked the witness if the plaintiff had been informed at an early stage of the alleged shortcomings in his work, and

[1] The plaintiff in this case was a well-educated man and highly articulate: an ordinary worker would have been well advised to have legal representation in such a case.

the reply was that he had been. The procurator then asked the witness whether in view of the admittedly unsatisfactory state of affairs when the plaintiff had commenced this work, the plaintiff had had a fair chance to do the work properly, and the witness said that he had. The procurator then intervened further to say that the plaintiff ought to state exactly what he was claiming, whether it was reinstatement, or damages for wrongful dismissal, or revocation of the testimonial. The plaintiff said he wanted whatever relief the court could give, and that he was not bound to particularize; the court accepted this, and over-ruled the procurator's intervention, the judge saying that the plaintiff was entitled to claim these remedies in the alternative or cumulatively. The procurator then intervened further to point out that much of the first witness's evidence had been hearsay, and that the second witness was not really qualified to judge of the quality of the plaintiff's work: he therefore asked the court to adjourn so that the defendant might call a witness properly qualified to give useful evidence on the matter, and this was done.

It will be noticed that the interventions by the procurator were all designed to assist the court in reaching a correct decision: they were not intended to influence it either way. Thus, the first intervention was intended to make it quite clear to the court that, although the witness had, under cross-examination by the plaintiff, admitted that conditions were unfavourable, nevertheless the witness still thought the plain-tiff's work unsatisfactory. The second intervention was an attempt to simplify matters, though the court ruled against it. In the third inter-vention, the procurator pointed out (as the judge had already noticed) that the first witness's evidence was largely hearsay. This is significant, because Soviet lawyers have always disliked rules of law laying down that certain evidence cannot be given in court, or that a certain weight should be given to certain types of evidence, doubtless by way of reaction to the artificial rules of evidence which prevailed in Tsarist times: nevertheless, certain types of evidence, such as hear-say, which would be inadmissible in England, are regarded with suspicion, and the case was therefore adjourned so that direct evidence could be called.

If the dispute arose as a result of a defect in organization, the court can, after giving judgment, make a supplemental direction ordering that the defect be remedied. Thus in a case which I heard in a Moscow People's Court in 1939, also an action for wrongful dismissal and for wages due, one of the points in issue concerned the times at which the plaintiff had left work on certain days. The court believed the plaintiff and his action was successful, but the conflict of evidence had revealed the fact that the factory had no adequate system of recording the time at which people stopped work, and in a supplemental direction it was ordered to install a proper system of timekeeping which not only recorded the time at which workers arrived but also the time at which they left.

SOCIAL SECURITY

The administration of the social security system is to a very large extent in the hands of the trade unions, though the rules governing the system are laid down by law and supplemented by regulations issued by the Ministries of Social Security of the Union Republics. The social insurance system is financed by contributions paid by employers, supplemented by payments from the state budget. The employer has to register with the local office of the trade union to which his employees belong. As most unions in the USSR are organized on industrial lines, it seldom happens that the employees belong to different unions, though where this does occur he must register with each union. Most employers of labour are of course public corporations or state institutions, though private persons and religious organizations may employ domestic workers, secretaries, chauffeurs and other personal servants. Under a decree of 1961 priests are now deemed to be the employees of their parish councils, a measure which has caused some resentment in Orthodox Church circles, for legally it puts the priest in the same position as vergers, cleaners and other workers.

Benefits are payable in cases of temporary disability, and pensions in cases of permanent disability, old age, and death of a breadwinner.

Temporary disability benefits are paid in cases where a worker cannot do his usual work because of illness or injury, or because he is in quarantine. They are also paid in cases of pregnancy and childbirth, and in cases where a person cannot work because he is needed at home to nurse a sick relative. Entitlement has to be established by means of a medical certificate issued by an approved doctor. Payments last until the disability is removed, or until the worker is classified as permanently disabled. Where absence from work is due to a domestic accident, payment of benefit commences only on the sixth day of absence: in other cases it runs from the day when the disability arose.

Where the disability was due to an industrial accident or to a scheduled occupational disease the benefit amounts to full compensation for the earnings lost: in other cases the amount of the benefit depends on whether the worker is a member of a trade union or not, and on his period of continuous service, and is subject to a maximum and a minimum figure. Thus a union member with three years' continuous service receives 50 per cent of his wages, and one with twelve years' service 90 per cent of his wages, subject to a maximum of ten roubles a day. Workers under eighteen receive 60 per cent of their wages irrespective of length of service. A non-unionist receives half what a union member would receive, subject to a minimum payment of 30 roubles a month for urban and 27 roubles a month for rural workers. There are detailed rules about when service is regarded as continuous and when it is regarded as interrupted, and we need not go into these, except to note that continuous service is not broken where a worker moves to undertake some specially favoured kind of work, such as work in the far north, under a contract of limited duration, and that it is not broken when a worker changes his job because his spouse has moved to another district. Arrears of benefit must be claimed within six months from the date when they accrued due.

Benefits are not payable to malingerers or persons whose injuries were self-inflicted, and entitlement to benefit ceases should the person concerned refuse to follow his doctor's instructions. Where an illness is due to excessive consumption of alcohol a single worker receives no benefits: a worker with dependents receives half the benefit which would otherwise be payable but nothing in respect of the first ten days of the illness.

Pregnancy and confinement benefits amount to 100 per cent of wages in the case of women union members with three years' continuous service including two years with the employer at the date of the onset of pregnancy, and in the case of women under eighteen with one year's continuous service with the present employer: in other cases there are deductions depending on the length of service. Non-union members get a benefit amounting to two-thirds of their wages in all cases.

The collective farms have their own social security funds which are responsible for making payments in the case of temporary disability: pregnancy and confinement benefits, however, are payable to women collective farmers under the general scheme.

In the case of pensions payable on account of old age, permanent disability, and death of a breadwinner, the law is contained in an All-Union enactment of 14 July 1956, as amended by an enactment of 15 July 1964 (which extended the scheme, with some modifications, to collective farmers), and regulations made under these enactments. Apart from wage and salary earners, and, since 1 January 1965, collective farmers, the law also covers members of the armed forces, students, and other persons who suffer disability in the fulfilment of state or social obligations.

Old age pensions are payable to men who have attained the age of 60 and 25 years of service, and to women who have attained 55 and have 20 years' service. Once awarded they are payable for life. The maximum rate of the pension (depending on former earnings) is 120 roubles a month and the minimum 30 roubles a month. Certain additions can be made in the case of a pensioner with dependants, and those who continue to work suffer certain deductions. Those who do not have the prescribed length of service, but have worked for at least five years, of which three must immediately precede the application for a pension, are awarded pensions at reduced rates.

Collective farmers have to fulfil somewhat different conditions, and the maximum pension in their case is 102 roubles a month, and the minimum 12 roubles a month. In view of the way in which their pensions are calculated, it seems unlikely that many will receive pensions near the maximum: from the estimates given when the bill extending the scheme to collective farmers was presented to the Supreme Soviet, it seems that it was anticipated that the average old age pension for a collective farmer would be 18 roubles a month.

Disability pensions are payable in the case of permanent or indefinite loss of working capacity. Loss of working capacity is established by a committee of medical and labour experts, which places a disabled worker into one of three categories: Group I, invalids who require constant attendance on account of their inability to look after themselves; Group II, invalids who can look after themselves, but are able to work only in exceptional circumstances; Group III, those whose ability to work is seriously diminished, and who cannot carry on their former occupation, but who can work part-time or at some less exacting occupation.

In the case of disability due to industrial accident or occupational disease, the amount of the pension is determined in accordance with the amount of former earnings and the category into which the pensioner falls, subject to maxima and minima: the maximum for Group I invalids is 120 roubles a month and the minimum for Group III invalids 21 roubles a month.

In the case of industrial accidents and occupational diseases no length of service is required, but where the disability arises from other accidents or illness a period of service which varies with the age of the applicant is required to establish entitlement to a disability pension. Where a person is entitled, supplements may be made for dependants, subject to the general maxima: in the case of accident and sickness pensions, the maximum pension is 90 roubles a month for Grade I invalids and the minimum 16 roubles a month for Grade III invalids.

In the case of collective farmers, no benefits are payable to Grade III invalids, and other benefits are on a less generous scale than those for industrial workers.

Disability pensions may be reviewed at any time before retiring age: when a disability pensioner reaches retiring age, he may elect either to receive an old age pension or to continue drawing his disability pension. If he opts for the disability pension, it can thereafter be reviewed only at his own request.

Where a worker, collective farmer or pensioner dies leaving dependants, that is, members of his family unable to work because they are too young or too old or are themselves disabled, a loss of breadwinner pension may be claimed. The amount of the pension varies according to the number of dependants, whether death was due to an industrial accident or not, and whether the deceased was a worker, pensioner or collective farmer.

It will be noted that housewives are outside the social security scheme, except that they may receive death of breadwinner benefits if they are over the age of fifty-five, or engaged in looking after a child, grandchild, brother or sister of the deceased breadwinner under the age of eight.

No unemployment benefits are payable, for officially unemployment does not exist. Another general feature of the scheme is that the benefits and pensions are not high, and this means that serious financial loss may be incurred by the worker who falls sick or is disabled. The prudent Soviet citizen, like his fellows elsewhere, voluntarily takes out additional cover; *Gosstrakh*, the State Insurance Corporation, does a flourishing business in accident, disability, life and endowment policies. The low rates of benefits and pensions also explain the survival of tort actions in Soviet law, as the loss of wages may then be recovered from the person responsible for the disability.[1]

FURTHER READING

R. Schlesinger, 'The New Pension Law' (1957), 8 *Soviet Studies*, p. 307.
R. Schlesinger, 'The Statute on Settlement of Labour Disputes' (1957), 9 *Soviet Studies*, p. 99.

[1] See p. 166 *infra*.

CHAPTER TEN

The Collective Farms

In this chapter we shall consider one of the most typically Soviet institutions, the Collective Farm, which is the most important agricultural unit in the USSR. In addition to the collective farms, however, agriculture is also carried on by State farms (*sovkhozy*) and by individual peasants.

A Soviet farm or State farm, is a farm owned and controlled by the state, and managed on factory principles, by a salaried manager with his assistants, and worked by labourers who receive an ordinary wage. Although agricultural rather than industrial products are produced, the whole organization is factory-inspired. A number of Soviet farms were established shortly after the Revolution; these were mainly farms which were highly specialized and required highly trained managers and agricultural experts to run. Soviet farms represent a type of agriculture which is to be expanded in the future, and account for an ever increasing proportion of Soviet agricultural production.

Individual peasant farming is still allowed by law; the individual private peasant no longer exists in European Russia, but a few scattered peasant farms still exist in the more isolated parts of Siberia. Such farms are worked by a peasant household (*dvor*), consisting in principle of a peasant family, though it is possible for persons not related by blood to be admitted. Hired labour cannot be employed. In 1959 the contribution of the individual peasant to Soviet agricultural production was given as 0·01 per cent of the total.

FORMS OF COLLECTIVE FARMING

In theory there are three possible forms of collective farming, though only one type exists in practice. The different forms vary according to the amount of collectivization involved.

1. The agricultural association, commonly known as the TOZ (*tovarishchestvo po sovmestnoy obrabotke zemli*), the association for the co-operative cultivation of the land. Under this form of association, the

peasants pool their land, but not their animals or farm buildings or farm stock. The communal element consists in the collective working of the pooled land, and in the use of any machinery or equipment bought by the association out of its funds, constituted by the entrance fees and subscriptions of the members. However, there are no longer any of these associations left, though on paper Soviet law still permits their formation. The official view at the present time is that the TOZ was a useful form of collectivization at an earlier date, which prepared the way for the fuller stage represented by the collective farm. After 1929 the number fell off rapidly; at the end of 1930 there were about 14,000, and at the end of 1933 little more than 4,000. During the nineteen-thirties almost all the remaining ones were converted into collective farms, though a few TOZ were still in existence in 1941. There is no reason for thinking that any have existed since the Second World War.

2. The collective farm proper, sometimes called an *artel*, but usually known as *kolkhoz*, from *kollektivnoe khozyaystvo* (collective economy). This is the form of agricultural collective which has always been most favoured by the Soviet authorities. In this form of association the peasants pool their land and most of their cattle and livestock, but retain individual dwellings and small plots of their own on which they can carry out subsidiary household farming.

By the end of 1919 there were already some 3,000 collective farms in existence, and with the encouragement of the authorities the number had reached nearly 10,000 by the end of 1921. However, the peasants were not really prepared for collectivization; there were disastrous famines, many of the collective farms formed during these early years were later disbanded, and the number of collective farms gradually diminished during the years of the New Economic Policy, falling to something like 7,000 in 1927. In 1928 there began the great movement for the collectivization of agriculture, with much pressure on the peasants to join collective farms, and their number again rapidly increased, and by the end of 1933 there were over 200,000 of them.

3. The commune. This represents the highest stage of collectivization, where the members share almost everything, have communal kitchens and dining-rooms, and own virtually no private property; children are brought up in common nurseries, and all members of the commune are regarded as equal, no matter what function they fulfil in the running of the commune. The communes were always popular with the extreme left wing of the communist movement, but they were never much liked by the Soviet authorities for various reasons; they were inclined to be too independent, and their communal way of living, though it may have

appealed to their individual members, tended to antagonize the peasants who feared that it might be forced upon them against their will. A large number were formed by enthusiasts in the early years of the Soviet régime,' and by the end of 1921 there were over 3,000 of them. Many of them, however, were unsuccessful; many members wanted their equal share of the produce but did not want to do a fair share of the work, and during the period of the New Economic Policy their number steadily shrank until by the end of 1927 they numbered only 1,300. However, the drive towards collectivization of the period 1928–33 led to many more being formed; some of them were highly successful, and the left-wing element among the communists took advantage of the collectivization drive to create this form of collective. By the end of 1931, there were well over 7,500 communes, but after that date the number rapidly decreased. During the nineteen-thirties the vast majority of the communes were converted into ordinary collective farms. A few survived into the nineteen-forties, but since the Second World War there has been no reference to them as still existing in the USSR. However, it is still possible in theory to form them, and the official view at present seems to be that communes may develop at a later stage, for they demand for their successful functioning both a highly skilled personnel and a highly developed 'socialist conscience'.

The various ideological trends, which in Russia facilitated the transition to collective farming, were by no means all of Marxist inspiration: there was no strong tradition of individual peasant farming in many parts of Russia as there had been in other countries. In Poland, for example, the system of individual peasant ownership was very strong, the efforts made after the Second World War to force the Polish peasants into collective farms broke down completely, and Poland has largely returned to the system of individual peasant farming. In many parts of Russia most peasants had been serfs until the Emancipation of the Serfs in 1861, and after the Emancipation the peasant association, known as the *mir* or the *obshchina*, which represented the peasants in their dealings with the authorities, encouraged a certain amount of co-operation. Pasture land and woods were held in common, and agricultural land redistributed among the households forming the *mir* every ten or twelve years, so that the idea of individual ownership of a particular plot of land did not become highly developed. The *mir* also often kept a common granary, and came to the aid of its members in times of trouble. The Russian peasant was much less of an individualist than peasants in many other countries.

Secondly, there was a religious element. Communes had been formed

P

years before the Revolution by dissident religious groups such as the Old Believers, the Dukhobors, and various evangelical sects. Many were failures, but some were highly successful. During the nineteen-twenties some of the most successful of the communes were those established by religious sects, for the common religious belief of their members held them together.

Thirdly, there was a political element. In Tsarist times, the principle of co-operative agriculture was one of the main points of some of the non-communist radical groups, such as the Populists, the Social-Revolutionaries, and the Anarchists. It may well be that one of the reasons why the Soviet authorities frowned on the communes was the fact that the most successful ones were often inspired by non-communist ideology.

It is worth noting here that these radical political beliefs, advocating democratic and communal living, were very much in the air in later Tsarist times, especially among persecuted minorities, and that it was a group of Russian Jews who founded the first *kibbutz* (agricultural commune) in Palestine in 1909. The modern Israeli *kibbutz* is very like the Russian commune, and its ideological inspiration is mainly socialist and secular rather than religious, although there are now religious as well as secular *kibbutzim* in Israel. The *kibbutzim* in Israel have mostly been extremely successful; they have advantages that some of the Russian communes lacked: they use highly developed scientific techniques, the members of the *kibbutzim* are often intellectuals with scientific training, unhampered by backward peasant traditions; as membership is entirely voluntary, the ideological element acts as a binding force. Only people who want to lead a communal life join them. The *kibbutzim* are relevant to Soviet agriculture in two ways, first, as being inspired by a similar ideology of communal living without the use of money, on the basis of full equality, and secondly, because they may represent the future pattern of Soviet agriculture.

Fourthly, there was what we may call the semantic element. The Soviet authorities have always been adept at finding names bearing popular associations for their institutions, and the collective farm is often called an *artel*. An *artel* in Russia before the Revolution was a group of workmen, usually peasants from the same village, who formed a sort of gang which hired themselves out for labouring jobs, often for unskilled but sometimes semi-skilled labour, lived together and sometimes pooled their earnings. Membership of course was quite voluntary, and was often fluctuating; if the *artel* got a contract for a big job, say clearing a large site for building, they would send back to the village for more volunteers; if work fell off, some of the members would return to the village. So in an *artel* the leader of the group and some associates would commonly be more or less permanently resident in a town, and other members would join and leave as they felt inclined, or as work was available. The *artel* was quite a popular feature of Russian life, because it enabled the peasant to earn money in the towns during periods when farm labour was not in demand.

THE COLLECTIVE FARM (*kolkhoz*)

The principle on which the collective farm system is based is that the members bring into a common pool their land tenure rights, their agricultural equipment and their livestock. The land remains, as before, vested in the State, but the collective farm is given 'perpetual use' of it. However, the farm cannot sell or lease this land or the use of it, even to state enterprises. Apart from exceptional circumstances for which there are special provisions, e.g. when land occupied by a collective farm is required for the construction of a railway, the land, of which a collective farm has the use, cannot be taken away from it, or disposed of by it; but more land may be added to it. The original members joined voluntarily in theory, though as has long been known in the West and is now admitted by Soviet writers, very considerable pressure was put on them to join. The more prosperous peasants often refused to join, and sometimes were refused admission: they were known as *Kulaks*, or Fists, and they were not usually, as is sometimes thought, people who objected to handing over ancestral farms to common use, peasant proprietors with long attachment to the soil, but rather people who had been most successful in the general seizure of land which took place in the early days after the Revolution, or who had benefited from the agricultural reforms carried out by Stolypin in the first decade of the twentieth century.

Each member contributed his land, animals, farming implements, farm buildings, stocks and seeds, and was credited with half their value, the other half going into what is termed the non-divisible fund, into which the nominal entrance fee was also paid. If a founding member leaves, he is entitled in theory to receive back the half that has been credited to him, but this no longer occurs. The children of members of collective farmers are automatically enrolled as members when they reach the age of sixteen, and although the enrolment has to be subsequently endorsed by a general meeting, this is normally a pure formality.

The non-divisible fund is really the farm's capital: the term 'non-divisible' indicates that in no circumstances will it be divided among the members. Originally it consisted of the property brought into the community by the original members, together with their entrance fees. Any other capital assets are credited to it, as is the value of animal increase, and each year a payment is made to it from the farm's income. Thus the non-divisible fund can never decrease, but must always increase. Assets forming part of the non-divisible fund may be used for capital outlay only.

Although in theory the collective farm is a voluntary association of members, in practice the collective farms are subjected to a good deal of what is officially known as 'guidance' from the authorities, mainly the Ministries of Agriculture of the Union Republics, and the local authorities. Before 1958, the Machine and Tractor Stations, from which collective farms had to hire tractors and combine harvesters, played an important part in state supervision of the farms. Since 1958 the now larger farms have been allowed to buy such equipment themselves.

Most collective farms are governed by model rules, which, however, may be varied to suit the special needs of some particular locality, or some specialized form of farming in which a particular farm may be engaged. The model rules, adopted in 1935, provide that the main organ is the general meeting of members, which meets annually (in some cases quarterly) and which elects the chairman, members of the governing board, and the members of the auditing committee.[1] The general meeting admits or confirms the admission of new members, expels members, and confirms the plans laid down for the following year, including the scheme in accordance with which the members are to be remunerated for their work, and the minimum number of workdays each member of the collective farm must perform. These are matters for the general meeting, and the board cannot take decisions on them; on everything else the board has executive authority to take decisions in between the general meetings.

General meetings were feasible in the early days of the collective

[1] Early in 1966 it was announced that new Model Rules for collective farms were to be adopted. None had been published, however, by the summer of 1968, though it is understood that they are in the course of preparation. It is thought that they will give collective farms greater freedom to manage their own affairs, and will clarify the position of individual collective farms in unions of collective farms. Probably the collective farms will be allowed to establish handicraft industries working for the market, to absorb labour that is redundant at certain times of the year.

farm system, when in most cases a collective farm covered roughly the same area as a village with the surrounding land; it was no more difficult to call a general meeting of collective farmers than it is to call a general meeting of villagers. However, since the early nineteen-fifties many collective farms were amalgamated to form bigger units, and many of them now cover an area of fifty square miles or more; under these circumstances it is by no means easy to call a general meeting, particularly when a special general meeting has to be called to deal with some emergency. A practice has grown up of calling meetings of representatives; each representative can represent five members, and representatives are elected by the various brigades into which the collective farmers are divided.

During the last fifteen years, not only have the collective farms been increased in size, but groups or unions of collective farms have been formed, and more of the important decisions are taken by the boards of the collective farms forming the union, and then later ratified by the general meetings of the individual farms in the union. These unions have been established for the purpose of running common services for the farms, such as establishing electric power stations, brick and tile factories, canning factories, bottle factories and bottling plants in areas where fruit and wine is grown, and so on.

Members of a collective farm are remunerated according to the work done, each type of work having its own grading; the basic unit of work being the labour-day (*Trudoden*). This, which once represented a day's work, has now become merely an accounting device; for some kinds of work one day's work will count as two or three labour-days. Members were paid, in cash or in kind, for the number of labour-days to their credit. Since 1966 farms have adopted a system of paying direct money wages. Wages are the first charge on a farm's income. They are guaranteed, and, where a collective farm would otherwise be unable to pay them, loans are made to the farm by the State Bank. This is a step in the direction of assimilating the collective farms to the Soviet farms, or state farms.[1]

Out of its produce the farm must sell specified quantities to the State at prices fixed by the State. The rest is either sold by the collective farm or distributed to members in kind as part of their remuneration. The cash income of the farm goes in meeting the farm's obligations to the State (taxes, insurance premiums, repayment of loans) and in paying

[1] This is borne out by the New Basic Principles of Land Use approved at the end of 1968.

its obligations and covering its administrative expenses. After an amount fixed by its rules has been paid into the non-divisible fund, the remainder is distributed among the members in accordance with the 'labour-days' to their credit or in direct wages.

A collective farm may also employ at fixed wage-rates, specialists of various kinds, but the hiring of casual labour for agricultural operations is allowed only in case of emergencies. Where members receive their share of the profits in kind instead of cash they can sell the produce on the open market, that is, at the collective farm markets to be found in the towns. And at these markets they also sell the produce obtained from work on their own individual plots.

These individual plots are usually about an acre or more; the exact size varies in different districts according to the nature and quality of the soil. On these plots, which are allocated to households rather than members as such, they can keep poultry, and limited quantities of sheep, goats and horses. As explained in an earlier chapter,[2] the collective farm household (*dvor*) is regarded as a unit, the property being owned by the household rather than by the individual members, so that when the head of the household dies the property still belongs to the same household, and the household continues, though with varying membership as members die and new ones are born. When the last surviving member of a collective farm household dies, the property passes according to the laws of succession contained in the Civil Code, or according to the will left by the deceased. The property owned by the household commonly consists of a house, its furniture and furnishings, the livestock on the plot, and other property used in common: but the members of the household may own as individuals their clothes and personal belongings and anything bought for themselves, as distinct from something bought for the use of the household.

If a member of a collective farm household leaves for good, as when he goes to a town to work in industry, he can claim that his share of the household property should be allocated to him, and he can take it or its value away. This is known as separation.

Distinct from separation is partition. This occurs when a household divides to form two new households, as may happen on the marriage of one of its members. Here the property is usually divided in proportion to the number of adult members in each of the new households; the old household comes to an end, being replaced by two or more new households. The rules about the division of property on a separation or partition of a collective farm household come from traditional peasant

[2] See p. 86 *ante*.

customary law; this is one of the few fields where custom has any real place in the Soviet legal system.

FURTHER READING

R. G. Wesson, 'The Soviet Communes' (1962), 13 *Soviet Studies*, p. 341.

CHAPTER ELEVEN

Legal Aspects of Economic Organization

PUBLIC CORPORATIONS AND THE ARBITRATION TRIBUNALS

In the Western world one of the most important branches of law is that concerned with business relationships, the law governing the sale of goods, hire, hire-purchase, carriage of goods by rail, sea and air, company law, partnership, law governing banking operations, cheques, law relating to commercial agencies, law relating to insurance, and so on. In the Western world the law on all these matters is based on the assumption that industry and commerce are to a large extent run by private enterprise. It is true that industry and commerce are these days regulated to a considerable extent by the State in most capitalist countries, and it is also true that in most countries public or publicly controlled bodies operate in commercial fields, such as nationally owned airlines or railway undertakings and public utility corporations for the supply of commodities like gas and electricity. In Great Britain the coal mines have been nationalized and are run by publicly owned Coal Boards; and these bodies, running nationalized commercial or industrial organizations, are usually termed Public Corporations. They differ from government departments, in that their functions are primarily commercial or industrial, and not governmental or administrative, and they differ from other commercial or industrial undertakings in that they are not operated for private profit. In Great Britain we have a mixed economy, in that there is a private sector and a public sector, but in general the public corporations operate under the same rules of commercial law that govern other commercial and industrial undertakings. For example, much the same rules apply with regard to compensation if you are injured, or lose your luggage, whether you are travelling in a coach operated by a privately owned coach company, or in a train operated by British Rail or in an aeroplane operated by B.E.A. or B.O.A.C. The rules of commercial law, in general, apply

equally to privately owned and to state-owned commercial and industrial undertakings. And they apply equally to relations between these
public corporations themselves; if the National Coal Board supplies
British Railways with coal of a quality inferior to that stipulated for
in the contract, they can be sued by British Railways in the ordinary
courts for breach of contract in the ordinary way.

On the other hand, in the USSR virtually all industry and commerce
is in the hands of bodies that we could call public corporations, and
disputes between these bodies are decided not by the ordinary civil
courts, but by a special system of arbitration tribunals.

The Soviet public corporation is a separate entity in the eyes of the
law, a legal or a juridical person, as lawyers say. It has a certain amount
of capital allocated to it on its formation, mostly in the form of fixed
assets such as buildings, machinery, etc., and it is under an obligation
to preserve these fixed assets intact, but apart from this obligation, it
operates as an individual entity, and the corporation itself is solely liable
for its debts. During the period of the New Economic Policy, public
corporations were often in competition with privately owned enterprises. After the adoption of the First Five Year Plan in 1927/8 the
privately owned concerns disappeared from the field; the main feature
of these Plans was the introduction of a centralized planning of the
economic life of the country; the public corporations were allotted
quotas of materials, and given planning directives about the commodities
they were to produce and their quantities, and the concerns to which
the finished products were to be sold.

However, the allocation of quotas of raw materials and stocks, and
the imposition of planning directives by the State Planning Authorities,
did not do away with the need for contracts between industrial concerns
themselves, and between manufacturing concerns and distributing concerns, for the plans and the planning directives were often of a generalized nature only. For example, a boot and shoe factory would be
given a quota of leather, and a planning directive to manufacture, say,
10,000 pairs of footwear a year, and to sell them to a trading corporation
at prices fixed by the planning authorities. But a contract between the
manufacturing corporation and the trading corporation would still be
necessary to fix the details, to determine the respective proportions of
shoes and boots, and of men's shoes and women's shoes, and the proportions of different qualities and styles, what proportions of different lines
were to be included in each delivery, when the delivery dates were to
be, and similar matters. So when a contract was signed, containing
agreement on all such details, the obligation to deliver 10,000 pairs of

footwear, which already existed in principle in administrative law, was supplemented by an obligation operating under civil law; a contractual obligation had been created on the basis of an administrative law obligation. The prompt negotiation of contracts between public corporations became essential to the proper fulfilment of the Plan.

Together with the introduction of the large-scale planning of economic activity by the State came the introduction of the principle known as *khozraschët* (*khozyaystvenniy raschët*), called at an earlier period *kommercheski raschët*, sometimes translated as 'cost-accounting', that is, the introduction of ordinary accountancy principles into the operation of the public corporations, and the preparation of proper balance sheets and profit and loss accounts on traditional commercial lines, the purpose of this being to ensure that they were managed properly and economically, and that waste, inefficiency and mismanagement would be reflected in their accounts; this is also sometimes known as 'control by the rouble'.

It followed that if a corporation's efficiency were to be judged on ordinary commercial principles, one corporation could not be allowed to suffer as a result of the inefficiency or mismanagement of another: and as premiums and other benefits were awarded to the workers of enterprises that had fulfilled their plans, or over-fulfilled them, it would have been very unfair if they had had to suffer for delays and under-production for which they were not responsible, e.g. in cases where they could not carry out their planned tasks because some other concern that was to have supplied them with the necessary raw material or with components had failed to do so, or because the material supplied was faulty and so could not be used.

Therefore a special set of tribunals, the arbitration tribunals, was set up in 1931 to deal with disputes between public corporations. Many of the disputes heard by these tribunals are very similar to the commercial cases that can be heard in the courts of Western countries, for example actions for damages for breach of contract for failure to deliver goods contracted for, or for failure to deliver them on the agreed date, or for the delivery of goods not corresponding to the contract specifications, or which are otherwise defective.

But there is another type of dispute which comes before the arbitration tribunals to which there is no real analogy in the West, and this is known as a pre-contract dispute. This arises from the fact that contracts between public corporations are, in the main, merely agreements setting out in greater detail obligations already imposed on the parties by planning directives. So two particular corporations may be under an obligation to conclude a contract in order to give effect to a planning directive binding on them both, but be unable to agree on the detailed terms, for example whether the goods should be delivered in weekly or monthly instalments, or what range of goods should be included in each instalment.

There are two types of arbitration tribunal, departmental and state. Departmental arbitration tribunals exist in ministries and other government departments and decide disputes where both the contesting parties are ultimately subject to that department. (During the period of the *sovnarkhozy*, the councils of national economy, from 1957 to 1965, each *sovnarkhoz* had an arbitration tribunal to decide disputes between corporations that were subject to its authority.)

State Arbitration is called for when the two contesting parties are subordinate to different Ministries, or other authorities. The state arbitration tribunals are organized on three levels, at city or *oblast* level, at Union Republic level, and at All-Union level in the Arbitration Tribunal attached to the Council of Ministers of the USSR. Altogether there are 132 state arbitration tribunals in the USSR, viz. 116 local tribunals at city or *oblast* level, 15 at Union Republic level (one attached to the Council of Ministers of each of the 15 Union Republics) and the one attached to the Council of Ministers of the USSR.

Among Soviet jurists there has been a good deal of controversy, of a rather theoretical nature, whether these arbitration tribunals should be considered as essentially courts, or as essentially administrative authorities. They seem in some ways to partake of the nature of each, so we can consider how they resemble ordinary civil courts and how they differ from these.

They are like courts in four ways:

1. cases before them must be decided in accordance with the evidence submitted and in accordance with the rules of law, and not arbitrarily or on the basis of administrative expediency;

2. there is an established procedure to be followed in the making of claims and defences. We could summarize these two points by saying that cases are decided judicially;

3. the hearing is in the presence of the parties' representatives, usually their directors or their legal advisers (*yurisconsults*) who submit evidence and argue their case;

4. their awards, if not complied with voluntarily, can be executed by court bailiffs in the same way that judgments of civil courts are executed. However, it is seldom necessary to call in the bailiffs, because most judgments are for a sum of money, and can be executed by notifying

the State Bank of the award; the Bank will simply debit the account of the party against whom damages were awarded, and credit the account of the successful party. But sometimes this will not meet the case. For example, if one corporation hires property such as a crane or a lorry to another, and the latter fails to return it at the end of the period agreed on in the contract, the corporation that owns the crane may take the case to the arbitration tribunal, and get an award that the crane or the lorry should be returned at once. If such an award is not complied with the court bailiff will have to seize the crane or lorry and return it to its proper owner.

The state arbitration tribunals, however, also differ from civil courts in certain ways:

1. Administratively, they form part of the administrative authority to which they are attached and are directly subordinate; local Soviet, Republican Council of Ministers, Council of Ministers of the USSR. They are not, like the civil courts, independent and subject only to the law.

2. The proceedings are intended to have something of the nature of conciliation about them; the arbitrator's task is to get the representatives of the parties together, and to see how far they can agree on the facts and on the terms of the award to be given, and only to make an award himself if the representatives of the parties fail to agree.

3. The hearing is not in public.

4. Unlike courts, the arbitration tribunals can themselves take the initiative in directing cases to be tried, if facts appear to suggest that there is something that should be investigated. For example, if a trading corporation is suing a manufacturing corporation for failure to deliver goods agreed to be supplied, the manufacturing corporation may say that it could not make the goods because some third corporation had failed to supply the raw materials. The arbitrator could then direct an issue to be tried between the manufacturing corporation and its supplier, even though no formal claim had been made by the manufacturing corporation. This power in fact is quite widely used. (There is only one case in which a civil court can direct proceedings to be started and that is where it appears that someone who should be contributing to the support of a child is not doing so; even though the mother, say, of a child does not wish to make a claim against her husband who has deserted her, or against her divorced husband, if it appears in the interest of the child that its father should contribute to its support, the court may direct a claim to be filed for that purpose.)

5. The arbitration tribunals are called on, in deciding pre-contract

disputes, to decide disputes which are not primarily disputes on fact or law, but which are to be determined rather by economic or adminis-trative policy. In deciding pre-contract disputes the arbitration tribunals seem to be exercising an administrative function, but in deciding dis-putes over breaches, or alleged breaches of contract, they seem to be exercising a judicial function.

In the early nineteen-thirties the arbitration tribunals took the view that they were primarily administrative bodies, and that they were not strictly bound, in deciding disputes, to adhere to the ordinary rules of contract law contained in the Civil Code. They considered themselves free to decide disputes according to what seemed to them to be the economic requirements of the situation. However, this attitude, to a large extent, defeated the purpose of the state arbitration tribunals, and by the end of the nineteen-thirties it was accepted that, except where otherwise laid down, the rules of contract law contained in the Civil Code applied to contracts between public corporations, and should be applied by the arbitration tribunals in deciding disputes. There is a wealth of special legislation in the USSR on commercial contracts and detailed rules in a number of cases have been laid down by the arbitra-tion tribunal of the Council of Ministers of the USSR, which is em-powered by statute to make practice directions binding on all other arbitration tribunals, both state and departmental.

As far as the state arbitration tribunals are concerned, there are three basic principles governing their jurisdiction:

1. They are concerned only with disputes between public corporations, and if it appears that a citizen ought to be joined in the proceedings as co-plaintiff or co-defendant, or third party, or that he might be in any way prejudiced by a decision given, they must not exercise jurisdiction; citizens' rights are to be adjudicated on by the courts, not the state arbitration tribunals.

2. They have no jurisdiction over matters relating to administrative law, but only over contract, pre-contract and property disputes. For example, they could not adjudicate on a dispute between two public corporations as to how a planning directive, binding on them both, should be interpreted; the interpretation of a planning directive is a matter of administrative law, and should be determined by the adminis-trative authorities.

3. They have no jurisdiction where both parties are subject to the same Ministry or other authority; the case is then one for departmental arbitration, not state arbitration.

The procedure in the arbitration tribunals is laid down by rules, and various formalities have to be complied with in connection with the filing of claims, but once these have been complied with, the procedure is quite speedy, and the great majority of cases are dealt with within a month from the time when the claim was filed. The evidence consists mostly of written statements, for example, reports by experts who examined the goods on delivery and found them to be faulty.

Where arbitration proceedings show that a particular corporation is inefficient, for example, when numbers of claims are constantly brought against it on account of goods delivered by it being defective, the tribunals report the matter to the body to which the corporation is directly subordinate, so that its work can be investigated and defects eliminated.

Appeals and reviews are possible, as in the civil courts, and the arbitration tribunal attached to the Council of Ministers of the USSR can give directives on the interpretation of the law to all other arbitration tribunals in the country.

The number of cases coming before the arbitration tribunals is extremely large, and various reasons have been given by Soviet writers to account for this. One is that in large concerns one department may not always know what another is doing, and communications between departments may not always be effective, so that cases occur in which one corporation sues another for the price of goods delivered, and it appears that the goods had already been paid for at the time when the claim was made, but this information has not filtered through from the accounts department to the legal department.

A more probable explanation is that many managers of corporations will, in doubtful cases, play for safety, and will not risk paying an account if there seems to be any doubt about the legal position; they wait to be sued, and then if the award goes against their corporation, they can pay under the award, and if the matter is later questioned they have the award to rely on. This might account for the number of cases where accounts that seem due are not paid. Another reason may be that the managers of public corporations have little power to compromise disputes, and are afraid of exercising what powers they have, preferring to rely on arbitration awards.

THE ROLE OF THE STATE BANK

The State Bank of the USSR occupies rather a special place, for the relations between the State Bank and a public corporation engaged in industry or commerce are governed partly by civil law, the law of contract, applying as between banker and customer, in the way in which we are accustomed in the West, but partly also by administrative law, for the State Bank is in effect a governmental administrative agency concerned, among other things, with ensuring that the state economic plans are properly carried out. Besides providing ordinary banking services for Soviet public corporations, government departments, and organizations, clubs and societies of various kinds, the State Bank also acts as an administrative body to see that they carry out their proper functions.

The operation of the banking system is a matter coming within the jurisdiction of the federal or All-Union authorities, and not within that of the individual Union Republics. This is provided for by article 14 of the Constitution of the USSR which sets out the powers of the Union; and paragraph '1' of article 14 says 'administration of the banks, industrial and agricultural institutions and enterprises and trading enterprises of an All-Union character'; and article 6 of the Constitution makes it clear that banking is a state monopoly.

However, the State Bank of the USSR is not the only bank in the country. There is also the Foreign Trade Bank, which is concerned with the financing of foreign trade, and up to 1959 there were some other banks: the Industrial Bank, concerned with granting credits to industry, the Agricultural Bank, concerned with granting credits to collective farms, and the Central Communal Bank, concerned mainly with granting credits to local authorities for financing local services, such as the building of schools, and local government office blocks. And there were also local communal banks operated by the local government authorities, charged with matters such as collecting payment from citizens for services rendered by the local authority, collecting rent from citizens living in houses or flats rented to them by local authorities, and collecting money due on electricity and gas bills. However, in 1959 all these other banks were consolidated into one bank now known as the All-Union Capital Investments Bank.

The Foreign Trade Bank can only grant short-term loans which must be repaid within one year from the date of the loan. It grants these to Soviet organizations concerned with the export trade, so that they can export goods to foreign countries, and receive a loan from the Bank which is repaid when they receive payment from the importer of the goods abroad.

The All-Union Capital Investments Bank is concerned only with long-term loans, that is, loans for a period of more than one year, and it lends money to industrial enterprises, State and collective farms, and to local government authorities for financing capital construction, for building houses, factories, etc., and the loan is usually to be repaid over a number of years.

The State Bank of the USSR can make long- or short-term loans to State authorities, public corporations, or citizens; loans to citizens are made primarily for the purpose of enabling them to build their own houses.

The importance of the banking system in the control of credit is due to its monopoly position, for state bodies and public corporations are not allowed to give credit themselves on their own authority or initiative, or to lend money at all, except in cases expressly provided for by law: so if one institution is selling goods to another, for example an industrial corporation is selling goods to a retail trading corporation, it cannot of its own authority allow the buyer credit; if the retail trading organization needs funds to finance the purchase, to carry it over until it has recouped itself by selling the goods retail to the public, it must borrow the money from the State Bank. This prohibition of the granting of credit by industrial and commercial undertakings goes back to a decree of the Council of People's Commissars of 1930 which is still in force and is commonly known as the Reform of the Credit System. Another aspect of the Reform is a rule which requires all government departments, public corporations, social organizations and collective farms to keep current accounts with the State Bank, which of course has branches all over the country; all surplus cash must be banked, and organizations must not accumulate hoards of coins and banknotes on their own premises surplus to their ordinary everyday needs. These two rules give the State Bank very close control over the whole economic system, and especially over the granting of credit.

Credits are normally granted to a public corporation only when it has fulfilled its production plans, and is carrying on in a normal way; so the banking system, by withholding credit in cases where there have been irregularities, acts as a powerful economic administrative authority for ensuring compliance with the state economic plans.

The functions of the State Bank of the USSR are:

1. The acceptance of deposits from state institutions, government departments, collective farms and social organizations, which, as we have seen, must bank surplus cash with the State Bank. Private citizens may also bank their surplus cash in savings bank departments under the control of the State Bank. Through these deposits the State Bank accumulates large funds.

2. With the funds so accumulated, the State Bank makes short-term loans to industrial and trading corporations to cover their expenses

before any particular expenditure is recovered; for example, an industrial corporation has to buy its raw materials, but before it receives cash for its finished products it requires money for paying wages, light and heating, so it needs a short-term loan, which can be repaid when it sells its products.

3. Industrial and commercial organizations keep current accounts at the State Bank, and their transactions with each other are settled through the debiting and crediting of their respective accounts at the State Bank.

4. The State Bank implements the budget of the USSR by making available short- or long-term credits as required for the expenditure provided by the budget of the USSR.

5. The State Bank controls the monetary system in the same way that most other national central banks do, by issuing paper money and coinage; and one of its duties is to see that sufficient is available in any particular district to meet its needs, and that no more is issued than is necessary, that is, it must guard against inflation by not issuing more money than can be used for the purchase of goods available.

6. The State Bank may itself give long-term credits, and it supervises the work of the All-Union Capital Investment Bank, in particular by granting or withholding credits to that Bank as appears to be necessary; in effect the All-Union Capital Investment Bank could be regarded almost as a department of the State Bank.

7. The State Bank has a monopoly of dealing with foreign currency. It fixes the official Soviet exchange rate of the rouble for various foreign currencies, and all foreign currencies received by trading organizations or by private citizens should be handed over to the State Bank for exchange into roubles at the official Soviet rate. It also operates the exchange control system, allowing foreign exchange to Soviet institutions or private citizens for expenditure abroad.

The State Bank is an All-Union institution, and is directly subordinated to the Council of Ministers of the USSR; in fact, the President of the State Bank is a member of the Council of Ministers of the USSR, the State Bank is in effect very like a Ministry, or Government Department, though it is not termed a Ministry. It is itself both an administrative authority and a public corporation. As far as its administrative and banking functions are concerned, it is not subject to the jurisdiction of the state arbitration tribunals that were referred to earlier; the arbitration tribunals have no jurisdiction over matters involving banking or credit, which are matters for the State Bank itself; but in ordinary commercial matters the State Bank is subject to the

Q

arbitration tribunals; for example, if the State Bank orders calculating machines or office equipment from a factory, and then refuses to pay for it on the ground that the machinery or equipment delivered is defective or does not comply with the contract specifications, there is a dispute over which the arbitration tribunals would have jurisdiction, for this is not a dispute about banking matters, and so the State Bank is subject to the jurisdiction of the arbitration tribunals just as any other public corporation would be.

And now we must look in a little more detail at some of the work of the State Bank. It acts as a general supervisor of the soundness of the economy in various parts of the country. For example, suppose that a branch of the State Bank in a particular *oblast* finds, that of the bank-notes issued by it to the enterprises of the region for payment of wages, only a small proportion are coming back to the branch through the accounts of the various retail trading establishments in the *oblast*. Something seems to be wrong: perhaps the shops are understocked so that people cannot buy what they want with their wages, or perhaps the shops are full of defective goods or goods that are not wanted by people; or perhaps there is a large-scale speculation by black-marketeers in the neighbourhood, and the notes are going into their pockets and perhaps being transferred to another region. The State Bank will take steps to remedy this.

Moreover every public corporation has to submit to the State Bank monthly, quarterly and annual balance sheets, and the State Bank conducts spot stock-takings at various enterprises to ensure that the amount given in the balance sheet as representing current stocks actually exists in the warehouses of the corporations concerned, and is not merely a fictitious figure.

The Bank is required to give special facilities to efficient enterprises that fulfil their production plans on time, and to apply financial sanctions to inefficient enterprises that are lagging behind or are in economic or financial difficulties.

The financial sanctions that may be applied by the Bank will now be considered.

The most severe sanction that can be applied by the State Bank is to declare an enterprise insolvent. This step is only taken after lesser sanctions have been applied without result, when it is clear that the enterprise cannot get itself out of its difficulties by the assistance of the Bank or other organizations, and that there is really no other method open to it to overcome its difficulties. If the State Bank intends declaring an enterprise insolvent, it must give fifteen days' notice to the organization or Ministry to which the enterprise is administratively subordinate. The declaration of insolvency having been made, a special commission will be appointed containing representatives both of the Bank and of the Government Department known as the Commission of People's Control, and they will conduct a full investigation into the affairs of the enterprise declared insolvent. The enterprise will not be allowed any further credit, its movable assets may be sold by the Bank to enable payment to be made to its creditors, and the question will arise whether the enterprise should be dissolved altogether and its operations consolidated with those of some other enterprise, or whether it will ultimately be possible to rehabilitate the insolvent enterprise. Usually rehabilitation seems possible; according to an announcement made in July 1958, during the previous four years 454 enterprises had been declared insolvent by the State Bank, and of these 292 had ultimately been rehabilitated, 74 had been dissolved altogether and their functions transferred to some other enterprise, and 88 were at the date of the announcement (1 July 1958) still under insolvency proceedings with their ultimate fate not yet determined. The great majority of enterprises declared insolvent were quite small local concerns, but some of them were large concerns operating throughout the Soviet Union.

A second sanction, less drastic than a declaration of insolvency, but sometimes a prelude to it, is for the State Bank to put an enterprise under what is termed a 'special credit régime'. Before doing this, the enterprise and the authority to which it is directly subordinated will be warned, and the Bank may suggest ways in which its working could be improved so as to prevent the necessity of imposing this special régime. Once the order is made, it means that any advances previously made by the Bank immediately fall due, for whatever period they may originally have been made, and no new credit will be allowed. The responsibility for running the enterprise is then thrown on to the body to which it is subordinated; it will have to consider measures to improve its work, and to see if the defects which caused the difficulties can be eliminated, and if that body can satisfy the Bank that proper steps have been taken, loans may again be granted. If real improvements take place in the course of the next few months, the régime will be lifted, but if six months later the enterprise is still in difficulties the State Bank may then proceed to declare the enterprise insolvent. This 'special credit régime' was first introduced in August 1954, and as at 1 July 1958 12,446 enterprises had been subjected to it; in 82 per cent of cases the enterprises concerned were put on their feet again by their superior authorities within a few months. Of the remaining 18 per cent, in about three-quarters of these cases it took longer to restore the enterprises to normal working conditions, and in the other quarter insolvency proceedings followed.

But there are a number of other minor sanctions that can be applied by the State Bank to enterprises, either in an isolated case with reference to one transaction, or generally. By far the most common sanction applied when the State Bank suspects that an enterprise may be running into trouble, is to agree to advance a loan to the enterprise only on condition that its superior body guarantees the repayment of the loan. This acts as a sort of notice to the superior body that the work of the enterprise concerned may need investigation; if the superior body is satisfied with the working of the enterprise concerned, it will of course guarantee the repayment of the loan and there should then be no further difficulties.

In other cases the Bank may agree to advance a loan, but at a rate of interest exceeding the normal rate of interest for loans to public corporations, which is 2 per cent per annum.

Another possibility is that the Bank may refuse to make any further loans until all existing obligations are settled.

THE TAX SYSTEM OF THE USSR

The basic source of income of the Soviet State is the turnover tax paid by public corporations engaged in industry or trade. The tax rates are determined by the Council of Ministers of the USSR and vary with different kinds of goods. The tax is levied on the monies received by the enterprise for its products. Each enterprise has to account to the tax office at frequent intervals, commonly weekly or fortnightly, and at the end of every month liabilities are adjusted and any overpayment refunded.

Other taxes levied on public bodies include entertainments tax payable by organizations such as cinemas and circuses. A small amount is added to the price of the ticket and paid to the tax office by the organization concerned (theatres, however, are exempt from entertainment tax, presumably on the ground that the type of entertainment provided is of a higher cultural level and so should be encouraged). There are also taxes on collective farms which are paid partially in money and partially in kind.

As far as individuals are concerned, there is an income tax, though at rates much lower than those prevailing in Great Britain, and heavy taxes on individual (i.e. non-collectivized) peasants, though most peasants are now in the collective farms.

An important point about the tax system is that by far the greater part of the money collected in taxation goes to the All-Union authorities, who then allocate sums to the individual Union Republics. The Union Republics do not have their own tax system, and are almost entirely dependent for revenue on the allocations made to them by the All-Union authorities. Similarly, local Soviets are mainly dependent for revenue on sums allocated to them by the authorities of the Union Republic concerned, for although there are some local taxes, such as a sales tax on goods sold in collective farm markets, a tax equivalent to rates on house property occupied, and a few other imposts, these form only a very minor item in their budgets. As far as finance is concerned, the system is therefore a highly centralized one, with the lower authorities dependent on the higher ones for the money necessary to carry out their functions.

FURTHER READING

R. Beerman, 'Gosbank Procedures in the case of Economic Difficulties of Enterprises' (1961), 12 *Soviet Studies*, p. 273.
E. L. Johnson, 'Planning and Contract Law' (1961), 12 *Soviet Studies*, p. 263.

CHAPTER TWELVE

The Soviet Lawyer

By a lawyer we mean a member of the legal profession. In many countries, however, the legal profession is divided into different branches or there is more than one profession concerned with the law; for example, in England there are barristers and solicitors, and in France *avocats*, *avoués* and *notaires*, and therefore it is not always easy to say whether any particular occupation should be classified as a 'legal profession', for many persons in the course of their professional activities are concerned in one way or another with the law.

The Russians use the word *yurist* to denote anyone who has taken a degree in law at a university, or has received a similar education in some other way, such as by attending some higher educational institute or by means of a correspondence course. (The term *yurist* may also be applied to law students.) All *yuristy* thus have a common educational background which differentiates them from those who have not had such a training, and this creates a certain common bond between them, even though their professional occupations may be quite different.

The Soviet law graduate will usually have decided before the end of his course the career which he wishes to follow, and four in particular will be open to him: the procuracy (*prokuratura*), the bar (*advokatura*), the notaries' profession (*notariat*) and acting as a legal adviser to a government department or public corporation (*yurisconsult*). It seems that the best graduates from the Soviet Law Faculties usually opt for a career in the procuracy, though women often prefer the notaries' profession. Sufficient has been said in other parts of this book to give an idea of the functions of a Soviet procurator: the other three legal professions will therefore now be considered.

THE BAR

Before considering the functions of the Soviet Bar, it will first be convenient to consider the position of the Bar in Russia before the Revolution.

The Judicial Reforms of 1864 had given Russia a modern judicial system, based on Western principles, and operated in the main by highly educated and cultured men. But the fact that Russia was given a Western judicial system, similar in many respects to the French system, did not mean that the principle of autocracy was modified. As far as the legislative and executive spheres of government were concerned, Russia was still a complete autocracy. The laws were often very oppressive. So there was a rather unusual situation; an autocratic and oppressive government operating with a judicial system based on liberal and enlightened principles.

This put the lawyer, especially counsel for the defence in criminal proceedings, in a very unusual position. In court he was free to say, indeed he had a duty to say, what he considered the facts of the case to be and he had a duty to defend his client in the same way as a defence counsel anywhere else. But to do this he had to dispute and contradict evidence brought by the prosecution in the name of the State, and prosecuting counsel were normally officials of the Government. A French writer, writing on Russia in a book published in France in 1889, said:

> Every Russian who has been taken to court has seen a man rise to defend him who has dared to oppose, on his behalf, the representative of state authority who is bringing the charge against him. In this vast Empire, which has no political assemblies, the honour of having been the first to speak up freely belongs to the lawyers. In a country where military courage is quite common, the lawyers were the first to be called upon to give an example of something hitherto unknown: civic courage.[1]

The lawyers in Russia, from 1864 until 1906, were virtually the only people free to criticize the administration and the Government. The great Russian novelists and dramatists of the nineteenth century, of course, often criticized the Government and the bureaucracy, but they did it obliquely, and by implication; if they were too outspoken, their books were banned by the censorship. But the lawyer, as defence counsel, could stand up in court, contradict the state prosecutor face to face, tear his arguments to shreds, and bring evidence to show that witnesses called by the state prosecutor were lying or were mistaken, and this contradiction of official authority was something that could hardly be done anywhere else in Russia but in a court of justice. Although in some ways the régime became more liberal after 1906, political

[1] Leroy-Beaulieu, *L'Empire des Tsars et les Russes*, Paris, 1881, cited in Kucherov, *Courts, Lawyers and Trials under the Last Three Tsars*, p. 212.

prosecutions became much more common, and lawyers who defended people charged with political offences sometimes encountered serious difficulties. But lawyers concerned with defence in criminal cases were commonly of a liberal and progressive outlook, and so the legal profession, or at any rate a large part of it, became associated in Russia with a liberal political outlook, based on the defence of the rights of the individual.

In consequence the legal profession as a whole was rather suspect to the Soviet authorities after the Revolution. It was admitted that the lawyers had done useful work in defending revolutionaries accused before Tsarist courts, but their attitude was felt to be bourgeois and liberal, rather than revolutionary and communist, and they were felt to be too concerned with the individual and too little concerned with the interests of society as a whole. The organizations of the pre-revolutionary lawyers were dissolved in 1918, and new organizations set up.

But although his position has been improving for many years, the lawyer still does not have the prestige in the Soviet Union that he had in Tsarist times, or that he has in Western countries. The defence in court of persons accused of criminal offences is not a very lucrative profession. And the best law school graduates still usually prefer a career in the procuracy, where they will be concerned among other things with prosecuting in the courts rather than defending and where they will have a safe salaried job with good prospects of promotion for able people, or else a career as a legal adviser to government departments or public corporations.

A career in private practice, advising and defending citizens who had fallen foul of the law, involves little prestige, and on occasion some danger, especially for the lawyer concerned in defending people charged with counter-revolutionary offences; pleading mitigating circumstances with a view to trying to obtain a light punishment for his client is still sometimes regarded as condoning such offences.

The position has changed considerably in the last twenty years, and in particular since the death of Stalin, but lawyers even in recent years have had to fight for their rights, and the best of them are today showing the courage and high principles which were characteristic of the Russian Bar in pre-revolutionary times.

Each Union Republic enacts its own legislation governing the bar, and the enactment of the RSFSR now in force is an enactment of 25 July 1962. This enactment replaces the law formerly in force, an All-Union enactment of 16 August 1939. There is now no All-Union enactment, but only the enactments of the various Union Republics, and we can take that of the RSFSR as being typical.

The lawyers of a particular area, usually of an *oblast*, sometimes of a larger area, become members of an association, termed a College, and it is now impossible to become a member of a College without a university degree in law, which was not the case previously. The University Law Faculties have expanded very considerably since 1945, and there is now a sufficient number of people with university degrees to justify this rule.

The College, in effect a sort of Bar Association, is responsible for the discipline of its members. The average membership of a College is about 150. Each College elects a Praesidium or Committee which has the task of establishing Legal Advice Bureaux in the main centres in its area, and allocating individual lawyers to work at particular bureaux. The Praesidium ensures that at each Bureau there are specialists in the various branches of law. The client who comes to a Legal Advice Bureau may ask for a particular lawyer by name, or if he does not know of one he particularly wants, for one specializing in a particular kind of case. Fees are paid according to certain scales by the client directly to the Bureau; the lawyer concerned then receives them from the Bureau subject to a deduction of about one-third; these deductions are made to cover the cost of running the Bureau, and also to establish a fund from which payment can be made to lawyers who do work which is required to be done free of charge to the client, for example, when a lawyer is allocated by the court to defend a person without means, or to act for a wife claiming maintenance, or for a person claiming social insurance benefits. Each Legal Advice Bureau has a salaried manager to direct its work, a secretary-treasurer, at least one typist, and generally a calendar clerk to watch the court calendars and advise the lawyers concerned when their cases will be heard in court. In any particular Legal Advice Bureau there may be about twenty lawyers working, and usually there are some probationers, that is, young men with law degrees who are required to undergo two years' practical training under the supervision of the senior members of the Bureau before being admitted to full membership of the College; they also have to pass further examinations in civil and criminal procedure before being admitted to full membership.

The College, while it exercises strict discipline over its members, also supports them if they are in difficulties over doing their work properly, for example, if they are subjected to insults by judges or prosecuting counsel, as still occasionally happens.

R

There has been a great deal of discussion among Soviet lawyers about the lengths to which they may go in defending clients. As in other countries, they must not mislead the court deliberately, or assist the accused in faking a defence, such as an alibi, that they know is untrue. But far more pressure has been put on them to 'assist the court in discovering all the facts of the case' than in other countries, even to the extent of trying to make them incriminate their clients. Indeed, in 1940 it was even suggested that the legal professional privilege of lawyers to refuse to divulge information received from them in confidence from clients, which is recognized in almost all countries, should be withdrawn in the USSR so that a lawyer could be required to give evidence of what his client had told him. This proposal, however, was strenuously resisted by the legal profession, who cited article 111 of the Constitution, which says 'The accused is guaranteed the right to defence' and they argued that this 'right' would be worthless if, in his attempts to obtain defence, he might prejudice his position; he could not really obtain defence at all unless he could be assured that nothing he said to his counsel in confidence would be repeated. The attack on the integrity of the legal profession failed.

The stand taken by pre-revolutionary lawyers is well known in the USSR; most of them took the view that they represented not only their particular client, but also society at large, and society at large was often conceived as being in opposition to the State. Therefore, in pre-revolutionary times, in defending people accused of offences against the State, counsel would often assert that the accused was merely doing something he had a moral right to do, and would be allowed to do in most other countries, or he would assert that the prosecution was acting harshly and unjustly, whatever the legal technicalities of the matter might be. Clearly the Soviet authorities do not want Soviet defence counsel to take this kind of line, so they deny that there is any opposition, under Soviet conditions, between the State and society, as there was in Tsarist times. The interests of the State and society do not conflict, and the Soviet defence counsel has an obligation to society just as his pre-revolutionary predecessor did; but as society is now represented by the State, this is considered to limit him in his defence; he must defend only the legitimate interests of his client. Clearly he can argue that the offence charged is more serious than the one actually committed, or he can plead mitigating circumstances, but, it is said, he must not try to obtain an acquittal if he believes his client to be guilty; his client may well be interested in securing an acquittal, but if he is really guilty this is not a *legitimate* interest. Nor must he try to mitigate the offence by suggesting that backward or uncultured attitudes are not really very blameworthy. For example, in a case before the Second World War where a man was charged with disturbing public order by abusive and insulting language to an attendant in a fun-fair, his counsel argued that people visiting fun-fairs were often in an hilarious mood, and that anyone who took a job as attendant in a fun-fair must expect a certain amount of banter from the crowds visiting the fun-fair. He was later reprimanded by his College, on the ground that in the USSR all labour is equally dignified, and that his line of defence was condoning backward or hooligan elements who think it amusing to insult people in comparatively humble occupations, such as attendants in charge of roundabouts. The lawyer concerned was an elderly man who had been in practice before the Revolution, and he was told that if he wanted to practice in Soviet courts he must learn to adapt himself to Soviet conditions.

However, it is generally accepted that the basic task of defence counsel is to see that no fact that speaks in favour of the accused is overlooked. The evidence offered by the procurator may be selective, biased, or mistaken, and then it is the task of defence counsel to expose it. Moreover, Soviet lawyers firmly rejected a suggestion made during the Stalin era, that in cases where it was clear that a crime had been committed, and the accused asserted his innocence, it was his counsel's duty to suggest who the guilty party might be. This suggestion was never accepted; it is the task of the police and the procurator's office to find the persons guilty of committing criminal offences, not the Bar.

In the main, however, in practice counsel's duty is to point out any procedural irregularities that may have been committed; there are still a number of investigators and judges with little or no legal training, and sometimes even very elementary rules are ignored, so the defence of the accused person's procedural position may often be very important. Indeed, because of the standards prevailing in many People's Courts, some Soviet counsel prefer to say as little as possible at that stage, and to reserve their main arguments for an appeal, treating the hearing at first instance as a mere formality. If they feel that the people's judges and assessors are too ignorant to appreciate any legal points which may arise, it is difficult to blame them for this attitude, which some clearly think is in the best interests of their clients. In the appellate courts, as we have already seen,[1] the case comes before a bench of three professional judges, so legal points can be taken with a reasonable expectation that they will be understood and appreciated.

[1] See p. 124 ante.

Under the Soviet system, witnesses called in court are questioned mainly by the judge (and the people's assessors, if they wish) and if defence counsel wishes to ask a question of a witness, he has to ask it through the judge, who may disallow it. This greatly reduces the scope for the examination and cross-examination of witnesses which is such an important part of proceedings in English and American courts, and so the most important part of the Soviet defence counsel's task in court is his concluding speech to the court after all the evidence has been heard. At this stage he sometimes appears, as his predecessor in Tsarist times did, as the one person freely entitled to criticize the activities of a state official, the procurator or the investigator who carried out the investigation, and occasionally advantage is taken of the opportunity, for example, where it has become clear that the prosecution was brought merely because of the procurator's desire to find a scapegoat for some offence that had aroused public indignation, without any substantial basis for thinking that the person accused was really responsible; but Soviet defence counsel do not do this as often as was done by defence counsel before the Revolution. Nor may he do what was often done before the Revolution in murder cases, namely attempt to blacken the character of the victim as much as possible in order to obtain the sympathy of the jury for his client; this was often done in Tsarist times when government officials such as policemen had been murdered, and the jury, which itself probably had no great love for the police, would be delighted to hear what a scoundrel the State employed, and would probably acquit. But in the USSR there is no jury, and general blackening of the character of the victim is not allowed; matters relative to the killing, such as provocation offered by the deceased, can of course be given as mitigating circumstances, but not his general bad character.

THE NOTARIAT

Generally speaking, it may be said that in the USSR as in other continental countries, one goes to an advocate for matters which will or may involve litigation, and one goes to a notary in non-contentious matters. But whereas the Soviet Bar is a relatively free profession and resembles the bar in other countries to a considerable extent, in the USSR the notaries are civil servants. Before considering the organization of the *notariat* it may be useful first of all to consider its functions.

The functions of the notaries fall into three main categories: first, in connection with contracts and other legal documents such as powers of attorney; secondly, in connection with inheritance; and thirdly, in connection with the provision of certified copies of documents.

a. Contracts

Soviet law requires a large variety of contracts, including tenancy agreements and contracts of loan, to be notarially authenticated: and even when the law does not require notarial authentication, the parties may have a contract notarially authenticated if they wish; this provides certain advantages, for if a contract is notarially authenticated this constitutes *prima facie* evidence of the identity and capacity of the parties, and of the truth of any facts recited in the contract. Moreover as the contract notarially authenticated is prepared in triplicate and one copy is retained at the notarial office, if one party loses his part a certified copy can be obtained from the office without much difficulty.

The fact that copies of contracts and other legal transactions are retained in the notarial offices gives the authorities a great deal of information about transactions between private citizens, all the more so as many types of contracts have to be notarially certified. It also gives the notarial offices an opportunity of detecting evasions of the law. For example, in March 1961 it was provided that all sales of cars between private citizens must be conducted through special commission shops. (One purpose was to prevent speculation; another was to prevent cars falling into the hands of people without driving licences.) This produced, in the words of a Soviet writer, an 'epidemic of donations' of cars; notarial authentication of the gifts was necessary to obtain the donee's registration as owner. Of course many of these donations were merely concealed sales in evasion of the law, and the notaries found that many people who professed a desire to give a car to someone collapsed under the simplest questioning. Thus a man who said his motive was to reward an old army comrade who had saved his life during the war, on being asked where this had happened and in which unit the parties had been serving, left the office in a hurry. Another even appeared to have staged a fake accident so that he could be rescued, in order to use the rescue as a 'motive' for the so-called gift of a car.

What we would term conveyancing is conducted by the contracts departments of the notarial offices. Subject to certain stringent requirements, dwellinghouses may be bought, sold, leased and mortgaged by private citizens, but before authenticating any such contract the notary will see that the requirements of the law have been complied with. For example, on a sale the notary must not only verify the identity and capacity of the parties and the vendor's title but also the purchaser's entitlement to buy, for under Soviet law a person may not buy a dwellinghouse if he already owns one, or if his wife or any of his children living with him already own one.

Another important function in connection with contracts arises in cases of breach where the debtor does not dispute his liability or offer any defence, but simply fails to pay. As there is no disputed question of fact or law, there is no question for a court to decide, and so the creditor can, if the contract has been notarially authenticated and in certain other cases, obtain execution through a writ of execution issued by the notarial office. If the notary is satisfied that the debt is due and unpaid, he issues a notice to the debtor requiring him to pay the debt forthwith or to give his reasons for not paying. If the debtor gives some reason which, if true, would amount to a valid defence, the notary cannot proceed any further and the creditor will have to bring an action in court to recover, but if the debtor gives no valid reason, or does not reply to the notice, the notary can issue a writ of execution for the amount due. The writ of execution will be forwarded to the court bailiff for the area in which the debtor resides, and execution will be levied just as though there had been a civil judgment obtained against him. In practice, this notarial procedure is frequently used by local and other authorities against people who do not pay their rent, or their gas or electricity or telephone bills, but it is equally available to private citizens who cannot recover under contracts of loan that have been notarially authenticated. In the event of any irregularity, or if the debtor has not received the notice, the debtor may appeal to the People's Court if he claims to have a defence, and this indeed is a general rule; there is always a right of appeal to the court against any decision of a notary; for example, if the notary refuses to authenticate a contract an appeal will also lie.

b. Inheritance

Wills are among the documents required to be authenticated by Soviet law. The testator gives his instructions to the notary who drafts the will in appropriate legal terminology, and who will refuse to include any provision which could not take effect in law. Of course the testator can appeal to the court against a refusal if he thinks or is advised that the notary's refusal was wrongful, and this has the advantage that in any doubtful case the litigation can take place in the testator's lifetime, and not, as with us, after his death. Powers of testation were very limited until 1962; they are now much wider, and it may well be that will-making will become more common in the USSR as a result.

As there are no death duties, and as the property of a deceased person devolves immediately on his heirs, whether they are entitled under a will or under the law of intestate succession, there are no executors or administrators as we know them in England, and in many cases there will be no need to obtain a formal grant of representation. However, in some cases evidence of entitlement will be necessary, for example, to obtain money standing to the credit of the deceased in a bank account or to recover debts which were due to the deceased, and notarial offices therefore issue certificates of inheritance, which in practice serve much the same purpose as our probates and letters of administration. Where, as often happens, there are joint heirs and they agree on the division of the estate, certificates covering particular assets can be issued to them in accordance with their agreement. In many cases notaries have to explain to the heirs their rights and liabilities, and perhaps decide disputes between them, subject, of course, to a right to appeal to a People's Court. In fact in the People's Courts cases relating to inheritance normally originate in an appeal against the decision of a notary to issue or not to issue an inheritance certificate to a particular person, or against a decision to issue it in a form which the plaintiff regards as unsatisfactory.

In explaining to the parties their rights and liabilities, Soviet notaries do not limit themselves to the purely legal aspects, but also consider it part of their duty to give moral advice as well. We have already seen that one of the interesting things about the Soviet system is the way in which an endeavour is being made to eradicate a strict line of demarcation between the spheres of law and morality,[1] as can be seen from provisions such as article 130 of the Constitution of the USSR which says: 'It is the duty of every citizen of the USSR to abide by the Constitution of the USSR, to observe the laws to maintain labour discipline, honestly to perform public duties, and to respect the rules of socialist intercourse', and in article 5 of the Civil Code of the RSFSR, which says:

Civil rights are protected by Law except in cases where they are enforced in a manner which would be inconsistent with the purposes of such rights in a socialist society during the period of the establishment of communism. In enforcing rights and performing duties citizens and organizations must comply with the laws and observe the rules of socialist community life and the moral principles of a society building communism.

[1] See p. 156 *ante.*

An example of how such attitudes may work out in practice was given in an article in a Soviet law journal in 1963.

A woman came to the inheritance department of a notarial office in great distress. Her son had died a few days before. She was living alone, her husband had long ago left her and was living with another woman, and she was an invalid. She was in great need, and her son had left 220 roubles in a savings bank account. Strictly there should have been an interval of three months to allow other claimants to come in, but in view of her obvious need the notary decided to issue an inheritance certificate at once to allow her to draw the money from the bank. A few days later the office received a claim from the father for an inheritance certificate, also to enable him to draw out the money in the son's savings bank account. The father was a college teacher, which meant under Soviet conditions that he was one of a somewhat favoured élite, and apparently had a weakness for drink. Clearly, in law, he and the mother were equally entitled as joint heirs to the deceased son. The notarial office, however, did not consider that he had an equal moral claim, for the mother had brought up the son by herself, and was in very poor circumstances. The notarial office sent one of its inspectors to investigate, and he found the situation of the mother to be as she had described it. He also found out about the father's predilection for drinking parties, and that he had never bothered about the son, or visited him in hospital during his last illness. Clearly the notarial office had no power to deprive him of his inheritance rights under the law, but they explained the situation to his college authorities, who promised to 'have a talk with him'. What happened at this 'talk' is not recorded, but at any rate the next day he came into the notarial office to renounce his inheritance rights. Clearly some sort of pressure was put on him by his colleagues; but it was the notarial office which decided to inform his college. This is an interesting illustration of the Soviet attitude that nothing is really 'private' and outside other people's concern, an attitude which Westerners find difficult to appreciate. The attitude of the notaries concerned in the case was cited with approval by the author of the article. Doubtless on the merits of the case the final result achieved was in accordance with ordinary decency and justice, though the manner in which this result was achieved seems highly questionable.

c. Certified Copies

A notarial office also has a department for certifying copies of documents. This would seem a fairly routine matter, but in fact the notaries concerned with it quite often detect forgeries, in which case they detain the suspect document and inform the police. The main documents which are forged and of which certified copies are required are diplomas showing academic attainments, which are usually needed when applying for a job requiring special qualifications.

d. Organization of the Notarial Service

The Soviet notarial service was first set up by a decree of the Council of People's Commissars of 4 October 1922, and later an All-Union decree on the Basic Principles of the Organization of the State Notarial Service was promulgated on 14 May 1926. In accordance with these Basic Principles each Union Republic enacts its own legislation on the notarial service: that of the RSFSR currently in force is the decree of 30 September 1965.

In accordance with the principle of dual subordination which prevails throughout Soviet administration, notarial offices are subordinate both to the local authority (city or *oblast* Soviet) and to the Supreme Court of the RSFSR.

Under the decree of 1965 a person can be employed as a notary only if he has a university law degree, though in exceptional cases a person may be employed if he has had three years' experience of legal work. Over 85 per cent of Soviet notaries are women, and it seems that the notarial service is regarded as a normal career for the woman law graduate with a good degree.

Notarial offices exist only in the towns; in country areas most notarial functions are performed by village Soviets under the supervision of the notarial office in the nearest town.

THE JURISCONSULTS

The jurisconsults are the legal advisers to ministries and other government departments and to public corporations. They are really a separate branch of the legal profession, but until recently there was no legal regulation of this branch in the USSR, and there were constant complaints by jurisconsults that their legal position was not clearly defined. As far as the RSFSR is concerned, the matter has been put right by a decree of 29 March 1963 which lays down model rules for legal departments of public organizations and public corporations, though deviations from the model rules are permitted in cases where there are special circumstances. We will consider certain points in these model rules.

Paragraph 4 of the Model Rules says that the head of the legal department is bound (not merely entitled) to refuse to act in court or before arbitration tribunals where the claim submitted by his organization does not appear to be justified, or where his organization has no valid defence to a claim made against it by another organization. It had been a long-standing complaint among the jurisconsults that the managers of the organizations they worked for considered that their job was to win cases, good or bad, and that they therefore had to fight cases which they knew were bad. The fact that they are now bound and not merely entitled to refuse to fight cases which they think are bad in law may help to reduce the enormous volume of cases that come before the arbitration tribunals.

Rule 5 of the Model Rules also seems intended to serve this purpose. It says that where a jurisconsult finds that some legal rule is being infringed by persons in the organization he is working for, he must inform the director of this, and in the event that the director takes no steps to prevent it, he must inform the management of the organization to which his organization is directly subordinate. This would cover not only cases of breaches of safety or fire regulations and other such matters, but also practices such as regularly forwarding goods late because this happened to suit the convenience of the dispatch department.

To be a jurisconsult it is necessary to have a university law degree, though in exceptional cases persons with five years' practical experience of legal work may be appointed. This perhaps will meet some of the complaints of managers that persons sent to them for work in this capacity did not have the necessary qualifications.

Rule 10 provides that the head of the legal department of an organization is directly responsible only to the director of the enterprise. In some cases the head of the legal department of a concern was responsible, not to the director, but to the head of another department, usually the finance department, so that the legal department was in effect a sub-department of the finance department and this caused a good deal of confusion where the head of the finance department was not well versed in legal matters. Rule 11 prohibits the use of staff of the legal department for other duties, and rule 12 provides that the management of a concern must supply the legal department with copies of legal enactments and other materials necessary for their work; again, this deals with a matter of complaint, in that in some cases managers of enterprises did not see the need for subscription to legal periodicals, and so the jurisconsults were not always able, especially in outlying parts of the country, to get copies of the relevant rules and regulations.

An important part of the work of the jurisconsults, apart from dealing with claims brought by the organization against other organizations, and in defending claims, lies in supervising the legality of acts done within the organization itself. In many organizations it is provided that all rules and instructions given to subordinate organizations must first receive the 'visa' or *fiat* of the jurisconsult, in order to prevent *ultra vires* instructions being given. Many purely administrative acts are first submitted to him, for example, if there is a question of transferring a worker from one kind of work to another, the jurisconsult will advise on the extent to which, and the conditions under which this may be done without violation of the rules contained in the Labour Code. Sometimes these things are not done, and irregularities occur; for example, it was reported that in one case an enterprise was employing workers such as porters and canteen staff on the terms laid down for managerial staff. The jurisconsult, or the head of the legal department in a large concern, may, if he insists on seeing all administrative papers, prevent illegalities of this kind arising. In some enterprises a useful rule has been introduced that the director signs nothing without the prior 'visa' of the jurist.

Moreover, the jurisconsult is now entitled to require from any other department any necessary papers or information, and to view operations in progress. For example, if complaints are received from customers that goods are arriving damaged, the jurisconsult may inspect the actual packing of the goods to see what is going wrong.

In short, it may be said that the decree of 29 March 1963 has had the effect of giving a proper status to a profession that in the past was often regarded as a comparatively unimportant one but is today of vital importance in state-controlled industry and commerce.

FURTHER READING

E. L. Johnson, 'The Soviet Notary' (1964), 2 *The Legal Executive*, p. 124.
I. Lapenna, 'The Bar in the Soviet Union and Yugoslavia' (1963), 12 *International & Comparative Law Quarterly*, p. 631.
R. Schlesinger, 'The Tasks of Defence Counsel' (1957), 9 *Soviet Studies*, p. 200.
Y. Zaitsev & A. Poltorak, *The Soviet Bar* ;Moscow ;1959.

Glossary of Russian terms

Advocatura	the Bar
Arest	detention in custody
Artel	collective farm
Chastnaya Sobstvennost	private property
Chastny	private
Dvor	peasant household
Gosplan	Central Planning Authority
Gosstrakh	State Insurance Corporation
Grazhdanski	bourgeois or civil
Grivna	coin
Gubernia	province or provincial
Instruktsia	Decree of individual Ministry or other central or local authority
Khlysty	flagellants
Khozraschët (*Khozyaystvenniy raschët*)	cost-accounting
Kolkhoz	collective farm
Kollektivnoe khozyaystvo	collective economy
Komitet Gosudarstvennay Rezopastnosti (KGB)	State Security Police
Kommercheski raschët	cost-accounting
Krai	region
Kulaks	(literally 'fists') richer peasants
Kuryadniki	nickname for the mounted police
Kuryatnitsy	chicken-stealing foxes
Lichnaya sobstvennost	personal property
Lichny	personal
Militsia	militia
Mir	local communal peasant organization
Nadzor	revision or review
Nakaz	peasants' instruction
Narodynaya militsia	people's militia
Notariat	notaries' profession
Oblast	district
Obshchina	peasants' association or peasant communities
Obvinyayemy	the accused
OGPU	All-Union State Political Board
Podozrevayemy	a suspect

Podsudimy	person before the court
Politseyschina	police bureaucracy or police brutality
Politsia	police
Polnoye Sobraniye Zakonov Rossiikoi Imperii	complete collection of the Laws of the Russian Empire
Postanovleniye	Decree of the Council of Ministers of the USSR or of the Council of Ministers of a Union Republic
Pravitelstvuyushchi Senate	Ruling Senate
Prigovor	verdict or sentence
Prikaz	Decree of an individual Ministry or other central or local authority
Prikazi	special boards set up under the council of Nobles
Prokuratura	Procuracy
Propiska	residence permit
Raion	district
Rasproyazheniye	Decree of the Council of Ministers of the USSR or of the Council of Ministers of a Union Republic
Rayon	sub-division of a district
Russkaya Pravda	Russian Code
Skoptsy	practisers of self-castration
Sovkhozy	State Farms
Sovnarkhozy	councils of national economy
Ssylka	exile
Sudennik	revised version of Ulozheniye published in 1554
Sudimost	criminal record
Svod Zakonov	Imperial Russian Code
Svod Zakonov Rossiikoi Imperii	Code of Laws of the Russian Empire
TOZ (Tovarishchestvo po sovmestnoy obrabotke zemli)	Association of the co-operative cultivation of the land
Trudoden	labour-day
Ukaz	Decree issued by the Praesidium of the Supreme Soviet of the USSR and by the Praesidia of the Supreme Soviets of the Union Republics
Upravlenye Militsii	police board
Uryadniki	mounted police
Volost (courts)	peasant (courts)
vysylka	banishment
Yurisconsult	legal adviser to government department or public corporation
Yurist	law student or person with degree in law
Zakon	law of Supreme Soviet of the USSR or of the Supreme Soviets of the Union Republics
Zemstvo	local authorities

Index

For Product Safety Concerns and Information please contact our EU
representative GPSR@taylorandfrancis.com
Taylor & Francis Verlag GmbH, Kaufingerstraße 24, 80331 München, Germany